ENGLAND

A travel journal by
NIKOS KAZANTZAKIS

SIMON AND SCHUSTER
NEW YORK

CONTENTS

◼ PROLOGUE

◼ THIS PRESENT JOURNEY is, of necessity, a difficult one. It leaves behind the serene atmosphere of free and irresponsible beauty and stirs sanguinary modern anxieties.

Involuntarily, in the course of facing passions that are still bubbling, still unrefined, you must reveal your own opinion. And this opinion of yours, whatever it is, will enrage the people opposed to it. And if you attempt to discern and criticize by creating a great distance of time and space, disinterestedly and painstakingly, then both opposing camps will lunge at you in fury.

For to discern and criticize today's unhaltered passions with an independent mind and spirit is considered a mortal sin. There are two legions composing the solid, simpleminded, bleating herd of the articulate masses. For these people, "Yes" and "No" are the only permissible and feasible answers. White or black. Between these two extremes, comprehensible only to militant men of action, the free-thinking man cannot even attempt synthesis.

You must look with unclouded eye (unclouded by either hate or love) upon present-day reality in the world at large. You must admit the infamy as well as the virtues, the dark as well as the light, for here on this earth every living thing—human beings and ideas too—has always been composed of both. In a word, you must be a free person. This becomes an increasingly dangerous feat for the

7

spirit. And indeed the times require that in this critical moment of history, when the two worlds stand fully armed, clashing with dire necessity, intellectual hairsplitting should be regarded as suspect and dangerous. This is not the moment for innocent reflection and investigation. For a few more generations, the mind is going to be obliged by the pressure of history to forget its independent theoretical function. It will have to be enlisted in the service of the most immediate and imperative need: that of making propaganda for one of the two great competing slogans and that of preparing techniques—by inventing lethal weapons and poison gases—for annihilating brothers and fellow human beings fighting on the opposite side.

Science, on which poor miserable man has based so much hope for deliverance from poverty, passion, and the brute beast, and for an answer to the agonizing questions of his spirit, has become the most formidable and immoral weapon of a new form of barbarism, the most horrifying form, the scientific.

At the present time we are experiencing and witnessing the moral bankruptcy of science before our very eyes, in the mounds of corpses piling up. It is not just that science and morality are failing to walk hand in hand, but (and this is what is most terrifying) we have also seen the possibility of the following abomination: the more science progresses, the more morality retrogresses, until the moral degradation of man reaches a state of primitive bestiality. Vaunted progress has also proved one of the most menacing myths of the modern world.

This is why our era hates the spirit. It has seen that theoretical thought has gone bankrupt and has turned into a tool applied for destructive purposes, or an aimless, foolish toy in the hands of a magician. In our time the young people no longer have confidence in the old faded moral

systems, or so-called freedom, or bombastic idealistic theories. They have seen that all these are convenient masks
for camouflaging immoral materialistic greed.

The masks have been rent. Belief has collapsed. The trap
doors have sprung open which used to hold the inhuman
forces dammed up within us. And when the mask of a
civilization is rent, chaos follows at once. The demons inside us have surged forth, a savage madness of destruction
and self-destruction. Good and evil, honorable and dishonorable, gluttony and starvation, are all collaborating
for catastrophe and decomposition.

Before our very eyes, every hour, every second, the
world is crumbling. Our heart, linked with the past, is
lamenting, mourning. Let it lament, let it mourn. That is
its function. And let us try to see with clear vision this
astonishing moment of bloodshed we are passing through.

Humanity finds itself at an abrupt turning point in its
course. And as always at such sudden turns, we must not
hope to find salvation just by creating a better adjustment
between ideals and reality, and by patching up the laws
and making them work more efficiently. Improvement, re-
assessment, continuation are not enough! By now modern man is aware of the need for a radical reversal, a
change of front, a new hierarchy in values, a new evalua-
tion of virtue.

A grand era. Never before have heroism, scorn of death,
the squandering and sacrifice of life attained these dimensions of a lofty mass delirium. Every second, thousands of
young men in both camps are risking their youth with superhuman fury. "*Agon eschatos kai megistos tais psychais
prokeitai*—the final and greatest struggle for all souls is at
hand."

And at the present time, who can stand aloof from
this horrifying diabolical contest? Even the finest spirits,
even the most dispassionate ones, are gradually being swept

away by the whirlwind, gradually forced to enter the struggle.

Only a mind capable of viewing our age from a very great height could do equal justice to all the people involved in the struggle. Your position in the fight, whether you were on the left or on the right, would not matter to this non-human mind. The only thing that would matter would be the purity and intensity with which you fought—that is, sacrifice.

But it is difficult for such a mind to exist today. Inevitably, in following the individual's own idiosyncratic rhythm, thought is disposed to veer with greater eagerness toward some particular side. It is very hard nowadays to acquire the "spherical glance" enabling you to see the truth simultaneously from all sides, like a sphere, and to confront all those involved in the struggle with the same respect . . . And not just with respect, but with some obscure strange love as well. At the present moment we find it hard to realize and experience the quite simple fact that we are all secret collaborators striving for the same great purpose.

What purpose? The two deepest impulses of man are firstly *hunger*, which drives him to expand his power as far as he can, to seize and conquer, to appropriate and to eat; and secondly, *fear* that what he has acquired may be taken from him, and therefrom arises the urge to preserve it as comfortably and for as long a time as possible.

A youthful organism, strong and vigorous, that is still hungry and in its upward surge, is impelled by necessity to expand its power, to disregard danger and to break loose in all directions in order to find nourishment and stay alive —to make war! A mature organism that has eaten and had its fill has only one desire left: not to have its possessions taken from it and not to let the consecrated order be overturned. This world is good and pleasant for it, and it wants peace.

And both are right; and both, by following necessity, are collaborating in the same great purpose. What purpose? That the human soul be stirred. That the human soul be stirred and that one further step be taken toward escape from the old moralities, freedoms, customs, which have ended up as immorality, slavery, death . . . and toward the creation of a new vision, a new civilization.

All our hopes today rest upon the fact that the times we are passing through (and still more, the times that our children and our grandchildren will pass through) are difficult. Since life began, difficulty has always been the great incentive that has aroused and goaded the whole range of impulses, good and bad alike, to leap over the hurdles looming ahead. And so we summon all our forces, which otherwise would have lain dormant or operated sluggishly or at random, and so we sometimes progress much further than we had hoped. For the forces we summon are not only our own individual forces. Nor are they merely human. While man is recoiling like a spring to attempt the leap, the life of the entire planet is gathering momentum within us. And we become clearly aware of the simple truth we so often forget in our moments of fruitless ease: that, though man is not immortal, he is forging something or some one that is immortal.

That is why in these creative moments it is impossible to make any predictions. The law of analogy or historical precedent or learning by experience are inapplicable at this point in time when man—humanity, Life; call it what you will—is rushing for the leap. Here the unforeseeable is the only thing that can be foreseen. Here history loses its force. Its mask falls and its true face becomes visible. A tale told to tiny, tiny children as well as to big children by the three gossipy dames, Imagination, Vanity, Insolence.

In these grand moments we are experiencing, some other force has intervened to guide us: faith, the faith that we are capable of molding a new world all over from the beginning; of emptying out our memory; of liberating ourselves from unnecessary, imbecilic burdens; of giving our spirits a new virginity. Naturally, we believe in something that does not exist, but by believing it, we can create it. What does not exist is what we have not desired strongly enough, or nourished with enough of our own blood to enable it to cross the mystic dark threshold of nonexistence. By faith and love, or by force, out of our blood—that is, out of human materials—the nonexistent is molded and the great leap from one civilization to the next occurs.

In order for this leap to occur, it is indispensable that catastrophe come first. Many respected and beloved objects must crumble and from among the ruins the spirit must forge its new path.

Our age has very definite and very active elements of decomposition, and it has, as well, still unidentified and uncertain but unsubduable elements of synthesis. At this very moment myriads of people struggling throughout the five continents are performing the sacred, trail-blazing task of decomposition in a perfect fashion. The elements of synthesis must be nurtured from now on by the best efforts of all men of the spirit.

More than ever before, men of the spirit have a tremendous responsibility. They are duty-bound to let themselves be flooded by the destiny of their times. They must not seek escape. They must stand at the crossroads where all anxieties and all hopes blow, the rose of the winds. They have these duties: (1) among all the conflicting directions of the present time, to distinguish the positive good each one has to offer and to see how each one helps modern man's frenzied yearning to create a new and more just world; (2) to try to make their own classification of all these positive contributions, and within their own minds to forge the design of the coming world; (3) to experience man's contemporary agony on a deep level and to strive to express it not only in art and thought (nowadays these by themselves do not suffice) but by the example of their own life as well—and this is the hardest thing of all!

Escapism is a cowardly desertion. Yet the way in which men of the spirit strive is utterly different from the way in which the "world leaders" strive. Their duty is different, on a different level. They must convoke within themselves all the heterogeneous modern struggles and bring order into the chaos; they must transform their internal chaos into cosmos. And they must keep their personal independence unimpaired in order to find themselves impeccable and upright when their time comes. For it will most certainly come. Endurance, understanding, internal tension, the attempt to express in their own life and work the dominant chord of the future civilization. Within the universal delirium, to find how to articulate a simple right word, a Good Tiding.

Such was my train of thought as I wandered for several months over English soil at this apocalyptic moment, breathing in the air of England.

I loved these people, admired their virtues, so fundamental for man: pride, dignity, determination, power of resistance, discipline—few words, many deeds, great humanity.

Man has fought decisive battles in this damp green island of the North, far away from the blessed Mediterranean. There were the same enemies here as in all human struggles—man against the beast inside himself, light against the darkness in him. And as everywhere, here too human blood flowed in rivers. Here too even the most insignificant victory was heavily paid for.

But after centuries, over the rocks and green hills and harbors of England, three great English monuments were erected: Magna Carta, the Gentleman, and Shakespeare. These are the three great triumphs of man *made in England*. And all three of these triumphs constitute great stages in the ascent of freedom.

We should try to see them with as independent a spirit as possible. And we must accept with equanimity, that is, without joy or grief, the risk of satisfying no one. It doesn't matter. There are periods teeming with passions and interests and a host of desires, wherein the most honorable title a free man can aspire to is the title that Basil the Great gave Saint Ephraim: Professor of the Desert.

Aegina, summer of 1940

◾ ENGLAND

◾ TENDER GREENERY; a gentle, elongated un-
dulation of land; a springtime joyfulness; a damp, dense,
pleasant touch of autumn in the heart of summer. A
ceaseless, noiseless drizzle; a smell of cut grass. Flocks of
well-fed cows, the color of cinnamon with splotches of
white, raising their heads lazily, masticating. The steam
seeping out from their nostrils, blue and peaceful, floating up toward the sky and turning into a warm summer
rain.

Beneath your feet the earth elastic and flourishing, and
even your walking stick, should you plant it there, would
sprout leaves, like the staff of Mary's bridegroom. Whenever the earth lies stretched out like this and serene, as
though with folded hands, and the rain falls on it, making
it moist, the same image comes to me from my innermost
depths. Not an image, but an icon: "The Dormition of the
Virgin." Stretched out, with her conscience at peace because she has done her duty (having given birth to a son
more lofty than herself), she rests with folded hands. And
enveloping her from overhead, the blue wings of the angels, a slightly denser air, enfold and carry off her soul like
mist.

I opened the rain-soaked wooden gate of a country
house and strolled to a hill over the way. Cows, plump
sheep with thick, curly wool, the little houses set like red
brush strokes against the greenery, and the tar-paved road

15

all shiny like steel. Solitary. Inexpressibly pleasant and silent. A silence not like silence in our own sunny lands, spun of crickets crying so loudly that the human ear cannot hear them, that stealthy, dangerous silence where all your nerves are shaken, straining to grasp the ungraspable. Here the silence is honest, guileless, empty of echoes, comfortable, smoothing your brow with thick honey.

"Is this England? Is this England?" I cried to myself in surprise.

Another day, in London. The railway station hummed with people. The King, First Gentleman of the Empire, was returning from Canada today. The English people love official processions, medieval costumes, wigs, lords' ermines, the antiquated gold royal coaches driving their King to Westminster for the opening of Parliament, the heavy keys handed by the Lord Mayor to the King as he enters the City.

The English proletarian rushes eagerly to gape in admiration at those who stand on a higher social scale. He feels organically connected with all these taciturn lords and rosy-cheeked, wealthy aristocrats. The Englishman has no cosmic theories aimed at fashioning the world according to his own design. He is not led astray by abstractions. He proceeds step by step, seeking everywhere for reality, submitting to it in order to make it submit to him, questioning it, attempting to discover its rhythm and to produce simple, sure conclusions. He does not want to generalize them into universal principles. On the contrary, he wants to make rules in order to be able to act and to have his action bear immediate, tangible fruits.

He knows (not knows, but feels and sees and experiences) that a social hierarchy exists and that on it, the entire history of his race has been based. But he also knows that the doors are open, and that if he has will power, determination, luck, and if he plays the game well and offers significant services to the community, he will be able to stride through these doors and rise. "England is an aristocracy with open doors." The Englishman looks upon his superiors in a proud, dignified way, thinking to himself: "I too am like these people and I'll be able to climb up there where they are." Whereas the Frenchman, enslaved by the general universal principles imposed on him by logic, looks on his superiors and his whole spirit rebels against the injustice of it; "These people are just like me," he thinks to himself, "so why should I have them standing over my head?"

The train arrived. The King appeared, smiling, slender, slightly weary. All the Englishmen thundered and waved their arms and opened their mouths to sing. Some sang the royal anthem, others sang gay, simple little tunes. And a few of them chanted psalms from the Gospels. There was no slavish uniformity here. Everyone was expressing his joy, but freely, in his own separate way. In England the masses manage to save their independence and individual dignity from getting completely drowned. They are no herd, dully and monolithically following a slogan. They know how to take the same slogan and adapt it to a completely different entity. They bestow a nuance of freedom upon necessity, and they chant religious hymns or gay songs or national anthems, each group with its own spirit, to welcome back their King.

I was standing in a corner of the railway station, listening—a hubbub as in a beehive. Occasionally in springtime, there are throngs of bees buzzing mournfully, when they are left orphaned, without their queen. Then suddenly they bring back their queen and at once the buzzing changes its tone, becoming a rich, joyous, profound song, so profound that we forget the way the song had begun, and we too seem to be singing inside ourselves, as though welcoming some age-old hope.

The King of England is a sacred personage, like the Mikado. He is an indivisible part of the totality, like the queen bee in the beehive. But he is not motionless or unapproachable, no slab of granite. He too is a living organism, developing in time. He absorbs and is absorbed, adapting himself, subduing reality and submitting to it. The King and the people felt each other out and in the deep stream of their historic development, with patience and compliance to one another and love, they gradually became reconciled. As individual liberty became more and more aroused, so too the monarch kept changing form, modifying his power. They entered into agreements with him and they received from him. He gave and bestowed. New forms were discovered: the Privy Council, the House of Lords, the House of Commons, responsible ministers, constitutional liberties. And in this way, by keeping his eyes wide open and adapting himself to time, he conquered time.

The moment the King mounted his carriage, all the people began running along behind him, singing as they went. All their faces became suffused with a curious glint of royal purple, a curious Royal Communion! I did not join the procession. I just stood there avidly observing this extraordinary Royal "sacrament."

"You're a foreigner? You don't want to join in? You're not singing?" an old man asked me, as he rushed by on his way to join the crowd.

"No," I answered, "I don't want to join. I'm not singing. I am a foreigner."

"Well, if you stay long here in England," he laughed, "you'll turn royalist too!"

I shuddered.

"Is this England? Is this England?" I cried again inside myself in surprise.

Another day, in Hyde Park. Saturday evening. Delicate clouds in the sky, an unexpectedly pleasant warm spell, crowds of people. It had rained that morning, and the earth still smelled of rain. Perched up on their wooden scaffolds, about thirty orators were jabbering away. Apostles of all possible ideas: Mormons, Irish patriots, Salvation Army preachers, Christians, Catholics, Buddhists, Seventh Day Adventists, Democrats, Fascists, Communists, Vegetarians. They were all shouting and gesturing furiously. The audience kept shifting from one frenzied zone to the next.

A bony young man with gold teeth was ranting about Danzig, Hitler, the Peoples' Freedom. Next to him a fat, flabby silenus with ecstatic blue eyes gasped for breath as he climbed up to his wooden box. He looked down with compassion on his neighbor, who was crying his lungs out against Hitler. He shook his head:

"These things are all so insignificant!" he barked. "They are ephemeral. Hear ye the Word of God, the Eternal!"

He opened an enormous Bible and started turning the pages. They were thumbworn and smudged with fingerprints.

"Hear ye the Word of God!"

He discoursed on heaven and hell, but no one approached. He insisted, groaning and moaning away. The veins in his neck puffed up. I felt sorry for him and stopped there in front of him a while. Gradually other people began gathering around me—old women, old men, kind-hearted middle-class people, young girls with corn-yellow braids. A fat plebeian next to me felt his blood throbbing angrily as he interrupted the orator. He had doubts. He was racked by terrifying questions:

"Do I or do I not have free will, yes or no? Does God do as He wants, or do I do as I want? And if I do *not* have free will, then why hell and why paradise? How am I to blame? Why should I be rewarded? Why should I be punished?"

He was sweating and gesticulating, his mouth hanging open. All his front teeth, upper and lower, were missing. He lisped, and his efforts to get the better of his lisp were all the more repulsive for their absurdity.

Soon quite a crowd of men and women had collected around him, and with shouts, smiles, nods they were encouraging him, agreeing with him. But at once another chorus of equally impassioned men and women was formed around the orator across the way. The two choruses were now confronting each other like enemies.

The man of the people mounted a rock. He seemed to feel that he had taken on his own back all the souls gathered around him there. He was aware of his responsibility. The two leaders of the chorus began their dialogue, conversing on God and His passion, conversing on man and his passions, conversing on salvation. Here and there the choruses intervened noisily. And an invisible hero passed back and forth from one chorus to the other, laden with wounds and kisses: Christ.

Within this boundless English park, once again the eternal elements of the tragedy were unfolding: Dionysos (now called Christ) and man engaged in a battle to find his salvation. What salvation? The becoming identified with God, the living of His passion and His sacred resurrection.

Then suddenly, at the moment I was happily thinking about this periodic rediscovery of eternal themes, there emerged from behind the leader of the second chorus a dried-up, flat-chested old maid—the kind that used to be depicted in the Middle Ages as the Plague.

She unfurled a blue banner covered with white capital letters: AFTER DEATH THE SECOND COMING. Her cold little blue eyes stared at the man of the people who longed for discourse. He closed his mouth and fell silent. The *deus ex machina* had put an end to the tragedy.

The evening fell slowly, slowly; a light fog; the trees enveloped in white mist. The women's faces took on a satanic glint. The girls giggled and squealed as the young toughs perched up on the wrought-iron gates teased them. An erotic breeze began to blow as night fell and the audience began to thin. The young men and women hurried off under the rows of trees, melting into the fog.

But the Apostles with their swollen throats were still roaring on. Communists, Fascists, Democrats, all deifying their own panaceas. An Irishman was cursing the English government, demanding liberation for all Ireland. Further along, a consumptive Indian student with gold eyeglasses and huge front teeth and long pliant raven-black hair, was describing the martyrdoms of his country. He too was demanding freedom: "We are three hundred fifty million souls," he shrieked. "We have a great civilization, older and greater than yours. Why are you tyrannizing over us? We've had enough!"

Next to him, an aged Seventh Day Adventist spread out his steamy, transparent palms, smiling and reassuring his audience: "The day is at hand when the dead will be resurrected," he muttered, short of breath. "It has come. Brothers, let us don white gowns and go out to meet them!"

Two or three policemen, complacent, well-dressed, with their blue-black helmets and their heavy white gloves, moved to and fro, indifferent, sure of themselves, with a smile on their lips.

"Freedom! This is what it means to be free!" the person next to me was saying, a goodhearted, enthusiastic young man. "Where else in the world could you see a sight like this?"

I was reminded of once in Crete when I had a talk with my father, who didn't know what Communism was and wanted me to explain it to him. After I had been talking to him a long time and he had been listening with great patience, he shook his head and answered:

"It's all very nice, what you're saying, nice and holy-sounding. But if it *happens?*"

Which is as much as to say: "Go on talking away, who cares? Talk away, you old jabber-brain, blow off steam! I have no objections—up to a point, so long as it remains words, chatter. ("Chatter" was his word for ideologies.) But if you dare to put it into action, beware! Then I'll show you!"

And this is what England says too.

Once an English naval officer told me this story:

"In the last war, three German warships hurled themselves against one of ours. We did our duty. But our ship was riddled with holes and began sinking. It was night. We only had one searchlight left in working condition. 'Abandon ship!' the captain ordered his officers and sailors. 'Man the boats.' 'Captain,' they answered him, 'we'll die along with the ship.'

" 'All right!' the Captain called back. 'Set the searchlight on our flag!'

"They set the searchlight, and so, with all those souls together, the ship sank in darkness, only the English flag brightly lit high up overhead."

■ ■

Simple, incongruous mosaics. But just as you can reconstruct the whole lion from a single claw, so, perhaps, a trained eye can discover the arrangement of all these simple but scattered mosaics in the whole, and find where the various limbs belong, and so be able to visualize the lion of Great Britain in its entirety.

But you must not be in a hurry. You are in the land of patience, persistence, slow sure thought, where modern science first found its firm foundations. No longer big clouds of abstract theory, but the small definite stones of everyday experience.

Here, prudence constitutes a virtue. Silence becomes the trap door of a great clamor, and the slow pace is the surest way to arrive. Beyond a doubt, the totem of this country is not the hare but the tortoise.

And so I let my five senses amble peacefully over the tender green grass, the heavy, grimy buildings, the lacy churches, the blond braids of England. My eyes reveled, my ears eavesdropped, my spirit absorbed passively like the earth, like a woman. I let myself be penetrated by England noiselessly, slowly, day in day out, without any logical program or erotic impatience.

From my first moment here, I had sensed that this was the only path to follow in this country. Other places I had plundered voraciously, grabbing whatever I could, as fast as I could, and then leaving. Here, this piratical approach would be superficial and fruitless. Here you must remain calm, silent, patient; you must give time to the English rhythm—her climate, sea, green grass, green ever since time began, her social life, old universities, tennis, golf, harbors, factories, contacts and conversations with people—you must let these set the rhythm of your blood.

You must transpose values, setting patience and stubborn determination higher than impulsiveness and rebel thought. And you must be aware that speech is a weighty, precious metal and that oath and speech are of the same essence.

You must learn to love and respect everyday petty events, and only in these events to have faith. You must know that only by obeying and following them punctiliously, can you transcend them. On them alone, upon this earth, can human liberty be based. Yoke and wing are of the same essence.

You must daydream and keep a firm grip on reality and at its topmost peak let the dream oscillate. Beware of any action that is not nourished on the chimera and encircled by it as by an aura! Beware of any chimera that sits idle and ecstatic, melting away at the feet of the Lord. Martha and Mary must become one. Martha and Mary, this is the name of the inviolable spirit.

A difficult, gallant rhythm, but utterly appropriate for a proud spirit, the only one it can be at ease with. To love and hate passionately, and yet keep your face unperturbed and your mouth shut. To win and not exclaim over it. To be defeated and only clench your fist and start all over again. To throw yourself wholeheartedly into the danger-ous game of life; to have violent desires, but learn that it is the height of boorishness to flaunt them; to learn that one of the supreme human virtues is self-control.

England is a temple to Upright Artemis. In this country, you flagellate yourself even to the point of bloodshed, in order to learn to bite your lips and move forward.

◼ THE SIX WAVES
OF CONQUERORS

◼ MY EYES SHONE when they first encountered
the coasts of England. The ocean was seething inhospita-
bly, angrily, with cold steel-gray reflections. You feel this
sea is no mere liquid element encompassing an island. It is
an untamed, unsleeping lioness with her mane forever
ruffled, guarding and isolating England.

Over beyond the waves, a white-and-green undulating
line is sketched delicately along the horizon—England.
The sun emerges from behind the transparent summer
clouds and caresses with gentle tenderness the distant
breasts of the land and the white rocks of the coast. Up
over this gloomy, xenophobic sea the land seems to smile
and beckon.

For centuries now this unexpected smile of the English
countryside has been enchanting incessant streams of avid
lovers. In the midst of that fierce sea, a pleasant bosom,
charming breasts, a warm embrace from the Gulf of Mexico.

I leaned over the prow of the vessel, admiring her white-
and-green coastline sparkling and smiling over there behind its fine veil of air and water. And as I gazed, I was
trying hard to penetrate time and relive the joys and terrors of all those impatient lovers who have passed over the
dew-fresh body of England. Calmly, in broad outlines, inside the dark chamber of my own skull, the six great waves
of conquerors passed, one after the other.

■ ■

1. Prehistoric ages; summertime. Wild, dressed in sheep-skins, uttering inarticulate screeches as they leaped from rock to rock, the few natives had gathered on this same seashore facing the sea. Further off toward the south, the Iberians had emerged in their light, multicolored ships. They were short, dark-haired, and had greedy eyes and hands.

They had left their fatherland, casting a curse behind them, as they headed due north. Hunger, profit, adventure guided their rudders. But when these delicately built, sun-burned pirates came in contact with the isolated island at the edge of the world, they were terrified. All their fairy tales spoke of some distant Thule teeming with gold and pearls and tin, full of wild beasts, inaccessible. Flanking its one side, to the west, a boundless mysterious ocean, and to the north, blocks of ice as old as time.

But the closer they came, the hotter it grew. The hills smiled and beckoned to them. These first lovers were over-joyed as they seized the rocks and made their conquest. A Mediterranean race with hooked noses, raven-black hair and black eyes, they brought with them oxen, pigs, goats, their own gods and legends. They erected great upright stones, constructed a broad megalithic threshing floor and offered sacrifices.

And the erotic labor of conquest began. They opened roads through the dense virgin forests and stagnant waters. They founded the first villages near the harbors and rivers—Winchester, Canterbury, London. They hunted wild animals, made friends with the natives, took their wives, begot children, spread their roots.

The skeletons still located beneath the artificial mounds have two kinds of skulls: round and oblong. They must be the first conquerors from both races. They intermingled with the natives and the future conquerors, but their own blood was not lost. Even to this day their traces can still be detected: upright, Cyclopean stones; a few words left like fossils in the English language; and then suddenly, even today, along the roads of Wales and Ireland, dark forms, crooked noses, short fantastic Englishmen emerging out of the depths of time.

2. Ten or twelve centuries passed. And now, about 500 B.C., the second great wave arrived: The Celts, once again from the south. From the Danube, the Alps, France, came shepherds and warriors, tall, strong, blond, with blue eyes. They painted their whole bodies with strange, colorful marks—religious, military, exotic.

They were split into two races: the Gaels who withdrew toward Ireland and Scotland, and the Britons who took root on the southwest shores, facing their brothers, the Bretons of France.

The Celts also brought new gods and demons in their ships. They loved music and dancing. They were poets and daydreamers, believed in ghosts, created legends of the Round Table, of Tristram and Isolde, and of the great King Arthur who, in dying, cast anchor on the magic island of Avalon, where heroes are eternally happy, eternally carousing with the Nereids.

These daydreamers burned human beings alive, in sacrifice to their gods and ancestors. For they believed in a future life, and murder was but the violent transition from Earth to Paradise.

Three centuries before Christ, the Greek man of Marseilles, Pythias, thirsting for wisdom and wealth, must have opened wide his eager eyes after sailing past the Pillars of Hercules up past the Iberian and Gallican coasts to reach the mysterious Thule. They say he found blond people who drank wine mixed with barley and honey, and who painted their bodies and brought tin down from the mountains, carrying it by donkey to the port.

3. Once again years passed. And once again the south wind puffed up the sails of the ships. The third wave broke against the cliffs of England—the Romans.

Julius Caesar was the first to labor at subduing the Celts. He describes them as clever, brave, divided into families, without any sense of the community or the government. They loved flamboyant colors, he tells us, and flags and ornaments. Their leaders were their priests, the Druids, bloodthirsty and intrepid, who sang their ancient religious and military exorcisms. They believed in a future life and in Fate.

The Roman legions could hardly control their terror when they saw the Druids, dressed all in white, dashing out at the head of the battle, with their fierce warriors shrieking behind them and the maddened women with their blond hair flowing loose, holding burning torches in their hands.

The Celts fought bravely. But in the long run, organized power won out. The Romans became masters of southern England, and after the Iberians and the Celts, they too brought their civilization: governmental organization, fortified strongholds, broad networks of communication, cities with straight streets, fields, temples, baths, aqueducts.

Londinium became a great port, the central knot where the roadways of the north and of the south met. The Celtic chaos became organized. Here too, Rome left her mark—straight lines serving government and private needs, order and discipline, and in the middle, an omnipotent god, the prosaic, sober mind.

But gradually time, women, habit conquered the conquerors. The Romans remained in England as workers or

legionnaires. They sensed how pleasant it was, its hidden
austere charm. They loved it and no longer had the heart
to leave. They married the native women, learned their
language, begot children, built houses reminiscent of Roman houses. On the walls, they painted their favorite myth-
ological themes: Orpheus taming the wild animals, the
blond Apollo with his lyre, Aphrodite with her belt loosed,
Bacchus with grape leaves—all the sacred Greek forms that
tamed life and saved humanity from bestiality.

The natives were enchanted by these strange conquerors, who had become pacified and did not upset their religion or their customs or their language. The only thing demanded was order and external discipline. Internally, they
were left free. The Celts no longer rebelled or reacted.
They approached the Romans with confidence. They too
learned Latin, and began to dress, eat, build houses, dance
and sing like these Latins from the distant land.

In time, their gods became fused with the gods of Rome,
and with their gods, their stories and their thought as
well. The Celts became more disciplined, more practical.
The prosaic Roman mind produced its supreme fructifica-
tion, the dream. And the children born of the two races,
half blond, half dark, learned the language of their mother.
They took root on English soil, and little by little forgot
Rome, until one day they reared their heads and ac-
claimed their own independent king. They were emancipated.

Peace spread over the now tamed island, and peace
brought with it the usual bonuses: security, well-being,
enervation. The Romano-Celts lost their military virtues
and became ripe for the fourth wave.

4. Once nations start collapsing, they emit a mysterious
smell of carrion flesh that penetrates continents and seas.

Other hungry, greedy nations smell it from afar and surge forth.

From the dark forests of Germany and the harsh coasts of Denmark, the Saxons and the Angles caught wind of this fallen land and rushed upon it.

During the fifth, sixth and seventh centuries A.D., the new conquerors arrived, wave after wave. With their faces dyed blue and with long blond braids, they were fierce, stubborn daredevils and libertines; strong vehement beasts. "They feel no shame," comments one historian, "in eating and drinking day and night."

How could they feel ashamed? Like true daredevils, they both loved life irrationally and, at the same time, disdained it. They disdained their own lives and felt no pity for other people's lives. Their two chief delights were not women and poetry, not God and His Paradise, not the earth and the good and peaceful things thereof; their two delights were war and, as soon as the war was over, tremendous feasting. They used to eat mounds of meat and drink barrels of beer. In order to keep their love of slaughter and feasting constantly refreshed, they used to sing heroic legends to the music of the harp.

They were heavy peasants. They utterly lacked the cleverness and flexibility of the Celt, or the organized practical mind of the Roman who loathed superfluous kindness or cruelty, and had only one purpose—government. In unbridled fashion, they used to break out into joyful songs or laments. They lived and they killed in tune to their own superabundant heart. Their senses were coarse and heavy with mud. They needed much food, much drink, fierce blood-stained sport, in order to stir a bit and feel pleasure. "When I kill, I feel as happy as if I'm holding a girl on my knee."

They seized the English coasts, fell upon the villages, split open women's bellies, threw men into cauldrons of boiling water. Flocks of their favorite birds, the crows, used to follow them about.

"I do not want you," a Saxon princess tells her ruler, Egil, who was longing to sit by her side. "I want you not, for all this autumn, I have not seen the crow crying over your head!"

And he reassures her, singing:

"The blood was streaming from my sword, and in back of me the crows rushed out to devour. We set fire to the huts of men and slept in bloodshed!"

But these blond, bloodthirsty animals had two fundamental virtues: they were brave and at the same time faithful to their leader unto death.

They worshiped gods similar to themselves, cruel gods who punished ruthlessly all cowards and liars and rewarded the brave with rich banquets in their heroic paradise, Valhalla. They readily forgave any man who loved violence and abandoned himself to fury. They could forgive everything except cowardice and lying. To be a brave daredevil and to tell the truth were their supreme dictates, the only ones that could not be transgressed.

The Saxons also brought a great gift to their new land: a rudimentary but secure social and economic organization. They had no love for cities. They cut down trees and built simple sturdy houses. They knew how to cultivate the land better than the Celts and they allotted it better than the Romans—justly, so that all the families could live on it.

The old notables used to sit under a large tree or climb up to the top of a hill to choose their leader. They themselves passed judgment on their own differences and made the decisions on communal interests. Many villages made a joint election of a common military leader for their king. But this king was no absolute monarch. Around him convened the "Council of Elders," endowed with broad legal powers and the right to judge.

Faithfulness, honor, justice, freedom were the firm foundations of their individual and group life. Every man was absolute master in his own home and soul. He ceded nothing to society except when he himself wanted and approved it. The common people used to stand around the king and the notables, voting from an upright position, in full battle array.

The women were also free to stand alongside the men. They had precisely the same rights and duties as the men. They were free. They were entitled to have their own fortune, receive inheritances, attend the councils, voice their opinion. Husband and wife were bound to preserve their family honor unstained. Any man who seduced the wife would be killed. Any woman who seduced the husband would be condemned to hang or be killed by the honorable women. Women were not for pleasure and sport. They were comrades of the men in peace and war.

The Celts had a profound feeling for the beauty of the external world. These Anglo-Saxons were profoundly aware of the beauty of the inner world. They created a system of morality based on duty. And their religion had a strange fierce beauty, to this day enchanting proud spirits.

A militaristic religion, rife with awesome superhuman forces, wintry monsters struggling with the light, gods and heroes intermingling to fight the Wolf, the Snake, the Fire. They conquered and were conquered, and then the war would start up again. They refused to surrender, refused to demand mercy, refused to fold their arms and give in to fatalism. And yet they knew that the day would come when the powers of light would be vanquished and the sun turn black; when the stars would be quenched and the earth crumble into the sea, and everything would be consumed by fire. They knew this, and yet they were not panic-stricken.

Such was their religion—fierce, despairing, heroic, free

of undignified hopes. For they were strong spirits capable of resisting.

But one day the Pope, in the course of his perambulations around the slave markets of Rome, caught sight of some splendid young men with snow-white skin and long blond hair.

"Where are these young men from?" he asked. "What race?"

"Angles," came the answer.

"No, not Angles—Angels," the Pope corrected, gazing at them with admiration. "What a pity that such bright bodies should be burning in hell. I will send missionaries to their land to make Christians of them, comrades of the angels."

Several months later, for the first time, Christ landed on English shores. The very first people to be bewitched by the symbol of the crucified Saviour were the Celts, these sentimental daydreamers. This daydreaming God who loved birds, children, flowers, and who suffered and died on behalf of humanity, fulfilled their deepest and most sensitive feelings. They became Christians.

In time, even the barbarous Anglo-Saxons were enchanted by this idyllic strange god who forgave his enemies, preaching love and kindness throughout the world. This god offered them precisely what they lacked, enriching their spirits and opening the gates of heaven in their own inner world and coarse vitals. They cocked their hairy ears and listened to the new preaching.

The few descriptions of the conversion we still possess are steeped in patriarchal simplicity and poetry:

King Edwin was sitting on a high stool, amid his Senate. The missionary Paulinus came and began preaching the Good Tidings. Everyone listened seriously and attentively. When Paulinus had finished, the King turned toward his senators.

"My sages, you've heard the stranger's words. You've understood what this new religion preaches. Now I want to hear your own opinion as well. We must all take counsel here and come to a decision."

One of the elders, the oldest one of all, arose to speak:

"O King, the life of man is like the flight of a sparrow. In wintertime it enters the big room where you are sitting with your princes, eating and drinking by the lighted fire. Outside, the rain and snow are raging. An icy wind is blowing. And then the sparrow comes in quickly through one door, going out the other. For a moment, as long as he had been passing through the hall, he had been warm and content. He had escaped the winter. But then straightway he fell back into the dark icy night whence he had emerged . . .

"Such is the life of man, my king. Whence do we come and whither are we going? We know not. Well then, if this new religion tells us this, let us follow it!"

The High Priest of the old gods arose:

"Until this moment, I did not understand what I was worshiping," he exclaimed. "I was seeking God but not finding Him. Now I have found Him. Let the idols fall!" He seized his spear and began smashing the idols in the ancient temple of Odin.

Barbarous violent spirits tormented by metaphysical anguish. Whence have we come? Whither are we going? We descend into our "earthen home," the ground, and then? . . . And then? . . . They felt the need of a god who could answer these terrifying questions gnawing at their thick Anglo-Saxon innards.

This god arrived wearing his double mask—Jehovah and Christ—and swept them all off their feet. In the beginning, they had been attracted by the sweet-tempered face of Christ. But gradually, their fierce, still bellicose spirits turned wholeheartedly toward Jehovah, the merciless leader of the race. This is how they had always longed for their leader to be—harsh, unafraid of bloodshed, rushing to the fore to lead his race to conquer the world.

The Anglo-Saxons were not long deceived by the sweet temper of Christ. They did not succumb to the cult of the Virgin Mary. They were not touched by the sorrow and beauty of Mary. Their real god became the "Lord of the Powers," Jehovah, and their real Bible, the Old Testament.

With a leader like this, they became fierce fanatic Christians. Inhuman crimes, grand heroic deeds. Villages were sacked and whole counties, for having refused to accept baptism. In the course of doing away with war, these violent spirits were now fighting their own deepest desires, their own most primitive impulses. In spite of being dark libertines, they now gave up meat, beer, revenge. Bloodthirsty kings became monks.

The only thing they wanted to keep from dying out were their old heroic songs. But these too deserted and went over to the other camp, as accompaniments to the new Christian feast days. Minstrels sang of the old pagan heroes on their harps as they wandered from village to village, through the public squares and Christian festivals and aristocratic courts. The figure of the crucified Christ was nailed up and set in the snow. The more fanatical of the Christians were furious.

"What are these songs?" they exclaimed. "What connection can the god Thor have with Christ? Our house is small. There is no room for both. Thor must go!"

But these songs were the roots of the Anglo-Saxons, and it was not easy to eradicate them. Indeed, there was one bishop who used to don the clothes of a minstrel the moment the church service ended. He used to grab his harp and rush to a much-frequented bridge in order to sing

Beowulf, their beloved pagan epic. Who was it who remarked that when the idols were expelled from the temples, they took refuge in the human heart?

5. England was kind, her earth fat, the Celtic women exotic and attractive. And the Anglo-Saxons forgot their fatherland. The conquered people tried to stir up several more rebellions, but these were stifled after much bloodshed. Once again, peace reigned through the green island and the new masters could devote themselves, unimpeded, to cultivating the land and saving their souls.

But the military men were still restless. The peace was suffocating them. And they began squabbling among themselves. Families fought against families, and villages against villages. They shed blood and blew off steam. But they were growing weaker and weaker. If a new conqueror were to cast anchor suddenly on their shores, they would be ruined.

And apparently just at this very point, England uttered yet another cry, and one day, at the end of the eighth century, the new bridegrooms arrived. The Vikings and the Danes.

They too arrived in multicolored boats, with red sails and sea monsters carved on their prows. Their shields were painted yellow and black and they held heavy double axes. They landed on the island like raging pirates crashing a ship. They burned the villages and monasteries, killed the men and absconded with the women. Then they leaped back onto their ships and sailed off.

Years afterward, they returned and sailed up the Thames in three hundred ships to conquer London. This time they did not leave. They liked the place and they took root here. They had devil-may-care leaders and believed in rapacious, happy gods. They too had their warlike songs, full of the sea and bloodshed and adventure. They had left their own country because their power had expanded and they needed to wield it. Along their way they had found England and seized it. They were masters of the sea. They had superior armor: steel helmet, ironclad garment and an awesome hooked axe.

The Vikings built fortified cities. War was their profession. The conquered natives cultivated the land and worked for the masters. The conquerors took responsibility for defending them in time of danger. The country people, the Celts and the Saxons, were delighted to have found protectors against the troublemakers and the pirates. They were relieved that their own internal dissensions were of necessity at an end, and they obeyed gratefully.

These were the solid initial foundations on which feudalism was based. The ruler assumed certain obligations. He had to train himself constantly in hunting, duels, festive group sports as well as in preparation for war. He was the man of power. He stuck his chest out and defended the masses. And under his powerful wing, the masses could work peacefully and live their little lives in security.

6. But time does its duty, devouring all things. And it devoured these strong spirits too. Peace lay heavy on them. There was less danger. The military men waned. The sons and grandsons of the man of power stopped going to war. They changed their habits, took a liking to good food, sumptuous clothes, beautiful women, the sweet-tongued minstrel. Once again a mighty neighbor caught wind of their decline. And the sixth and final wave arrived—the Norman.

Centuries earlier they too had come down from the Scandinavian countries to conquer northern France. They had cast their roots on her rich soil, built castles and towers in her harbors, along her rivers, in her harsh mountain passes and fertile fields. Here too, the conquered natives tilled the earth and the conqueror waged war. At that time, the common people were in a state of upheaval. They kept changing place like clouds of locusts, and any country deficient in strong warriors was foredoomed. In order to be prepared at every moment, many of the Normans used to keep their horses saddled inside the great halls of their towers where they slept with their wives.

They had divided the land among themselves. Out of anarchy they had created order, hanging the bandits and murderers. And now they lived the austere life of dedicated men. Unlike the Saxons, they did not eat and drink day and night. Nor did they daydream and dance like the Celts. They were frugal, economical, vain. The spirit was awaking inside them, unburdening the flesh. They erected tall churches, constructed in an unprecedentedly strong yet graceful style.

They married Frenchwomen and learned their language. Here too, the women subdued and tamed the fierce conquerors. They began writing simple chronicles, free of rhetoric, crystal-clearly thought out. They were men of action. They hated flamboyant diction, irrational ecstasy, dim, confused passions. They lived and thought securely, within the fortified walls of sobriety.

They were strong and happy on the rich soil of France. But in time their numbers increased enormously. There was no longer room for them. And then one day, the bold ambitious William, Duke of Normandy, summoned his barons:

"The old king of England, Edward, has died," he told them. "His wife's brother, Harold, has been proclaimed king. But at one point when I was holding him prisoner here, I made him swear on the holy altar to remain my subject. And on these terms, I agreed to free him. But now he's trampled on his oath. He has dared ascend the throne without my permission. So let us equip a huge fleet and take our weapons. We will conquer the island and depose him from the throne. My subject's throne belongs to me!"

And when he saw his barons hesitating, as though they found the enterprise too daring and difficult, the cunning Duke set them this great bait:

"England," he said, "is rich. She has boundless forests and fields, rivers and lakes and great cities. All these will fall into our hands, and I swear to share them with you. Here the land is too constricted for us. We don't have enough room. With God's help, let us set out to war!"

The prospect of all this booty kindled the imagination of the greedy barons. Their slaves and peasants were enlisted and sent to the forests. To this very day we can still see them as they were, woven in the old tapestries: hewing trees, preparing timber, fitting out the keels of ships. These multicolored threads of wool immortalized this grand moment in England's destiny.

Fifteen thousand ironclad warriors gathered and five thousand cavalry. For fifteen days, strong winds blew. The ships could not stir. Finally a headwind started blowing. 750 ships unfurled their sails, and one autumn morning, on the twenty-eighth of September, 1066, the green coasts of England came into sight, smiling and once again beckoning seductively to these new and last lovers.

The Normans landed, mounted their horses, and hurled themselves against the Anglo-Saxon foot soldiers, scattering them every which way. Everything came easily to the brave and cunning Norman general-in-chief, William the Conqueror. When he had got the upper hand of London, he issued an edict, his first act being to establish order:

"I, King William, hail all the citizens of London, French and English. I place you all under protection of the Law. I grant every child the right to inherit from his father upon the latter's death. I will not let anyone do you wrong. God be with you!"

This proclamation became England's first established charter.

Once again new blood surged through the veins of England. Her fate was enriched. The Normans brought with them a superior civilization, a sage, tightly integrated governmental and economic organization, as well as a strict hierarchy. At the peak of this hierarchy stood the Duke of Normandy; after him, the feudal barons; under them the knights, and under these last, the subjects and the slaves, classes subdivided in a perfect way, each with its own inviolable obligations and rights.

They found and kept two of the old Saxon statutes: the land tax and the recruiting of the freemen. They organized law courts, summoned councils, curbed individual freedom. They imposed their own laws, at the same time accepting whatever local laws they could absorb and adapt. Whatever did not suit them, they annulled. With architectural coherence, they created a firm governmental, economic and social organization.

In the midst of the Saxon peasants, these Normans appeared as superior beings, gentle, civilized, talking a more cultivated language—aristocratic people. And they brought a new virtue to this still barbarous, undisciplined island: strict control of passion.

They built churches as beautiful as palaces, as strong as fortresses. They lived in well-constructed fortified strongholds and did not drink to excess. The French language was spoken now by the aristocratic classes and the royal court and the princes. The higher clergy spoke French and Latin. At first the ordinances and laws were composed in Latin, then later in French. To this day several French words and phrases are still preserved in the official language of England. The common people spoke the heavy peasant Saxon tongue. As yet, it was not written and that is why it preserved its marvelous plasticity. It was in a state of constant flux. In each word the main syllables were emphasized. Then little by little, from mouth to mouth, the unemphasized syllables disappeared and the monosyllabic words multiplied. Thus the English language was forged and acquired its unique conciseness and force.

Simultaneously, a strong royal authority was being created. When William had conquered his kingdom by force, he proclaimed the entire land of England as his own property. He kept most of the fiefs and the richest of them, and the rest he distributed to his barons. Each baron in turn kept as much as he wanted of these and distributed the remaining fiefs to his own knights. But since the nobles were incapable of cultivating the land by themselves, they made their subject peasants and slaves till the land and give them the crops.

By virtue of this system, the King was incomparably stronger than his nobles. No one dared rear his head against him. But in order to be still more secure, the wily Conqueror granted the common people liberties. In this way, he would have them on his own side in case the barons should one day dare to come to blows with the royal authority.

The King imposed his authority on the Church as well. Without royal approval, no bishop could be appointed by the Pope. The royal officials and nobles could not be judged by the ecclesiastical councils without the King's consent. No one had the right to correspond with the Pope in secret. In this island, there was one supreme coordinator of each and every power: the King.

A logically integrated architectural structure without a

single crack. But time passed over it and began knocking it down slowly, methodically. Feudalism in England moved through three fatal stages:

The first stage, the high point: The feudal princes with their organized unspent dynamic offered great services to the community. They risked their own lives to defend it from foreign invaders and internal uprisings. Whatever privileges they had were their rightful deserts. For without them, the country would have relapsed into slavery and anarchy.

The second stage, tradition: The nobles still had their ancestral privileges, but ceased offering the great services which their ancestors had offered the community. There were no longer any invaders or rebels. Security reigned. And if any enemy power did emerge, the mercenaries were there to arm themselves and fight it. The nobles were no longer protecting their country with their own vitals. Yet they were still being rewarded with privileges and fiefs, acting as though if they had not been there, the land would have been in danger.

Last of all, its third and fatal stage, decline: The feudal lords were now incapable of either protecting or preserving their privileges. They became more and more supererogatory and harmful to the community. Other uncorrupted social classes arose who deserved these privileges and who now assumed the power.

Here too, mercilessly, patiently, time fulfilled its mysterious mission of helping the seed (be it human or divine or a great civilization) to grow and flower and bear fruit and finally to decay. This decay then turns to fecund fertilizer, and time, the great gardener, plants a new seed till once again the wheel of Fate is set in motion.

■ ENGLISH COASTS

■ By now we were grazing the shores of England. The symmetrical buildings of Folkstone and the cherry-red brick house tops lay spread out before us in straight monotonous lines, like a Froebel Institute toy. The day was pleasant. A transparent fog trailed over the stones and grass. The body of England steamed, warmed by the weak sun, in the midst of the cold gray seas.

I was thinking to myself, this was the seacoast where the six waves of conquerors had let loose the four races. Surrounded on all sides by the sea, they had lunged one after another over the island, over green plains, low mountains, peaceful hills, with a damp, rainy climate, not too hot, not too chilly; an unstable climate fatal to men of delicate constitution, a tonic to the strong.

The conquerors and the conquered tussled and compromised and intermingled to create Great Britain. The Saxons gave their coarse peasant qualities; they had a commonplace, secure way of thinking. They were stubborn materialists, heavy eaters and drinkers, and they loved their individual liberty. They used to raise their drawbridges so that no one could enter without their permission.

The Celts offered their poetry, love of music, dancing, singing. They were intoxicated with beauty, abandoned to daydreaming. Their blue eyes pulsed with desires and visions:

The Vikings and the Danes offered their love of the sea,

their nervousness and love of adventure. They could not adjust to houses and intangible dreams. Singing and dancing were all very well, so long as they came after the dangerous adventure. Beauty was not the essence of life; it was a mere embellishment thereof. They looked beyond the sky and sea and boarded their ships to discover at all costs what lay beyond, behind that sky and sea.

The Normans gave their organization, discipline, order. They were economical householders. They enjoyed bridling their power in order to use it for beneficial works at the right moment. Lovers of logic, they despised (despised and feared) all that was vague, undefined, unexpressed, all idle desires. Above all other things, they valued form.

Each race deposited its capital in the Bank of England. They all intermingled. None of them disappeared. None of them surrendered unconditionally. They all remained utterly alive, even to this day, both when fighting each other and when working together. That is why the English spirit is so rich, so full of opposing impulses—its practical mentality and its streak of daydreaming, its love of comfort and its love of adventure, its passion and its silence. For often all four races are vying within the same heart.

What is the central purpose common to all their endeavors? What is the synthesizing goal where all the ingredients of the English spirit were, and are still, aimed and united? What are they pursuing? Which bluebird?

Every great people that created a civilization had its own bluebird: Greece beauty, Rome the state, the Jews divinity, the Indians Nirvana, the Christian civilization kingdom come. The English people? Which is the bluebird hunted by Great Britain through the ages?

This was the question ruffling my innermost being from the moment I first set foot on the cliffs of England. Each new plot of earth we tread can and must become a catalyst for broadening our own spirits. The spirit too has its own imperialistic desires. It neither can nor should exist without conquest, for it too is akin to the great *Conquistadores*, considering mainland and sea alike as its own ancestral heritage, longing to occupy the entire surface of the world, both visible and invisible.

"What is the good of conquering the whole world without liberating your own soul?" the Christian ascetics used to query.

"How can you liberate your own soul unless you conquer the whole world," the avaricious spirits of the modern day retort.

A tremendous joy and a tremendous agony. And when my own spirit first came in contact with England, it was pinioned to her soil like a spear. What is the way to master a country? There is but one way: by discovering its meaning. So let us try to discover the meaning of England.

THE WHITE MAN'S BURDEN

I was walking in the port of Folkstone with a young Englishman I had just met in the course of crossing the Channel. He had been in Paris—a sort of spiritual honeymoon, a gift from his father upon finishing his studies at Oxford the previous year. He was on his way back now. His mind was dazzled by the playful sparkle of Paris, so superficial and yet so deep.

For a serious Englishman, such a journey was like a journey to Cythera. His imagination had set sail. As an inexperienced traveler, excited and in the springtime of his youth, he had ecstatically distorted French logic, metamorphosing it into carefree airiness. Now that he was coming back to Puritanical England, he was blushing a bit, smiling furtively, as though returning at dawn from some house of ill repute and opening the paternal gates like a thief, afraid that the stairs might creak as he went up them. In a happy, shamefaced way he was licking his lips.

He was not aware (and this was the whole charm of the journey—otherwise, would it have been a honeymoon?) that the house from which he was returning was the neatest, most rigorous and sober house in all Europe.

Here in this northern port, I felt pleased to find this youthful, downy-cheeked innocence, contrasting so sharply with the thousand-year-old rapacious soul of the Oriental, who has no innocence.

I sometimes think that we of the Oriental, tormented, pain-steeped ports, where the air has been permeated with desires for thousands of years, are like crafty old men going to the innocent, barbarous, ephebic North, our eyes forever seeking, greedy, yet slightly tired and derisive, as though knowing everything. These races of the Orient are old ladies, heavy and primordial. And even to the most insignificant Oriental child, life beckons in a way that transcends the short-lived experience of the individual and embraces the entire memory of the race.

The expression "How *old* are you?" should not be used, as English-speaking people do use it, when they ask the age of even a child. We are the ones who should use it, and it is the children of the Orient who should answer: "I'm an old man two years old . . . three years old . . ."

I turned toward this young, downy-cheeked Englishman. "And now," I asked him, "what are you planning to do? You've finished Oxford. You've been to Paris and enjoyed it. The romance is over now. Reality is starting. Which way will it go?"

He pointed toward the sea, southeastward.

"That way!" he answered calmly.

"India?"

"India. My father was in the service there, and I'll do the

same. I'll follow the same path. I was born over there in a tropical climate, in the shadow of huge banana trees—in Ceylon. The climate is hard on us. My father insisted it was better for me to go to Canada or Australia. But India attracts me. 'I'll go the same place you went,' I told my father. 'I'll carry on your way.' My father smiled. 'That's the same answer I gave my father,' he told me. 'He too was in the service in India.'"

The way Englishmen talk, their eyes penetrate all five continents. Later on, throughout my entire sojourn, I kept noticing that the English speak *sub specie globi*. Nothing seems far away to them—exile, the end of the world. They move easily from one continent to the other, with familiarity. You sense they are treading, bestriding the earth as though it belonged to them.

This unsophisticated young man talked of India, Canada, Australia, as though they were three adjacent points on the horizon and he had just stopped for a moment to choose among them. Other peoples move from country to country, mentally or on foot, or by donkey or barges, or at the very most, by boat or train. The English move in airplanes.

And what's more, wherever they go, even the most backward, distant country, they are able to settle down comfortably, because everywhere, they carry England with them.

From the time I was a small child I can remember when they came and settled in Herakleion, Crete. Immediately they set about clearing a wide field out beyond the army barracks. There they made a lawn and began playing tennis! Then when several of their officers climbed the peak of Mt. Psiloritis, their guide, a delightful old man from the village of Anóyia, informed me in amazement, "My dear lad, these men are stark raving mad. When we got up there on top of Psiloritis, it was so cold we thought our last hour had come. And, lad, they started shaving themselves up there on the rock. They undressed, changed their clothes, put on some black jackets, black trousers pressed just right, white waistcoats and starched shirts. And then they sat down and began eating, I made the sign of the cross. 'Good God Almighty,' said I, 'what men are these!' "

Very simply, they were Englishmen. Each Englishman is an England and moves as a whole in harmony with his island. They are rulers and can travel with much luggage. They are traveling with England.

I was still carried away by the thoughts I had had as I approached the English coasts—about the great races that had taken root on this soil and on these rocks. I scrutinized my young friend, trying to discover which of all the races was uppermost—Saxon? Norman? Celt? Or Viking?

"Which do you prefer?" I asked him. "The land or the sea?"

"I like the land," came his answer. "The green, well-trimmed grass. But—" He stood there watching the sea beating fiercely against the rocks now. He was silent. After a while he turned around. "Do you like our poet, Kipling?" he asked me.

"Very much!"

"Then you must know these words:

" *'Therefore, from job to job I've moved along.*
Pay couldn't 'old me, when my time was done,
For something in my 'ead upset it all,
Till I 'ad dropped whatever 'twas for good,
An', out at sea, be 'eld the dock-lights die,
An' met my mate—the wind that tramps the world!'

"They're from 'Sestina of the Tramp-Royal.' "

His voice had become suddenly warm. Paris had vanished, submerged inside him. The well-trimmed lawns had disappeared, and his spirit had set sail.

"Viking!" I murmured to myself contentedly.

No one feels so deeply as the Englishman the irrepressible, seductive call of the horizon. Inside the soul of even the most tight-lipped practical Englishman, there is a little window open toward the ocean. A mysterious charm, unsilenceable voices, a romantic yearning to board ship and plunge into adventures. The history of England—her commerce, her politics, her art, her glory—is drenched in the sea.

The English love the land, the green lawns, the wooden fences bordering the private estates. They love the pleasant tranquillity of the countryside. But deeper down, they feel the sea as their native land, their own domain. Ever since the night the awesome Armada crashed off the cliffs of England, the English people have held dominion over the sea. It has belonged to them. They struggled enormously, suffered enormously in order to acquire it, and now they can no longer do without it. The sea is the greatest graveyard for the English people—"Every wave conceals an Englishman."

Nothing is more enticing for the English than strange tales of the sea, pirate adventures, sea heroes. From the time they are small children, they dream of distant travels and sea-swashed glory. The sea satisfies the romantic, anxious necessities of the English spirit; the land, her practical, conservative, stubborn needs.

"You're a Viking," I said to my friend, as though trying to help him distinguish the historic roots within him. "You're a Viking, not a Saxon."

The young man shrugged his shoulders. "I've never been interested in analyzing the various bloods flowing through my veins," he remarked. "It's enough to have them flowing regularly and strongly. In case they ever vie among themselves, no one should learn of it. These are our own private affairs, of no use to anyone else. And even we ourselves should not scratch beneath the surface very much—because that way, we cannot act."

"But," I kept insisting, on purpose, "it's such a fine thing to be able to glance to the right and left, in the course of acting."

"Perhaps," the young man answered politely. "But I remember once at Oxford, I was running a race with a friend of mine up some hill. The winner would be given a branch of flowering lilac. We began running. He was better than me, out ahead of me. But the moment we'd nearly got there, I don't know how or why, I passed him, got there first, and I was given the lilac branch. Our professor asked him: 'What happened to you, Samuel? Why did you stop like that?' 'I was looking at the landscape,' my friend answered. 'It was so pleasant!'

" 'When you're running a race to reach a certain point,' the professor remarked severely, 'you must never look to the right or left!' "

When I am speaking with someone, nothing pleases me more than to see him contradicting me, so long as this contradiction is based on unshakable arguments. I know that he is right, and at the same time, that I too am right—each one on a different level.

There are two or three levels, perhaps four. Each level has its own purposes and, therefore, its own truths and ethics. So in the course of talking with a person, you may notice that he has suddenly climbed up or down a flight and is supporting a truth of no value outside its own sphere.

This young Englishman was satisfied with his answer and stood there smiling at me.

"What do you think of that?" he asked politely.

"You're right," I answered with the same politeness,

shifting down to his own level. Then to change the subject, "Was England always an island?" I asked.

"Apparently, a few thousand years ago, it was still part of continental Europe," he answered.

"I don't mean an island, geologically speaking. My question was if, psychologically speaking, England has always been an island."

The young man lowered his head to think. His cheeks turned crimson from the effort. "I don't entirely understand your question," he finally said.

"I mean this: At what point did the English begin to perceive that they were distinct from Europe? It seems to me it's been more than three or three and a half centuries—"

"You're right!" the young man answered, finally having understood what I was asking. "For many centuries we felt ourselves connected with Europe. We had continental ambitions; we wanted to *occupy* France. Yes, indeed, psychologically speaking, we were not always an island."

"When the Armada crashed and you formed your own great fleet; when you cut your chains and bonds with the Pope and liberated yourselves in the religious sphere as well. At that point, England became an island psychologically.

"What's more, her geographical position shifted too. Until then, she had lain at the outer edge of the universe, beyond which nothing existed—an unexplored wasteland of sea. But with the discovery of America, a shift of interests occurred. And England's geographical position shifted with them. The world widened, and instead of England's being cast off at the edge, she now acquired a central position in the inhabited world, between Europe and America. Before her stretched the boundless plantation of the Atlantic for her to plow."

I felt abashed for having gotten so carried away. My friend was thirsty. We passed a bar.

"Shall we have a whiskey?" he suggested.

We sat down. He stared out at the sea and the departing boats. And I said nothing, trying to complete my train of thought, for if it stopped short like that, it would bother me.

I drank my whiskey, feeling that as I drank this precious, disagreeable liquid, I was becoming mystically united with the English race. We drank another whiskey and yet another. My mind was inundated by the light giddiness, the dignified exhilaration this English drink induces.

Like fragments of the English coastlines, thousands of vessels sailing under the British flag to seize the five oceans flitted through my mind. Merchant-pirates forged new roads. Walter Raleigh founded the first colony in Virginia. The first cortege of ships set sail for the mysterious Indies, rich in precious stones, silks, spices and people. The English flag moved from sea to sea. From continent to continent it was hoisted up as it chased away the Spanish, Portuguese, Dutch, and French flags. The British Empire expanded over one fourth of the terrestrial globe.

The body and spirit of the nation expanded as well. At the universities, fiery nationalists preached grand imperialistic crusades to the young men.

"England," proclaimed Sir Charles Dilke in 1868, "must take Asia and Africa, the coasts of South America and the bridges between England and the Indies. A triple alliance: England, England's possessions, and the United States of America. Thus will the English aristocratic race dominate the earth and international peace reign throughout the world."

Then came the great poet of imperialism, Rudyard Kipling:

*Come up, come in from Eastward, from the guardports
of the Morn!*
Beat up, beat in from Southerly, O gipsies of the Horn!
*Swift shuttles of an Empire's loom that weave us main to
main,*
*The Coastwise lights of England give you welcome back
again.*

> —"The Coastwise Lights"

We are the sons of Martha, he cried, not the sons of
Mary! We create acts. We battle with reality and fashion it
in our own image and likeness. And what is the English
form of destiny? Duty. For this duty we live and work and
fight. Every Englishman must risk his own being for the
whole, must consider himself a representative of his whole
race and be aware of the great responsibility. Success, happiness, the salvation of the entire Empire—we must feel
that these are our right and duty.

Keep ye the Law—be swift in all obedience—
Clear the land of evil, drive the road and bridge the ford.
Make ye sure to each his own
That he reap where he hath sown;
*By the peace among our peoples let men know we serve
the Lord!*

> —"A Song of the English"

What does it mean in English to say, "We serve the
Lord"? It means: "We are working with human beings,
performing our human duty, struggling to organize the
chaos within us and outside us, to create order, to fight
against hunger, illness, injustice, laziness." Take up the
white man's burden.

For Kipling, the poet of the race, human beings—and
above all, the English—are duty-bound to kick against the

downstream current, to stand like alert watchmen over their own souls and over the world, to concentrate their power and never let themselves become panic-stricken. The spirit of the genuine person must ally itself with the rising international tide, must ally itself with the Lord of the Powers. It must not sit passively and idly at His feet like Mary, in ecstatic adoration. No, it must stand at His side like Martha to fight with her against fear, laziness, apathy.

The mind must not be considered as the highest acquisition. The brain is suspect. It betrays readily, moves deviously, and like a lawyer enjoys defending now the good, now the bad, just to revel in its own nimbleness and skill. The supreme human virtue is character. A strong will; an organized, disciplined power with a sure monolithic "Yes" to all that is light and a sure monolithic "No" to the darkness.

"What are you thinking?" my young friend asked me. "Shall we have another whiskey?"

"What is your favorite song? What has most helped you in the course of your life?" I asked, my mind very far away from the whiskey.

The young Englishman's eyes sparkled. He did not hesitate a moment:

"Kipling's 'If,' " he said. "I first read it when I was twelve years old. I understood it somewhat later. From then on, it's been my Gospel."

I recalled that stern and manly chant:

If you can keep your head when all about you
Are losing theirs and blaming it on you,
If you can trust yourself when all men doubt you,
But make allowance for their doubting too;
If you can wait and not be tired by waiting,
Or being lied about, don't deal in lies

Or being hated don't give way to hating,
And yet don't look too good, nor talk too wise,

. . . .

If you can dream—and not make dreams your master,
If you can think and not make thoughts your aim,

. . . .

If neither foes nor loving friends can hurt you,
If all men count with you, but none too much;
If you can fill the unforgiving minute
With sixty seconds' worth of distance run,
Yours is the Earth and everything that's in it,
    And—which is more—you'll be a Man, my son!

I shook my head in anger and grief. I was thinking of all those young Greeks to the south. How heavy such a gospel would lie on them. Force and discipline, passion and silence. To be all on fire and yet let out no smoke!

■ LONDON

HOA-HAKA-NAKA-YA

To enable the mind to conquer chaos, order must be imposed. The chaos must be pushed and twisted and worn down according to the laws of the mind. A simile, a symbol, a myth must be found to bury chaos in a convenient mold. Thus it becomes endowed with a human form, a familiar form our mind is capable of loving.

Just such an ideogram for imprisoning and subjecting the chaos of London in a human way to a symbolic framework I thought I had discovered one day in the entrance to the British Museum, off to the right where the columns are. An amazing stone statue from the distant, mysterious islands of the Pacific Ocean. The form of an exotic, omnipotent, slightly sad god, Hoa-Haka-Naka-Ya.

I never let a day go by all the time I was staying in London, without pausing for a moment to stand before it. In mute and motionless silence I used to greet it gratefully. For it saved me from the chaos. An enormous pointed head, carved in broad abrupt levels; a narrow forehead; heavy cheekbones; thick open nostrils pulsing with desire; deep-set eyes, like black springs in some ancient cave. And his mouth big, hungry, savage.

As long as I lived in that gigantic city, the more I entered its hidden, often repulsive charms, the more insistently a strange idea was crystallizing inside me . . . that this god

Hoa-Haka-Naka-Ya was the patron saint, the tutelary deity of London.

An invisible magic bond links this carved stone with the great city, just as the word London is linked magically with its meaning. To be sure, this connection I had made was only my own individual, irrational imagining. But for me it was useful and that was why I cultivated it—to understand London better. Every human being, whether consciously or unconsciously, takes a guide, visible or invisible, in order to become familiar with a city. For my own spirit, this god was the finest guide to London, and with a sly smile I followed him.

As I stood there before this primitive, crudely carved stone, I only needed to break through its comfortable human limits in order to plunge into a roaring flood—a slow-moving, broad, creative rhythm. I could let my own blood stream assume its rhythm, not caring at all about any operation of the human intellect. I felt precisely the same way as a person feels on entering a dark forest full of invisible dangers; on embarking upon sexual love; on pondering death or after-death; or on stretching the memory to the utmost (to a point where the cerebrum begins cracking) in an effort to recall how that primitive chaos had been before the mind had come to confine it and tidy it up into a cosmos, that is, into a human order.

I felt both afraid and happy, for I knew that I had only to solidify the lines again in order for the chaos to become subjected to the firm outline of my god.

So from the day I discovered my mystic guide, I could sink into a disconnected, wordless, irrational London devoid of a beginning, a middle and an end. I was no longer afraid of losing its meaning.

London is chaos . . . without any plan or logic; an omnipotent, slightly melancholy, insatiable chaos. A dark tropical forest whose sole architect, Time, is fussy, con-

tradictory, charmingly naïve, full of irrational append-
ages.

You walk without being able to foresee anything. There
is no logic here whose laws can be learned so that from the
premises, unerring results can be divined. You come to the
end of an avenue flooded with brilliant light and people,
only to fall unexpectedly into some poor antiquated little
village full of narrow lanes. You pass quickly through it
and there, rising before you, stands a modern building with
its reinforced concrete, electric advertisements and glass.
Wandering through the streets of London, you feel the
excitement of the hunter; from moment to moment, you
never know what prey may spring at you.

In her big streets, the rhythm of London is broad, deep,
almost silent like that of a big river. All those races that
we watched breaking like waves over the grassy meadows
of Great Britain, you can see here suddenly right before
you, after all these centuries, clearly reincarnated in the
highly diverse passersby. Blond, rosy-red Viking giants;
clever, lithe, daydreaming Celts with blue eyes; Norman
gentlemen with eagle eyes and a tranquil, steady gait.
Short, swarthy, ancient Iberians, restless and rapacious.

And more often than all the others, in the shops and
trams and pubs, you can see the thickset, well-built, abrupt
but kindhearted Saxons, with their athletic flesh, their
short bull-like necks, and the everlasting pipe wedged between their broken teeth.

Like tall lighthouses set plunk in the middle of this
human sea, the policemen keep the waves in order. And
amid those great throngs, occasionally one of them can be
seen striding with steady steps, holding a little dog in his
arms. The poor little thing had gotten dazed and couldn't
find its way across to the opposite bank. And so the dragon
with the child's heart had taken pity on it, picked it up and
carried it across.

A deep rumbling sound, an inexhaustible world, thousands of people rising and falling like inundating rivers. Then you turn around suddenly to find yourself in a silent cool park full of little sparrows and felicity. If you were to open the heart of an Englishman, you would find in its very center a plot of ancient grass. An Englishman's greatest joy is to live in the countryside. And when he is forced to live in the city, he is deeply nostalgic for the country. But since he cannot always go out to find it, he brings it back into the midst of his own dark, sooty, fog-enveloped purlieus.

The park is like the erotic haiku those formidable Samurai warriors used to hide in their bosoms in between their iron armor and their silk shirts—

> O *the nightingale's song*
> *and the flooding moon*
> *and my cup of spilled milk!*

These parks are remains of ruined monasteries, aristocratic gardens, old thickly wooded groves. They have their roots and drink in the swamps where the giant city of *Lon-don*, the "watch-tower of the swamps," had been built. The very first moment he can, an Englishman of the working classes or middle classes as well as the gentleman of leisure goes and sits by his ancestral totem, the tree—or stretches out on the grass or strolls calmly, mutely beneath the green foliage, wearing the ecstatic, controlled, slightly grief-worn expression of an aging lover.

They say a rose blooms in the midst of hell. Similarly idealized by contrast with the thankless struggle for life encircling them, the London parks induce an inexpressible delight, nostalgia for some past or future happiness. The paradise of the Englishman is bedizened with lawns. And over these felicitous lawns, the saints of Great

Britain stroll, smoking their pipes and holding their eternal umbrellas.

But the rhythm of the park—trees growing amid deep silence, drops of dew on the leaves, chipper blackbirds dipping their monkish heads in the water as they bathe themselves—all this seems contrary to nature nowadays. Neither our bodies nor our minds can find rest. These days, we find the foolish method of the ostrich utterly humiliating. Our hearts reject it. The natural climate of our spirits, willy-nilly, is the state of upheaval, rage, war.

After a brisk walk through the park, I came out into the din of Trafalgar Square. I stood there looking up at the bronze statute of Horatio Nelson, set on that gigantic pillar like a stylite upright against the clouds. After years and years have passed, it is the individual inner life of the hero that moves us most deeply. A hero's deeds have been embodied in history, indissolubly fused with his race. And if they are tremendously great deeds, they become impersonal and merge imperceptibly into the Chronicles of Man. Only in the ephemeral vivid events of his own everyday life does he preserve his own face, and this is usually bathed in tears.

For a moment there, looking up at Nelson, I could sense his victories rushing through my mind, his great achievements and brave contribution to the glory of England. But soon all this became one with English destiny. His own personal seal faded and only Nelson the man, remained, naked, bereft of his three-cornered hat and medals, alone with his own wounded heart.

How this hero loved! And what a tender heart this leonine warrior had, and how it trembled every time he thought about that disreputable woman in whose nets he had been trapped! "The thoughts of such happiness, my dearest only beloved, make the blood fly into my head."

In just such a way, his great adversary used to imagine Josephine making love with other men, and just at that point he was writing her those childish, heart-rending letters from his victory camp—"I care nought for the war. I care nought for victory! You are the only thing I think of!"

This hero Nelson, who today stands in the clouds, was dragged about by the beautiful but insufferable coquette Lady Hamilton as a bear might be dragged about by his trainer, one of his friends remarked bitterly. She decked him out in all his medals, pinned his three-cornered hat on him and the Sultan's aigrette. Then she would cart him about to the salons, making him happy but ridiculous.

His friend St. Vincent wrote: "This poor miserable great man, where has she landed him! She whose hair is never washed, who dresses so boorishly, and whose belt is always stuck between her shoulders!"

And to think this man had made "All or nothing!" the principle of his life! But one day he turned overwhelmingly bitter. Shortly after the Victory of the Nile, he wrote: "There is no true happiness in this life, and in my present state I could quit it with a smile . . . Believe me, my only wish is to sink with honour into the grave."

But once again Circe showered her sweet poisons on him, until one day the proud conqueror, trusting like all lovers that the woman he loved was the sole source of his greatness, sank to the point of writing: "Brave Emma!— Good Emma!—If there were more Emmas, there would be more Nelsons."

At Trafalgar he fell and died, and he was laid in the coffin (carved out of the mast of an enemy ship) that he carried with him always. And so he escaped.

Like some dense dream, this London mist is good for walking in and remolding Fate out of the wind and rain and frost. Damp and yellowish, the mist slips along, licking the walls, enveloping the trees and people, penetrating and settling in their lungs. In rising, it obliterates Nelson. In descending, it shrouds the details, softens the harshnesses, glorifies the rags and endows the ugliness with a mysterious, other-worldly grace.

A gray slow-rolling sea, where thousands of houses are drowned and the red avenues stir like gigantic goldfish, the electric lights all lit and the flocks of people moving like anchovies. London assumes the nobility and aristocratic atmosphere of a sunken city. She has sunk altogether, and out of the cataclysm, rising like motionless ghosts, only the Tower of London and the enormously tall column where Nelson rises and the finely carved stone walls of Westminster are still left standing.

From time to time the sun, like a bald Apollo, pierces the frost and the leaves of the trees and the people's noses. Here the sun often merges with the mist and rain. There is no abrupt break. Light plays incessantly with darkness. London weeps and smiles simultaneously. The smile conceals itself discreetly, half grief-worn, half mocking, flashing playfully through the thick tears. And the tears at the very moment they long to burst, control themselves out of pride and politeness, turning to a smile just as the smile begins to cloud. Thus suddenly for the first time, here in London, we sense that English humor was created unconsciously along with the weather, the climate, the pride.

THE BRITISH MUSEUM

If Time had a home—if it were some delicate aristocrat capable of cherishing and remembering its beautiful moments in the past, surely the British Museum would be its home!

What a joy to lose yourself in the endless corridors there, transported from the one pole of time and space to the other, so to revel in the most refined of human endeavors. After all, what is this clay we call man, who in spite of hunger and illness and death is able to lift his head, stretch out his hand and so create immortal works?

Only in works of art is the miracle revealed so clearly— that a worm is capable of creating immortality. In action, we can see many faces: dense masses; an often anonymous, shoving group; a rich, complex collaboration. In art, a human being sits with pen or hammer or a few paints, stooped over, cramped, all alone. Just as the silkworm spins silk out of its own vitals (or rather, takes out its own entrails in the process of making the silk) to weave the miracle of the cocoon, so the artist is able to transform earth into a divine, precious substance.

I recalled some verses that used to keep my spirit in good order:

Like the golden silkworm, Buddha has
cast anchor on the branches of flowerless silence.
He has eaten all its leaves.
He has eaten all the leaves of the mulberry tree of earth,
He has eaten all the leaves
and made them into silk.

Like Buddha, the artist lives completely liberated and completely liberating matter.

If there were suddenly a great catastrophe, I was thinking to myself as I wandered about this infinite treasure house of man, an earthquake, fire, barbarian invasion . . . and if I had it in my power, what would I save of all these numberless good things?

My heart stirred as though this imaginary hypothesis were a reality; as though havoc had actually broken loose and I were rushing frenziedly from room to room, from work to work, struggling to choose—To choose . . . Yes,

but here you find a superb Chinese painting, there a divine
Egyptian statuette, and over there a lacily carved gold ornament from Peru, and you feel the need to rush and save
it alone. Then all at once a lament rises from all those
rooms, and this game of the imagination becomes a nightmare, and a cold sweat runs over you, for you long to save
everything and are not able to.

According to the day (whether it happened to be
washed in sun or rain), according to your own spirit renewing itself each day (like the vitals of Prometheus),
you would choose. For months I had been experiment-
ing with this maddening torture, and finally, I had discovered my three most stable loves in the British Museum
—the Assyrian bas-reliefs, the Persian miniatures, and class-
sical Greek art.

When I first came face to face with the huge square
balcony where the Assyrian bas-reliefs hung, I shuddered.
A primeval, age-old jungle, exploding in the workshops of
God and deep within our own spirits. A weighty vision,
an archaic prehuman recollection, powerful and murderous.
Kings with curly, thick-knit beards hunting lions; darting
arrows, some still poised in mid-air, roaring in the heart of
that terrifying silence; others piercing the lion's flesh like
spears. And the lions falling back, struggling with all four
legs to remove the arrow, or stretching out their necks to
vomit up a river of blood.

And the proud lioness, our big sister, pierced by three
mortal arrows, one at the base of her neck and two in her
kidneys, dragging along on her belly, her hind legs paralyzed, she bellowing through the air. This awesome cortege
of Destiny, whose bridegroom is no human being. Here the
kings and the people, mountains of taut flesh, look like
genuine gods. They smile inhumanly through their thick,
bloodthirsty, sensual lips. And the eyes of the lions over-
flow with human grief.

After basking for hours on end in this abominable cosmic vision, I rushed to the out-of-the-way rooms where the rainbow-colored miniatures are hung—tiny, charming, sweet-tempered, tender, voluptuous. I was rushing not in order to catch my breath or to forget the Assyrian horror. I was only striving to bring my spirit to fulfillment. From the dark base of our vitals, with its inhuman slaughter, to the highpoint of our vitals, a delicate, bloodless, beautiful flower.

A youth dressed in yellow silks, with a finely embroidered blue turban, reading poems ecstatically beneath a flowering tree; the blossoms entwining him and choking him; he is like a nightingale caught in the branches of springtime, raising its throat about to warble.

An ethereal Moslem palace, a rose-colored gate, an arabesque arch as its lintel, the king sitting cross-legged outside it on a divan, rendering judgment. The old councilors to his right and left like brightly colored birds, and behind them the open garden with its torchlike cypress, its flowering almond tree, its little poplar sprouting a few leaves, and a partridgelike bird with red legs strutting along the gate . . .

Further along, slender Arab horses, black and tawny and white ones, with half-moons on their necks. Women with painted nails, ribbon-thin eyebrows, almond eyes, stepping lightly, their arched red soles inscribed with precious proverbs from the Koran.

Their gilded background gives the impression that all these creatures live and breathe in an eternal, motionless, paradisiacal atmosphere. Visions woven of silks and flowers and birds, mysterious smiles and red lips. Here substance never became spirit and so never scattered. It attained its most charming fruition, preserving only the lines and the colors from all that weight.

Such is the Paradise of Saadi and Fra Angelico: dream

and plaything, the towering desire of the heart that loves the earth and transposes it to heaven; the slight intoxication of the mind that rebels against trailing like a prudent worm among the other solid bodies, of the mind that sprouts wings and returns to its own land as a butterfly.

With the Assyrian bas-reliefs steeped in flesh and mud, I descended into the terrifying caverns of the unconscious. With these miniatures, I could rise and float like rose-colored down, like a dream. I lost my human face, part beast, part cloud. After that, I felt the need of catching a firm hold on earth, the surface of the earth; walking solidly yet lightly over the earth. Neither beast, nor cloud, nor man.

At that point I could go with steady gait toward the huge hall with the Greek marbles, knowing that I had found the right way. A pagan joy; naked, sun-baked bodies. My lungs breathed deeply. There is an air of spring blowing here. At long last, the poisoned lip of Fate could laugh. Greek vision, fantastic, exiled, hanging like a meteor here amid this smoky fog.

In her sooty vitals, London stores these marble moments of the gods, just as some unsmiling Puritan might store in the depths of his memory some past erotic moment, blissful and ecstatic sin.

I stood in the presence of the Parthenon reliefs: high-breasted maidens carrying their offerings to the goddess; young men on horseback; venerable old men . . . and I perceived that the great secret of perfection in life and art goes by the name of balance. Neither violent movement nor the serenity of Paradise. Great opposing forces that become balanced, but still remain forcefully, imperceptibly palpitating.

Here in Greek art, the flesh did not need to grow heavy in order to acquire force. Nor did it need to become ethereal in order to acquire grace. Here the flesh succeeded in

disencumbering matter without robbing it of its force—
disencumbering it up to the point where grace begins. If
it had gone slightly more in one direction, it would have
become strong but lacking in movement. A bit more in the
other direction, and it would have become charming but
insipid. But it discovered the superb, infinitely delicate
border line of perfect balance, invisible to the naked eye,
and there it stopped. This is the Greek miracle.

The Greek craftsman entered the forest of life with all
its tremendous confusion and darkness, where we cannot
see the sky, where we feel smothered. He entered the forest
of life and began working away. He cleared the chaos, expelled all the superfluous elements, made the forest into a
tree and the tree into a column. And when he emerged,
the whole forest had become concentrated into a Doric
column. This column was the essence of the forest, and
this essence was what he sought. And this column smelled
of pine or cypress. It was no abstract, odorless ideogram.
It bore the scent of wood and resin. When we touch it, we
are aware of its origin.

In moments of Dionysiac exaltation, we can make it
grow branches and leaves, turning it back into a tree. Moving further on into this state of ecstasy we can turn it into
a forest. We feel free. There is no fear of getting lost. For
it remains eternally sober, a never-moving border line between abstract thought and forest. And when we return to
our own human dominion, we confront it once again in its
immovable state as a Doric column.

If God were to demand an apologia from His peoples,
and require each nation to give an account of the several
(one or two or five) talents entrusted to it, then the
Greeks with their athletic nakedness and fresh-washed
hair and strong knees would have stood up to answer in a
free and manly voice (neither beseeching nor blaspheming):

"Before we came, men shrieked in shrill voices like birds and human desires raved, unable to articulate a sober word.

"We pursued the Word beyond chaos. We cut its wings and set it over the pediments of the mind as Wingless Victory.

"Before we came, Thought was an undisciplined throng, prattling and disorderly, terrified by thunder, lightning, dreams and death. It could not be mustered into an organized phalanx. At the first onslaught of darkness, it scattered.

"We are the ones who organized Thought. We created the syllogism—thesis, antithesis, synthesis—we opened roads, discovered laws, overcame chaos.

"Before we came, matter was the great enemy—heavy, miserable, gloomy. Born a slave, it had come to enslave man. Born without a brain, it had enslaved the brain.

"We wrestled with matter, stubbornly, purposefully, as man wrestles with woman. We discovered its secret doors and entered. And matter surrendered. We kissed its mouth, and its vitals filled with a son. The mind had found its mate.

"If each nation were to find its post in the government of the universe and assume a responsible position, we Greeks should have been appointed the architects of the world!"

This, I believe, is how the Greeks would have spoken if they had had to describe their use of the five talents entrusted to them by God—their five senses.

How long did the Greek miracle last? A moment, a lightning flash. But what does that matter?

Perfection lasts no more than that, nor is there any need for it to last more. It reveals the heights man is capable of attaining, and these heights now stand as the eternal landmark of human excellence. Soon the Doric column sprouted leaves, once again longing to return to the tree.

Hellenic art became Hellenistic, and Hellenistic Oriental. But what does that matter? Its mission was fulfilled, and it was free to go its way.

I remember that for days on end I used to visit the British Museum, wandering about in a trance, undecided between these three loves of mine—the Assyrian reliefs, the Oriental miniatures, and the Greek marbles. I was trying to discover the secret of each, to make a hierarchy of my desires, so as to organize my own inner disorder.

After several days of vacillation, in case I would have to choose one of those three visions, I finally felt certain of the one I would pick. Yet deep inside me, I felt that at the instant of the great disaster—earthquake, fire, barbarian invasion—I would not have chosen as I should have done. At the last moment, I would have chosen to save the wounded Assyrian lioness—my sister.

THE CITY

I was exhausted by the time I went out through the great wrought-iron gate of the Museum, out into the fresh air. I felt as though I had just escaped from a nightmare and was now able to breathe. But then one day I stumbled into another nightmare, this one modern, throbbingly alive—the City, the labyrinthine, profit-minded brain of London with its veins of gold. Narrow twisting lanes, the tension of the interests, the great temples of contemporary religion—the Stock Exchange, the Bank of England, Guildhall. And nearby along the riverbanks, loaded warehouses where all the good things of the entire earth are stored. As you stroll past, your nostrils fill with the scents rising from the barrels of wine and resin being lowered by pulleys down into the coal-cellars, as well as spices and coffee, mothballs and leather skins and exotic fruits.

The whole earth and sea collaborate in order to fill these warehouses. "Our slaves begin at Calais," an Englishman once remarked. The five continents carry their little presents to their master: Canada and Russia wheat; the Scandinavian countries wood; Australia wool and fruits; Egypt and the Indies and China cotton, rice, tea; Africa, sugar, coffee and tobacco. And even Mexico sends its great princess, the Gulf Stream, to warm her. The various countries of Europe sent their kings: the Normans, the French, Holland and Hanover. And Greece sends her tobacco, raisins, sponges, and her marble gods.

As I walked through the crooked narrow streets of the City, through all this fog, I kept thinking of a faraway, blazing day on the second of September, 1666. That day it was not the fog that gave London her beauty, but another savage element—fire. Thirteen thousand houses turned to ashes and one hundred churches. It was early one Sunday morning. Samuel Pepys, a high official in the Admiralty, famous for the cynical diary he has left us, was sleeping peacefully by his wife's side.

September 2nd (Lord's Day) Some of our mayds sitting up late last night to get things ready against our feast to-day, Jane called us up about three in the morning to tell us of a great fire they saw in the City. So I rose and slipped on my night-gowne and went to her window, and thought it to be on the back-side of Marke-lane at the farthest; but, being unused to such fires as followed, I thought it far enough off; and so went to bed again and to sleep. About seven rose again to dress myself, and there looked out at the window and saw the fire not so much as it was, and further off. . . . By and by Jane comes and tells me that she hears that above 300 houses have been burned down all Fish-Street, by London Bridge. So I made myself ready presently, and walked to the Tower, and there got up upon one of the high

places. . . . And there I did see the houses at that
end of the bridge all on fire, and an infinite great fire
on this and the other side the end of the bridge. So
with my heart full of trouble, I down to the water-
side, and there got a boat and through bridge and
there saw a lamentable fire. . . . Everybody endeav-
ouring to remove their goods, and flinging into the
river or bringing them into lighters that lay off. . . .
And among other things the poor pigeons, I perceived, were loth to leave their houses, but hovered
about the windows and balconys till they were, some
of them burned their wings. . . . And the wind
mighty high and driving it into the City, and everything after so long a drought proving combustible,
even the very stones of churches, I to Whitehall and
there up to the King's closett in the Chappell, where
people come about me and I did give them an account dismayed them all, and word was carried in to
the King. So I was called for and did tell the King
and Duke of Yorke what I saw, and that unless his
Majesty did command houses to be pulled down
nothing could stop the fire. They seemed much troubled, and the King commanded me to go to my Lord
Mayor from him and command him to spare no
houses, but to pull down before the fire every way
. . . At last met my Lord Mayor in Canning Street
like a man spent, with a handkerchev about his neck.
To the King's message he cried, like a fainting
woman, "Lord! what can I do? I am spent: people
will not obey me. I have been pulling down houses,
but the fire overtakes us faster than we can do it."
That he needed no more soldiers; and that for himself, he must go and refresh himself, having been up
all night. So he left me, and I him, and walked home,
seeing people all almost distracted; and no manner of

means used to quench the fire. The houses, too, so very thick thereabouts, and full of matter for burning, as pitch and tarr, in Thames-street; and warehouses of oyle, and wines, and brandy and other things. . . .

By this time it was about twelve o'clock; and so home, and there find my guests, which was Mr. Wood and his wife Barbary Sheldon, and also Mr. Moone: she mighty fine, and her husband, for aught I see, a likely man. . . . We had an extraordinary good dinner, and as merry as at this time we could be. . . . Soon as dined, I and Moone away, and walked through the City, the streets full of nothing but people and horses and carts loaden with goods, ready to run over one another, and removing goods from one burned house to another . . . River full of lighters and boats taking in goods, and goods swimming in the water, and only I observed that hardly one lighter or boat in three that had the goods of a house in, but there was a pair of virginalls in it . . . and the wind great. So near the fire as we could for smoke; and all over the Thames, with one's face in the wind, you were almost burned in a shower of fire-drops . . . and as it grew darker, appeared more and more, and in corners and upon steeples, and between churches and houses, as far as we could see up the hill of the City, in a most horrid malicious bloody flame, not like the fine flame of an ordinary fire. Barbary and her husband away before us. We staid till, it being darkish, we saw the fire as only one entire arch of fire from this to the other side the bridge, and in a bow up the hill for an arch of above a mile long: it made me weep to see it. The churches, houses, and all on fire and flaming at once; and a horrid noise the flames made, and the

cracking of houses at their ruine. So home with a
sad heart, and there find everybody discoursing and
lamenting the fire; and poor Tom Hater come with
some few of his goods saved out of his house, which
is burned upon Fish-streete Hill. . . . So we were
forced to begin to pack up our owne goods, and prepare for their removal; and did by moonshine (it being brave dry, and moonshine, and warm weather)
carry much of my goods into the garden, and Mr.
Hater and I did remove my money and iron chests
into my cellar (some 2350 pounds), as thinking that
the safest place.

A few days later, in the course of describing the terrible
catastrophe, Pepys recorded the petty circumstances of
his own life (of great importance to himself):

We dined on an earthen platter—a fried breast of
mutton; a great many of us, but very merry, and indeed as good a meal, though as ugly a one, as ever I
had in my life. . . .
I went the first time into a naked bed, only my
drawers on; and did sleep pretty well. . . . to Mar-
tin, and, there did *tout ce que je voudrais avec*
her, and drank, and away by water home and to dinner, Balty and his wife there. After dinner I took
him down with me to Deptford, and there by the
Bezan loaded above half my goods and sent them
away. So we back home, and then I found occasion
to return in the dark and to Bagwell, and there did
do all that I desired. . . .

In the heart of all that turmoil, poor miserable Life was
carrying on her own rhythm—like a singed cat, wounded
but still alive.

■ ■

The City was reduced to ashes. A grand joy for the architects, a unique opportunity for creating a new modernized city with broad streets, ventilation and lighting and squares and centers. And just in those very years, as though on purpose, the greatest architect England ever produced was living—Sir Christopher Wren. Delighted with his god-sent opportunity, this genius of an architect crystallized within a few days' time the logical plan of a comfortable city with all conveniences. Broad quays with enormous warehouses in the port of the Thames. The center was the Stock Exchange, and therefrom the great arteries would branch out: extra-wide roads, boulevards, squares, districts with identical spacious houses. The factories were to be built outside the walls. The old lady, London, would become rejuvenated.

Overjoyed at creating a new city, Sir Christopher presented his plans to the King. Everyone was amazed and began attacking them furiously. This logical reorganization of chaos, this sudden human intervention in reality, was contrary to the English spirit. Buildings, cities, institutions must be left like forests to grow and spread on their own. Man had only one right: to observe them faithfully and adjust to them peacefully, purposefully, without intrigue. Every single English law prescribed is a long-term, mute necessity, which has finally assumed a voice. The new law never annihilates the old by violence. Silently the two laws become interconnected until they fuse. There is no sudden break. And in time, the old law atrophies and withers without anyone's being aware of quite how and when.

Thus the English people neglected logic and left Nature to work by herself as she is accustomed to work—without plan. And the City remained as it had been—narrow, charming, disorderly, a work of chance. Once again new houses were built above ruins and new roads were paved faithfully following tradition, with Time as their architect.

Is this not the very way the British Empire was forged? Not by any systematic logical program, not by the inspired conception of one particular mind, but by tentative groping, by sporadic campaigns and assaults having no external relationship, by thoughtless inhuman religious persecutions that forced the Puritans to settle North America, by merchant ships transformed en route into pirate ships to attack and plunder the heavily laden ships passing by. Later on, these same merchant-pirate ships landed in distant ports and built commercial warehouses strong as fortresses. Then the soldiers followed with their weapons to protect the merchants and help them drain the country. Shortly afterward, the politicians arrived with their pens and papers, and so this chance landing turned into a permanent possession.

In all these disparate activities there was always an inner consistency—the Englishman's desire to satisfy his own greatest, deepest necessities of action, adventure, gain, and ultimately, of prosperity and nobility.

Great Britain is no logical organization; it is a living organism. In time, the mother beehive was divided into various swarms who carried their mother's habits and needs with them, moving across the oceans to make their wax and mature inside their own hives. Now they were independent. They had their own rhythm in harmony with the new circumstances imposed on them by the new climate, the food, the distance.

But the original physiognomy of the race was never lost. It acquired its own nuance and created a new type. The Englishman became an Australian, a Rhodesian, a North American, but he still remained an Englishman—an organic, not an organized, diffusion. That is why the unity of the race was preserved in such a deep, liberated manner.

■ ■

Trade, conquest, nobility—thus the British Empire began; thus it was created, and thus it crystallized.

I remember one evening in Covent Garden, the site of London's great vegetable market and opera. Beautiful ladies with bare bosoms, rich gowns and expensive furs, reeking of powder and perfume, were promenading through the vegetable market (their red or green or silver pumps sparkling), over the rotten oranges and shreds of carrots and cabbages. They were rushing to reach the door of the opera where the Russian ballet would be dancing that night.

An inexplicable, primitive sense of delight overcame me. These perfumed aristocrats looked panic-struck—as if by earthquake, fire or war—as though they had just awakened, screeching and half-naked, and had thrown on some heavy fur piece and begun racing through the market to save their skins.

Aristocrats and grocers, nobility and commerce—nowhere else in the world do these two theoretically opposed social classes cooperate so fruitfully as here in Great Britain. Here the aristocracy does not include only warriors and knights and grand firesides. Here the nobles do not form a closed class, refusing to open its gates to the bourgeoisie who have made their fortunes on piracy or commerce. The gates are open. And whoever so deserves is able to enter, no matter where he comes from.

This holds true not only if he comes from England, but if he comes from anywhere on earth and from any race. Here you are not asked where you come from, but what you have to offer. The Jews whom William the Conqueror brought over from Rouen in France made a comfortable living and took root in London. They became money-changers and bankers, grew wealthy, loaned money to the kings. And one day, their grandchildren and great-grand-children were destined to govern England.

Others came over as refugees from Flanders and taught the natives how their superb woolens were woven. Others came from Antwerp and taught the art of melting glass and forging their famous knives. The Huguenots were persecuted and left France to teach their skills in silk and gold-work and making weapons and paper. . . .

Everyone who brought an art enhancing England's power was welcome. And gradually the port of London outrivaled Bruges, Antwerp, Rotterdam, Genoa, and the ports of Portugal and Spain. The London merchants—insatiable, practical daredevils—penetrated the rich depths of Asia, the wastelands of North America, and the savage ports of Africa.

They made their fortunes, dressed up like great lords, built palaces, imported new customs from more civilized nations, making their everyday life more pleasant and comfortable. They stopped eating with their fingers. They imported forks from Italy and no longer drank like barbarians. They gave magnificent, lordly banquets, decorated their walls with beautiful paintings, used themes and costumes from Greek mythology for their carnivals and dances and theaters.

The doors of the nobility were open and they entered. They infused new, strong blood into blue veins; offered new, not yet exhausted abilities; added new zest to noble old hearthsides. And thus the English aristocracy did not become, as elsewhere, a parasite, a merely ornamental institution, a useless burden to the community. It remained an indestructible force continually renewing itself on English soil.

The aristocracy and the merchant class coexisted on such friendly terms that when they used to leave their country houses to stay in London a while, they never went to the Palace city, to Whitehall and Westminster, where the courtiers stayed. They preferred to stay in the noisy old City with the merchants. There, far from the Palace, these proud unyielding lords could breathe more freely.

For centuries, these two cities—the city of the King and the city of the merchants—clashed. The former had the great privileges; the unlimited, easy incomes and flamboyant processions, with all the feathers, swords and horses. The latter had the boldness, craftiness, constant toil—the fortunes accumulated by hard labor. Gradually, by great struggling, determination, cleverness, the merchants forced the Palace to grant them privileges: their own judges and councils to resolve their differences, their own police, their own keys to lock up the City.

They no longer scorned one another. They stood face to face on an equal footing, each with its own rhythm—the city of the King and the city of the merchants. And that is why the aristocratic ladies tonight, dressed in their heavy furs and their red or green or silver pumps, could walk through the vegetable market so familiarly and confidently, making no grimace, only smiling.

THE BANK OF ENGLAND

Once, Pelopides heard a practical-minded friend remark that all was well, only he was forgetting the most important thing—to hoard money. The great hero smiled, pointed to a cripple and answered: "This Nicodemus here is the one who needs money, by Zeus!"

A proud, but shortsighted answer. For even if the cripple did have money, he would never live to see any great progress. Money, the conventional value wherein great powers are concentrated, is needed by one person more than all others—the strong man. For he alone is able to achieve great deeds through using this material accumulation.

I was standing outside the Bank of England, where it rises like a fortress of the golden Knight of St. George, as if the Knight were striding forth on gold pounds to free the English spirit from the monster slavery.

A mighty undertaking. "The human heart," as an English baron once remarked, "can never be at peace. It longs for freedom." This heart kept waiting sleeplessly, anxiously, one hundred or one hundred fifty years after the Norman Conquest. It waited patiently because it knew that its time would come.

The City of London fought first for these freedoms. The bourgeoisie grew richer and richer. The merchants acquired power, becoming increasingly aware of the mystic union between might and right, for they coveted special privileges. Power sought power. The bourgeoisie, the merchants, the craftsmen and students and monks united to form societies. They knew that only in this way, by organizing their power, would they be able to acquire and keep their privileges.

Each society was a camp, and its members kept alert watch. The ruling class could no longer safely impose arbitrary taxes and unjust acts. For the whole society would rise up as a single man. The rulers were furious: "What is this cursed word 'Society?'" they fumed. "A vile invention. And so our subjects pay only regular, prescribed taxes and will not let us do as we like, as rulers should do!"

In vain, they raged. The societies grew rich, acquired power, and of necessity this power begot privileges. The nobles were now flanked by the guilds . . . legal personages with their own seal and emblem and their own "king," the mayor. These guilds became rulers too, like the lords. They too had their own senate, the House of Commons, to govern.

The ruler judged his subjects. But then one day in the twelfth century, two peasants who were quarreling over a plot of land were condemned by the ruler to wrestle with one another, and the winner would receive the land. They wrestled from dawn on. The lord sat on his broad throne amid his fluffy pillows and watched the furious battle, passing his time. By now, it was almost noon and the poor peasants were still wrestling violently. They were exhausted, but the ruler refused to let them rest. Finally, one of them toppled over near the edge of a precipice. If he had moved a bit more, he would have fallen to his death. His opponent felt pity on him and embraced him, dragging him away from that precipice.

The commoners who had gathered about the lord's feet to watch felt moved. A sense of human dignity was aroused inside them. They were no longer willing to let their overlord judge them and command them to wrestle like animals.

They rose up and uttered a cry:

"From this day on, master, we will judge our differences by ourselves!"

"How much will you give me?" came the lord's immediate rejoinder.

They came to an agreement. The commoners paid and got their privileges.

Thus with the golden Knight of St. George, the commoners bought their liberties—that is, their privileges. Now the cities had their own courts, their own banners, their own gallows. On their own initiative, they could impose and collect taxes, arm their citizens, recruit an army, help the barons control the king, and help the king strike the barons. They cast their swords into the balance scale that would be most profitable to themselves. And they kept the balance.

London was the first to set the example. The King got

poorer as she grew richer. In 1248, when Henry III was forced to sell his silver plates and jewels, London bought them. And the King was annoyed: "I know that if the treasures of Rome were sold," he cried, "this city could buy them! The clowns of London have pounds by the barrel-load!"

And at that time, what was London? Barely 30,000 souls! Garbage lay heaped up on the streets and the stench was unbearable. In vain, the mayor issued an ordinance that pigs should not be allowed to rove the streets. The first public well in London dates only from the thirteenth century. For only the poor people drank water. The rich people drank beer.

It was so filthy that every so often plagues descended, mowing the people down. The plague in the fourteenth century was terrible, the "Black Death." It started in Asia, stormed and destroyed Cyprus in 1347, then straggled over to Greece, Italy, Northern Africa, up to France in January of 1348, crossing the Channel in August. Whole countries were dismembered; in many places there were no people left alive to bury the dead. From the four million inhabitants of England, only two and a half million survived.

As is sometimes Destiny's wont, this horrible disaster became one of the main reasons for the formation of the British Empire. All the survivors from the ravaged villages made their fortunes, because now they could divide among themselves the abandoned communal forests, fields, and meadows. The lords could no longer find help to cultivate their estates, and so they rented them out for any amount they could get. Or else they sold them for a piece of bread. And the peasants, unable to cultivate all this land that had fallen their way so unexpectedly, plunged into sheep raising. The flocks of sheep multiplied. England was producing a large quantity of wool now, and of necessity had to turn to foreign markets in order to sell it. The island could no longer remain isolated as it had been; England had immediate economic need of the other countries. So she had to make merchant ships to transport the wool, and simultaneously a military fleet to protect the merchant ships and control the sea. Their life henceforth depended on their dominion over the sea.

This is how the Black Plague begot the need of raising sheep and the sheep begot the abundant wool and this abundance created the merchant and military fleets—and these fleets Great Britain!

This is the way Destiny works—not in hours, but in centuries. We cannot call the greatest disaster disaster or the greatest happiness happiness, for we are utterly incapable of guessing their consequences in the far reaches of time.

The Plague passed, debilitating the feudal lords and strengthening the commoners. With her gold pounds, London bought other privileges. And her example was followed by all the English communes, who purchased their liberties from the state.

For centuries, the English had considered one and only one thing as their supreme duty: to obey their own conscience alone. Internal pressure, not external. The sole purpose of the long struggle between individual and state was the freedom of the individual. That he should not be obliged to execute anything except the law imposed on him by his own inner voice.

The ancient philosopher, Xenocrates, taught his young men to do whatever the law bade them do. He gave the law the upper hand. The citizen must try to harmonize his own will unquestioningly with the law. But the English people gave the upper hand to the individual's conscience. Let the law try to accommodate itself to the individual conscience if it wants to be carried out. For the Englishman the law must first be ratified by the legislator within himself.

Throughout this difficult struggle, the city of London and all the cities of England had one omnipotent ally and protector: Saint George, armed with his spear and riding astride English sterling.

The golden-haired Saint George, enthroned in his monastery here, the Bank of England, had fought well all these centuries and given fine protection to his beloved class. The class that had acquired wealth and power and could no longer adjust to slavery had begun demanding privileges, confident that it deserved its emancipation.

Better than any other people, the English were aware of the mysterious connection between wealth and liberty. They considered it no disgrace to reward with gold the proudest of virtues and most noble of contributions. For they well knew that from this precious metal, the protective shield of virtue is most often forged.

A few steps farther along, the Thames flows calm and muddy, ferrying undreamed-of riches from the sea and sending undreamed-of riches back to the sea. . . . A summer day, a few naked bodies stretched out along the banks, on the coal-stained sand, swimming and sunbathing there in the midst of the tar and empty crates, tin cans and dirty newspapers. Young men wearing red scarves around their necks were sitting on the benches, their eyes heavy with all manner of dark desires. Others, old men, wasted away and slightly exhausted, with flabby, sagging chins, had sealed their eyelids, sunning themselves on the neighboring benches. Women kept flitting past from the pubs along the banks of the Thames. They had dyed flaxen hair and hoarse throats.

And in a window over the way, a green parrot with a yellow neck was turning its head sideways, staring at people with its round cruel eyes.

Suddenly a violent wish rushed through me like a sword. Whenever I find myself in a big city, wandering many hours through its streets and seeing thousands of people's greedy or idiotic faces, the same desire is always born violently inside me: to hurry to the zoo and look at the birds and wild animals and big snakes there and so find relief.

Animals preserve the seal of God more faithfully than we. They keep His secret open. They play, grow up, make war, unite with an indestructible urge, until they immortalize their own kind (this being their mission), and then they die with dignity. Most human beings are submerged in the inferno of hatred, barrenness, absurdity. They are like people who cannot read, who can make out only a few letters, but still try to read from the Divine Song. They mix up these letters and link words or phrases analogous to their own humble desires—food, women, wealth, logic. It is like reading some superb work in a drowsy state. Here and there they distinguish a word and then fall back to their sleep.

When I came to the iron cages of this green and harmless jungle, the lions and tigers were just being thrown their afternoon meal, thick chunks of meat. A fatty, nauseating smell—involving us and at the same time including some ancient nameless lust, as though the animalistic sense of smell in us can remember far more than our own human memory.

We fix our eyes on the tigers and leopards and are overcome by a mysterious sort of enchantment, as when watching the flames in a fireplace or staring at the sea—or gazing deep inside us at our own soul.

The rainbow-colored birds and fish, the arched and ornamental animals, the butterflies and insects all appear as patterns to mock superficial romantic spirits, like the fantasies of a man slightly drunk or some slightly weary creator. But the tigers are the most apocalyptic, the most characteristic creation of life. They are the pure quintessence of the awesome creative impulse, the naked, greedy, crafty, merciless force, supple and graceful in a surreptitiously dangerous way, that is identical with the spirit.

If the spirit were thus visible, it would walk like the tiger and eat of the same food—the chunks of meat. And thus, with the same blood-splattered yellow eye, it would look on people neither as enemies nor friends—just meat!

That evening when I went home and lay on my bed and closed my eyes, I saw the mysterious patron saint of London, Hoa-Haka-Naka-Ya, standing over me with an expression of discreet English humor and condescension, slightly sad.

His tight-sealed, enormous lips seemed to have opened slightly at the corners and two rows of snow-white, pointed teeth flashed. Like the tiger's—only his eyes were sad and tearless, like those of a proud human being.

GRIME-STAINED CITIES

"GOD holds the earth in His hands and gazes at it. And should He ever look astray, the earth would vanish." So runs a naïve popular saying of the Greeks. It haunted me during the whole of my trek through those appalling, depressing cities of England: Birmingham, Liverpool, Manchester, Sheffield.

I kept thinking about the forlorn scribe who, thousands of years ago, sat cross-legged and motionless where the roads met before Memphis; his wide-open eyes filled with angry, hopeless amazement as he stared at the massive, evil city. Wretched human beings would come along, aged fathers and mothers without enough to eat, women abandoned by their husbands; and he would go on writing the letters they wanted, telling about their miseries. The mighty would also pass in front of him, reclining in the arms of their slaves, weighted down with their own flesh, their expressions dim from drowsiness and much kissing. The scribe rolled his eyes and saw; and his outcry is carved upon the rocks: "I have seen! I have seen! I have seen!"

A new scribe with the same kind of eyes, a Dante, but a Dante who would love man more than God, ought to make a tour of all the factories in the world and begin shouting too. What for? Only in order that the dignity of man might be salvaged on some scrap of yellowed paper.

Had the scribe not seen and accused, injustice and fraud would have gone without punishment in this world, and

virtue without reward. After a little while, the whole thing
would have faded from the memory of man. But with his
magical arrangement of words the scribe conquered time,
and made reward and punishment immortal. Always when
a civilization is approaching dissolution, it is the scribe
alone who rises up and floats above the waves of time.
Would that this industrial age of ours could produce such
a scribe, before we sink into the abyss! For wherever we
turn there are frauds and lamentations that should be preserved forever.

According to that most sweet-tongued of mystics, Joa-
chim of Floris, human history passes through three stages.
The first is dominated by the Father (the law); the second
by the Son (faith); and the third by the Holy Ghost
(love). Mankind had entered the third historical stage,
he said, that of love.

Seven centuries have gone by since then, and we still
have not entered it. Today we have neither law nor faith
nor love. It is a jungle filled with machines and wily, repulsive people, a jungle more hazardous than any filled
with wild beasts. Worst of all, each of us feels in the
depths of his own being some bond with this jungle, some
dark, shameful complicity, some disquieting affinity, as if
we all belonged among the wild beasts.

BIRMINGHAM

"Do not condemn matter, or praise it. Rather call a
man's view of it blessed or ignoble according to whether
he makes good or bad use of matter." This wise statement,
by the fifth-century bishop Palladius, I bore carefully in
mind as I wandered through the four great circles of hell:
Birmingham, Liverpool, Manchester, Sheffield. I did my
best to overcome my profound revulsion, to find a balance
between honest admiration and horror, to give meaning
to whatever confronted my eyes.

These grime-stained cities boast no ancient fortresses or palaces or old churches or romantic legends. Time has not passed over them, leaving its blood-marked enchantment. These cities are all new and prosaic and ugly. Nevertheless, now that I've completed my tour of them, I have no doubt that they possess the grandeur of hell. And this I find far more moving than the romantic raptures we elicit from the older cities that have enjoyed so much worship and fame. When I think of the factory I saw, the sooty blackness of its walls, the streets, the faces of the people, the hum in the greasy air, my heart is stirred by a strange emotion and a sudden feeling of tenderness.

This is the contemporary visage of love, our mother. This is her face, bitter, grime-stained, covered with wrinkles. And such a mother penetrates far more deeply into our hearts than some well-dressed gentlewoman accustomed to the best of everything.

I arrived in Birmingham on a Sunday. Everything was closed tight—factories, shops, warehouses. The faces grim and fraught with grief, having the toil of the past week imprinted on them, as well as the horror of the week that would begin next day. The wheel, the torture wheel, the eternally rotating struggle. The wheel carved on the soles of Buddha's feet when they were liberated had the appearance of an open rose, they say. On the soles of these feet, it must surely look like a hanged man's noose drawn tight.

Today the sun was shining and the glare made the streets two or three times as ugly as before. I walked hastily through them, then climbed up to the famous Aston Park to get a breath of air. Marigolds, violets, flowers in every hue. I caught a smell of Greece. Of all the circular forms, the rose that blossoms in the heart of hell may be, who knows, the most pitiless and inhuman. Because it reminds the damned how life might be and isn't.

Young factory-girl mothers with their children. A little blond girl of three or four was holding a children's magazine with colored cartoons. She picked it up in her little hands and showed it to me.

"Comic!" she explained.

We chatted a bit, I tried to reach her childish soul. We laughed. When I left, she wrinkled her lips.

"Where are you going?" she asked me, with an amazingly precocious tone of reproach.

"To Greece," I answered her. "Far, far away."

"Goodbye! Goodbye!" she called to me, waving her hands.

In that infernal city, hers was the only voice I heard that spoke from the heart.

I set out for the countryside and sank into the inexpressibly lovely and tender English grass. With their blond, well-combed hair, white shirts, and gray flannel trousers, workingmen were playing golf and tennis, like princes. Nowhere but in the country can they forget their destiny for a moment and make the wheel stop.

The English worker plays like his master. Snobbery is always pretty ridiculous and shallow. But here in England it has become elevated into a great social virtue, bestowing genuine delights of a lordly nature upon humble, graceless people.

All week long the English worker saves his money in order to spend his weekend regally. All year long he saves his money in order to go to the country, put on clean clothes and play, as gentlemen do, tennis and golf. He raises his head, looks at the class above him and imitates it freely, as though he had been born on this upper level. For he feels in his blood that he too is a gentleman, and that these joys suit him as well. They are his own; needs of his own soul too. Only, unlike the upper class, he doesn't have time to enjoy them every day. So he enjoys them one day a week, one month a year.

The English people are naturally aristocratic. That is why snobbery here is something other than mere apishness. In the deepest sense imitation does not exist. When he does as the wealthy class does, the English worker finds a genuine satisfaction for an inner need identical with the need of the ruling class. So it is in England with all social progress; everything gets channeled down from the upper classes to the lower in a natural and mature way.

England has created a humane model that is open and accessible and requires no overly difficult spiritual or social feats for its realization. You don't need great education or wealth or lineage in order to be a gentleman; a certain loftiness of character is all that is demanded, along with a relatively comfortable interval of time. And these the Englishman frequently finds accessible to him. Finds them, or *did find* them *in the past?* These terrible days we are now living in will show.

It was evening by the time I got back to the city. I caught the sound of trumpets and drums, and I ran. Men and women of the Salvation Army with their dreadful blue costumes, their clumsy hats and red ribbons were standing in a circle outside a pub, singing and shrieking religious psalms.

All over England this odd army wages a desperate battle for temperance and virtue. They stride out in military style to save drunkards, criminals, and debauchees. They employ crude, flamboyant techniques of conversion: songs that have an elemental appeal, dances of their own invention, screeches, drums. From the depths of the ages they have resurrected magical arts to subdue the nerves.

And they have won great victories. They have founded hospitals, night refuges, popular canteens, workshops for handicrafts. They have gone into the prisons and preached.

They have organized popular groups which work together, play together and go on excursions. They take care of impecunious young girls, women of the streets, alcoholics.

All these miracles of patience and kindness I could see every day in England. But without my wishing it so, this philanthropy struck me—quite unjustly—as rather comic. The irritation I felt was not only spiritual. I felt a physical antipathy as well. Ostentatious virtue, inhuman fanaticism. I recalled the deeply sane advice of that ancient Christian: "Better to drink wine with reason than water with typhoid." And as I stooped through the doorway of the pub, I felt glad to see all the good, kindhearted topers drinking away, without a care in the world, and smoking, and with a dim, mocking eye surveying the garrulous blue-garbed magpies outside.

Take away all the imperfections from any soul and it becomes distorted and withered, because it loses some of the roots—possibly the deepest ones—that nourish it from the earth. These are what give a person strength to keep going and to endure the repulsive spectacle of daily decay and death. The Englishman is still strong enough so that he can permit himself the luxury of hanging on to a few barbarous defects. Only people who are faded, and most of all, the ones wholly faded, that is, the dead, have liberated themselves from all evil.

Early the next morning, Monday, I took to the streets again. Fortunately, that day the sun had vanished. A dense fog had descended, smearing the walls and concealing the ugliness. Once again the city had become transformed into an array of mythical symbols, a hyperborean scene; the people's eyes gleamed in the still frost. For a person born in the lands of the flaming sun, which lays all things bare without mercy, this veil-draped day exuded a discreet nobility and mystery.

In the enveloping fog throngs of working men and women scurried along, each holding a little package in his hands—his lunch—and disappeared behind the soaring pitch-black doors. A bitter Frankish song of the twelfth century seemed to arise from inside the factories—a dirge that constricted the human heart.

> *We will always be weaving silk cloth*
> *And we'll always be dressed in rags.*
> *We'll always be rotting in black poverty*
> *And we'll always be dying of hunger!*

As I roamed from factory to factory, the feeling of cramp in my heart grew sharper and sharper. "Merrie England" had ceased to be merry; the wheel had gained momentum, and no one could stop it. Gone was the simple patriarchal organization of the Middle Ages, when the work had been performed by craftsmen joined together in guilds. The guilds had been destroyed as the factories expanded.

Gripped in poverty, the many, the workingmen, had become more and more subjected to exploitation by the few, the capitalistic employers. Parallel with this, the population of England had grown in numbers. New markets had opened up. Machines had become ever more perfect, creating a need for far more abundant raw materials. Human hands had been thrown into the discard, replaced first by steam and later by the mysterious force of electricity. Modes of transportation had also grown constantly more effective. In the place of the horse and buggy had come railroads and automobiles; in the place of sailboats, steamships. The city had devoured the village, and the village population had begun to disappear.

Mercantilistic ideas and the old theories about the guilds had been set aside. Each man, acting on his own, without government intervention, had become free to produce whatever he chose and in whatever quantity he chose, since he could always find a market for his products. Banks had proliferated. Enormous fortunes had been founded. Wealth had come to the new industrialists, and they supplanted the old aristocracy of the countryside. The face of England had changed. It had ceased to be green like grass; it became black like coal.

The machines had triumphed. In his enthusiasm over his possession of his new iron slaves, the man of the nineteenth century, kindled by irrational hopes and naïve optimism, had rushed headlong to conquer matter. The young believed in the conquest of matter as the safest road to the conquest of happiness; the elect among them believed in it as the safest way to reach the spirit.

The eternal battle to replace the inhuman laws of the physical world by the laws of the heart is the emblem of man's nobility. Man has fashioned ideals that are entirely human, for they were created in man's own image and likeness: justice, equality, happiness for all men. But the jungle that has become man's heaven and earth is ruled by different laws diametrically opposed to these: injustice, inequality, happiness for the few—and even this happiness flits away and vanishes like a flash of lightning.

And still man battles against the laws of the physical world. He refuses to put his signature on them or to accept them. He regards the world as inferior to his heart, and so it is; and he wishes to create a world of his own that will be worthy of him.

The prudent and the prosperous resist. "We're well fixed," they shout. "The world is fine. Don't destroy it." But when did the flame that burns in the vitals of man ever become degraded to the point of heeding such people as these? This flame has never consorted with the well-off. A wayfarer traveling among human beings and in a hurry. Hungry, thirsty, he has seen mirages of cool oases in the desert—justice, equality, happiness—and he has hurried on.

He was impatient to arrive. The horses pulling him in the past had seemed to him to be dragging along at an intolerably slow rate; and he, as we said, was in a hurry. So he made new steel horses that crossed the continent, the sea, the air. Continents and seas shrank. Thick, invisible wires radiated through the atmosphere, and human thought flooded into it like currents of lightning.

The purpose of the machine was to provide a steed for the spirit to mount so that the spirit could pursue its chimera—pursue it not by idle wishing and hollow daydreaming but by practical methods. This was the only chimera anchored to the everyday world; it was going to bring greater ease into the economic life of man, and by easing it, to give man at last the sense that he had time and leisure to lift his head from necessity.

But, as sometimes happens in our nightmares, the horses gradually mounted the riders. With the machine, injustice multiplied and inequality and pain. Cities like Birmingham came into existence, permeating the air and man's vitals with ashes. These dreadful, monotonous, geometrically laid-out streets; these iron avenues of telephone poles; these grimy human faces.

We drove our iron horses toward justice and joy, but they took the opposite road. They ran their way and we with them. Perhaps the ancient Archidamos of Agesilaium was right. It was he who beat his hands in despair when he saw the first siege machine—the catapult—arriving from Sicily to replace the human methods of siege. "O Hercules," he shouted, "man's virtue is lost."

Who knows, perhaps the human soul, being limited in its capability, cannot subdue and use anything more than limited powers. If these alien powers which it summons to its aid exceed a certain strength, the spirit loses its capacity to tame them and propel them where it wants them to go; it falls into their clutches; its slaves and allies turn into its masters.

How shall we emancipate ourselves from our slaves? In man's profoundest despair, and indeed especially in his profoundest despair, he feels a strange inner joy that is hard to explain—as though some one inside him had confidence in victory. The greater the danger, the more difficult will be the victory, and therefore the more worthy of man. And by the same token the greater will be the joy. I walked through Birmingham looking at machines and factories, at the thin, atrophied shinbones on the children, at their sad smiles, at the rags hanging from the dark, dank windows of the working class. I was struggling to give nobility and meaning to the ugliness, to find hope for the hopeless, to locate the present horror—so far as I could —within the complete circle, and in that way to transmute it into joy. Since we can't change the world, let's change the eye that sees the world!

This is what my eyes did consciously during the three whole days that I roamed around Birmingham. This they did unconsciously also, I feel sure. One evening when the women were leaving work, I saw a young girl emerging from a factory. How her breasts heaved up and down, swelling with hopes, inside her transparent dimity bolero! The future of England, as well as that of the rest of the world, depended on these two dangling milk-bearing vessels. And it is a great misfortune that the word for "spirit" in the Greek language is neuter in gender. Had it been feminine, we should have had the correct Holy Trinity, the one that is universally human and deeper than any religious dogma: Father, Mother, Son.

LIVERPOOL

Liverpool, a still more hideous city. The second port of England, the first cotton market in Europe. Its warehouses make the most "beautiful" quays in the world. Beyond this modern organized ugliness you unexpectedly confront the immortal Greek harmony in a number of grave and graceful buildings with columns. But the endless uniform rows of smoke-stained brick houses present an unbearable spectacle, as do the streets bereft of charm and the faces without laughter.

Here, as in Birmingham, terror overcomes you when you see the people scurrying like ants; arid, as solemn as though they were hypnotized, wrapped in deep concentration as they stoop over their typewriters, telegraphing and telephoning, emitting frenzied shouts in the stock exchange. A tragic awe seizes your heart, far more hopeless than that produced by any ancient tragedy, for here there is no catharsis, and not even a great poet to lighten the horrible content with perfection of form.

My mind harked back to the picturesque economic life of medieval England with its still unmechanized, essentially human ethos. The shoemakers, butchers, fishermen, tradesmen, each group had its own special ways. At that time competition and free trade did not exist. You couldn't buy and then sell for purposes of profit. If one member of the guild bought a piece of merchandise, he was obliged to share with his fellow guildsmen without profit.

Retail dealers were not allowed. You didn't have the right to work for profit, to buy large stocks of merchandise in advance and sell afterward according to the demand. The law of supply and demand did not operate. Consumer came into direct contact with producer, and the cost of living was at a minimum. Woe to anyone who tried to cheat his client! If a butcher sold bad meat, they burned the meat under his nose, punishing him by making him inhale all the stench. If a tavernkeeper sold vinegary wine, they bathed his head in it.

Foreign merchants could not open shops in England to sell. They were immured behind walls in a fixed place for a fixed period until they completed their exchanges. The Germans took metals and wool and brought silks, spices and jewels that they had obtained in far-off exotic cities—Kiev, Novgorod, Trebizond, Baghdad. The Flemish brought precious woven goods and laces; the Venetians velvets and glassware; the Greeks raisins and almonds. The trade of that age had all the simple grace of the newborn. At the great trade fairs, buyers and foreign sellers mingled together, conversed, quarreled, drank and got drunk, and they all traveled to distant lands, inside the pub, as they listened to the merchants who had come from foreign parts.

But time is by no means a worshiper of the beautiful. It never says to any moment of history: "Stop, you are so beautiful!" Time swiftly annihilates the moment and brings another, being in a hurry. Well then, it annihilated the charming streets, the primitive ways of exchange, and the picturesque festivals. It also annihilated the simple craftsman and small merchant, and brought a new monster to England—capitalism.

Along unexpected paths, as always, the great change arrived. Till now England had been selling wool abroad and importing from Flanders the expensive woven goods that her own craftsmen did not know how to weave. The mysteries of the craft were kept with great secrecy by the Flemish. But suddenly in the fourteenth century the Flemish weavers and their masters got involved in war and were conquered. They sought refuge in England. Who could have guessed that these refugees, entering their new fatherland with pursuers at their heels, were bringing with them a great upheaval in English history?

King Edward III immediately sensed the great possibilities. In 1337 he issued the following decree: "It is no longer permitted to export wool from England; it is no longer permitted to import woven goods." His own kingdom now possessed the superb craftsmen. They had brought all their secrets. From now on, with the English wool, they could weave the precious woolen goods and would teach the English their famous art.

And everything seemed to converge in a comfortable way for the destiny of England. After ten years, at precisely the right moment, the great plague intervened, the Black Death. We have seen how the lords became impoverished, and leased or sold outright many of their estates. The peasants acquired the land, and not having time to cultivate all of it, they converted a large part into pasture for their flocks. Thus the amount of wool increased, and the Flemish, protected by the law, now had abundant raw materials.

The weaving industry was turned upside down; and many guilds along with it. Up to that time, in order to weave a single piece of woolen cloth, you had to belong to fifteen guilds, each of which carried out a prescribed process in the refinement of the wool until it became the finished material. Before any commission could be undertaken, all fifteen guilds had to agree.

A rhythm so leisurely as this could no longer continue. The operations became concentrated. In place of the employer of the weaving craft, the industrialist emerged and built workshops far from the centers. Soon hundreds of people were working under one and only one employing authority.

The attractive and slow-paced medieval period, with its

conservative distribution of wealth, came to an end. In-
dustrialism was born. The first crude machines were set
in motion by invisible hands. Women ceased to weave in
their homes with their primitive hand-operated instruments. Machinery developed. Levers and pulleys began
to move.

The English grew rich—country people, shepherds, craftsmen, tradesmen. The standard of living rose. The lords
were taken by surprise and raised complaints. "In my
time," one of them shouted, "peasants didn't eat whole-
wheat bread. They ate beans and barley. They drank nothing but water. Then was the world as it should be for that
sort of people. Three things become terrible when you let
them go free: floods, fire, and poor people. Ah, to what a
pass have we come? The people, whose sole duty is to
work, now has its head and wants to eat better than the
lords!"

All classes got rich. Well dressed in native woolen fab-
rics, men and women worked well, ate well, gained power,
became proud and scorned all other nations. They scorned
them for their poverty. "Their peasants," they said, "drink
only water, eat only apples and bread made out of rye,
never meat, sometimes only a bit of lard or the entrails
and heads of animals that have been slaughtered for nobles and merchants."

They scorned them also for their laws. "How could English laws fail to be better?" they said. "They are made not
by just one man, the monarch, but by the most outstanding commoners of the realm. In England the people
have the power, and they send the blood to the head and
to all the parts of the political organism. We English pay no
taxes except what we ourselves have consented to, and we
are judged by none except the established law courts. Our
king cannot wrap us up in a sack and throw us into the
Seine."

The mark of the weaver and the dyer was wealth. Rich craftsmen and merchants, mingling with the lower ranks of nobles, completed the composition of the enormously powerful House of Commons. Each commoner had his own weapons and in case of need immediately metamorphosed himself into a soldier.

Slowly but surely, as is her customary rhythm, England changed economically, socially, politically. New and very difficult problems were created. In the first place merchants and industrialists, speculating without restraint, were piling up treasure, and as they enriched themselves, they began dressing luxuriously, giving lavish feasts, making loans to kings, provisioning wars, interfering in politics, and playing an ever more prominent role in the authority of the state.

And simultaneously a new power, dangerous for the masters, was rising in torment and deprivation—the working class. It grew in numbers. From a jumble of heterogeneous members it gradually developed organization, became aware of its strength, reared its head, and it too demanded rights.

From the end of the fourteenth century on, England began to echo with great exhortations for justice and equality. A priest named John Ball, when his church service ended on Sunday, used to take his parishioners, men and women, over to the cemetery. There he would deliver fiery speeches on social reform.

"My good people," he used to tell them, "my children, things are not going well, nor will they go well in England so long as there is no public property; so long as some are slaves and others masters, and we are not equal. Why should we have masters standing over us? In what respect are they better than we are?

We are all descended from the same father, Adam, and from the same mother, Eve.

> When Adam dalf, and Eve span,
> Who was then the gentilman?

Why then is there such inequality and injustice? We sow and they reap. We are dressed in rags and they in velvet. They have the wines, the spices, the wheat bread—and we the rye, the bran, the hay, and water to drink. They have the rich towers and we the rain and wind. Let us go find the king. Let us tell him our sorrows. Let us tell him that we want this injustice to cease!"

The Cretans have an extraordinary proverb: "My God, withhold health from the rich man and the power of reflection from the poor man." When I asked the peasant who had told me this why the poor man should not be given the power of reflection or strength to rear his head, the peasant answered: "Because he'll eat the world!"

But in England the rich did have health and the poor did have the power of reflection. The clash was tremendous. When the king's men came to the villages to collect taxes, the enraged peasants beat them and chased them away. From church belfry to church belfry, the chimes gave the signal for rebellion. "John Ball greets you! Arise!" The peasants streamed forth, burned the nobles' towers, killed the king's men, entered the cities. The nobles, terrified, hid in the forests.

From village to village, from city to city, peasants, workmen and beggars marched shrieking, with their axes and rusted swords and archaic, almost arrowless bows. Eventually they reached London. King Richard II, still a child, along with his faithful followers, hid in the Tower. The rebels spilled out over the streets, opened the prisons,

freed villeins, plunged into looting and murder. They set
fire to the rich houses, and slaughtered hundreds of Flemish craftsmen because they were foreigners. Many commoners joined with them. London was in danger.

At that point the young king emerged from the Tower.
From a ship on the Thames he made a speech to the rebels,
and then collected them in a meadow outside the capital.
He summoned thirty scribes and began to dictate to them
the privileges he was granting the poor people. He sealed
the document with his royal seal, and the rebels, content
with these papers from the king, happily dispersed.

But precisely at the hour when the king was dictating
the emancipation papers, a crowd of the fiercest rebels
were invading the Tower, where they killed the Archbishop of Canterbury and the Treasurer of England.
Then they fixed the heads to a spear pole and set them up
on London Bridge. Drunk with blood, the rebels were unwilling to depart. The danger was acute; and the bravest
and most trustworthy barons rushed from all over England
to the king's side. They were bent on striking the rebellion down at all costs and stifling it in blood.

They had recourse to a ruse. The young king summoned the rebels to a big square. He advanced on horseback, and behind him followed the mayor and the noble-
men, well armed. At the other side of the square were
assembled the rebels with their antiquated weapons. Their
leader, Wat Tyler, also on horseback, rode out and halted
in front of the king.

He spoke to the king with boldness, demanding equality and justice. The mayor, in a fit of anger, drew his sword
and struck. At once the leader of the throng of poor men
collapsed on his saddle. Then the infuriated rebels grasped
their bows. But the king spurred his horse bravely and advanced all alone toward the rebels. "I am your king," he
said. "You have no other leader but me. Follow me!"

Magnetized by the audacity of this crowned child, the fierce rebels followed trustingly. He led them to the field beyond the square. When he got them there, he turned to the nobles surrounding him and commanded them to begin the massacre.* The rebels, in their disorganized state, with their crude weapons, could do little. They tried to escape, but it was too late. The nobles fell on them and annihilated them. The slaughter continued in the towns and on the countryside. The rebellion was drowned in blood.

The lords suffocated the voice of the peasant by cutting his windpipe. But the peasant class quickly revived, and went on ousting its old masters, until one day another great power emerged, much greater than the lords and armed in a fashion far more up-to-date—with the machine. Peasants were transformed into workingmen; villages were emptied. People flocked to the great cities. The machine swallowed the land.

In our own day the peasants have almost disappeared from England. This patient, industrious class that tilled the soil, built temples, carved stone and wood, embroidered cloth, sang, danced, created legends, has ceased to exist. The few peasants left are silenced and terror-stricken. As with the great prehistoric beasts, whose time was over when the earth's temperature altered, these survivors are no longer able to live under the new conditions. They feel themselves being destroyed by a mighty satanic power; and not only themselves, but their religion as well, and the entire world, visible and invisible, which they created with their knobby hands and steady brains.

"The world's going faster now. How can the peasant catch up with it?" That was the way one villager put it, with a shake of his head. The earth has changed its rhythm.

---

* On this particular occasion the rebels were dispersed, and the massacre did not take place.—TRANSLATOR.

It races on swift steel horses. How could the peasant, ambling along on mud-caked legs, ever catch up with them?

But how long will it be this way? The land always has the last word. Everything, it seems, is ephemeral, except this. The machines will pass; the land will remain. The peasant knows it, and patiently bides his time.

PETER VLASTOS

A rabbi once admonished a student thus: "When you pronounce a word, you must enter into that word with all your limbs." "How can a whole man enter into a word?" the student queried. "A person who thinks he's superior to the word," was the response, "doesn't deserve to have anyone speak with him."

Often in my life I have recalled the rabbi's counsel with pleasure. I have always conceived of the word as concentrated force, much the way that present-day sages think of matter. Matter, they tell us, is not dead, but rather has enormous powers imprisoned in it and merely appears inert because of the way these powers are held in balance. Words are the same. When a person reads something, if he wants to feel it, he must do one thing, and only one: He must crush each word's skin, be it hard or soft, and let the meaning explode inside his heart. The whole art of the creator consists in a magical squeezing of human essence into the letters of the alphabet. And the whole art of the reader consists in forcing these magic traps open and freeing the fire or sweetness locked inside them.

I was ruminating in such a vein as I walked through this graceless city in search of a great lover and master of the word, with whom I wanted to talk. Alongside a park dense with foliage and far removed from noise and smoke, in a noble house surrounded by tall trees, I had the great joy of finding him. Peter Vlastos.

A lofty, rugged, monolithic spirit, liberated from all the

idylls of youth. He reminds me of those Cretan rafters, where you climb, at high noon, in the blazing sun. There you have to have strong knees and kidneys to resist the thirst and solitude and not to yield to hope.

This man I liked because he expected nothing from either gods or human beings. He had succeeded in what I regard as the supreme human achievement—that is, in confronting the Nothing and not being overcome by panic. He was born, so he himself says, "with faith in the joyous tragedy." Without this "openhearted" sense of tragedy, he knows well that life is not worth living. He rejects the comforting shadow words that lull the "little lives" to sleep, as well as the soothing camomile of metaphysics and religious panacea. He dissects the Ten Commandments and clears out the rubbish of facile consolation, keeping for his own bread a brave, hopeless YES. Real bitterness makes him seal his lips, and when he hears a panicky laugh, he opens them. This is the way he puts it:

> Whoever feels a sunny force enlivening his vitals; whoever was born with faith in the joyous tragedy, with enthusiasm for the ironic mystery; whoever sings YES; whoever risks disharmony because he desires beauty—let him rise and come forward, in order to resurrect life and make it less harsh. Whoever mutters a feeble NO and wraps himself up in his "little life," whoever casts a shadow on the sun and salt, let him look for anchorage in escapes and forgiveness and narcotics . . . and let him fill up to the ears with the water of Lethe. We're from two different villages.

As Vlastos knows, the Muse most worthy of the real man is Difficulty. She chases the easy victory away from life and art: the kind of victories that humiliate the victor.

Life should not be comfortable; it isn't to a person's advantage to have it so. Nor should art. Never have the masterpieces of life or art been pleasant or easy. They are always rugged peaks to be ascended by the few. Prosperity, contentment, consolation, security are mortal sins. If you respect your own soul, you have to spend yourself without stint. You have to be willing at every moment to gamble all you have, so that you may practice your strength, so that you may never lose the assured feeling that you can do even without victory and are ready to begin again.

Vlastos' phrases sting; his language is rich, integrated, fearless. He brings big stones, cornerstones, to make the building; he is no apprentice builder fetching mud. He likes the Cyclopean way of joining boulder with boulder, without mortar or patchwork.

> *High*
> *with the hands and shoulders*
> *the word!*
> *Foundation, axe,*
> *scarf on the bosom of thought,*
> *with the movement of the heart*
> *high,*
> *for the sun to strike it!*
> *Light from the sun to take*
> *the word,*
> *hung from the sky*
> *like an immortal star!*

A true, proud song by Prevelakis, dedicated to the head mason, Vlastos. It suits him.

When I found him, he was bent over his desk writing down arrangements of demotic words, as though he were putting colored pebbles together to form some great mosaic. His appearance showed a secret fire, as well as scholarly attention. The work of the mosaic artist is difficult, for it requires a combination of opposites: the bold, free outline and the meticulous, studied fitting of parts.

He raised his head and stretched out his mason's hand, which had such precious value for Greece. We spoke about solitude and art. For many hours we stayed together, talking about our great love in life—the demotic language. He too has an unwavering passion for the best and deepest possession of our race: our great lady and at the same time, our fresh little virgin peasant girl. "Our demotic tongue is our country!" we were saying, hardly able to control our emotion. In the words of Solomos, "What else indeed do I have in my mind except freedom and language?" Our overwhelming love made us laugh, laugh in order to keep from crying. For we knew that great love can endure all things; it can survive even laughter and mockery.

To return to Greece with your ears cocked, to hear the word as it falls from the lips of the people, still virgin as it is and untouched by ink for thousands of years, and to carry it off with you with the gaiety of a buccaneer, as you would steal the woman you love! To climb mountains, be hungry and thirsty, utterly exhausted, and then suddenly to forget it all because you have met a shepherd and he has treated you to some glowing unfamiliar word! Only a person who loves our demotic language with a passion like that can know how little it matters that he was born—and is helplessly struggling still—in the midst of the ignorance, the indifference, and the laziness of his race. "It isn't right to suffer long for such a woman!"

The hours and days went swiftly by. "Six are the marks of friendship: giving and taking; confiding and having secrets; feeling well and making the other feel well." When we had clasped hands and parted, I felt that the Indian sage who had said that was right.

Ion Dragoumis and Peter Vlastos are, I believe, the two

people I have most respected and loved in my life. Companions in the great Hellenic solitude, champions in a struggle which transcends fatherland and language and mutely travels beyond their frontiers. Would that it might be the fate written for me that I should travel with them after my death!

MANCHESTER

"A dangerous marsh inhabited only by wild pigs, bulls and wolves"—this is the way an old chronicler describes the stretch of land where the enormous, monstrous city of Manchester sprawls. So it was then, and so it is today.

Here we see the face of our industrial civilization: fierce, bereft of human sweetness and tenderness, merciless, and bitter. As I gazed upon the thousands of human beings hurrying up and down the unsmiling streets, I felt overcome with anguish. Could I, I asked myself, be having some hideous dream? Or could it be that humanity was being destroyed in some collective nightmare? Why were they rushing? Why had people's lives ended in this dehumanization?

I remember an old Buddhist monk in a Chinese temple. In his orange cassock and broad-rimmed, funnel-shaped straw hat, he was sitting beneath a pine tree in the courtyard, a little vessel of water beside him. He started a conversation with me. When a young man, he had gone somewhere as a servant in a company of white men who were mountain-climbing in Tibet. He had seen famous monasteries, made pilgrimages to great ascetics. And in his broken English he told me of the marvels he had seen and heard. Of all the marvels, one that occurred on the sacred peaks far away had made a unique impression on him. He described it to me, and his calm voice hissed like a snake.

"Not so long ago," he began, "there was an ascetic who had been shut up for three years in a cave on the edge of an abyss. High up in the cave there was a hole, and through that a monk used to bring him a platter of rice and a cup of tea every morning. The ascetic sat cross-legged and motionless, concentrating his thought. He was struggling to impress the form he desired upon the air—to create a *tulpa*. Do you know what a *tulpa* means?" he asked with a shade of polite scorn.

"No," I replied humbly.

"How could you Franks know?" he murmured. "You know machines, railways, cannon. You have the power of the mind, but you lack the power of the spirit. The *tulpa* is the creature that the ascetic makes, by great concentration, out of air. He compels the air to assume the form he has in his own thought.

"Well then, the *tulpa* that this ascetic wanted to create was to be a monk—short and plump, clever and faithful— who would work for him. He was an old man by now, and couldn't bring water from the spring. He couldn't make tea, or spread his straw mat when he wanted to go to sleep. And he felt the need of a slave, who would be eager to serve him and would obey him gaily. He hadn't been able to find anyone like that in the monastery, and now he wanted to make his own, exactly to suit him.

"For six years he struggled to carry it off. He wrestled with the air, but it resisted. However, little by little, the air became obedient, began to grow dense, and to take on the form of a short, well-fed monk. And one morning just such a monk stood before him, smiling, arms folded, ready to carry out every command. When the regular monk who was in the habit of bringing him his tea came from the monastery, he bent over the hole in the cave, and saw inside not one monk but two. Some other monk must have come from faraway to visit him, he thought to himself. I'll run to fetch another cup of tea. He ran and in a little while he set the double portion on the stone.

"From that day on, the *tulpa* served its creator with mute obedience. Six months passed, then eight months. When the year was up, the *tulpa* began growing. It lost its fear of its master and began taking on new forms of its own. It ceased to run errands with the same eagerness. It reared its head against the master, got angry, grew rebellious. No longer short and plump, it got taller every day. Flames darted from its eyes. The ascetic was terrified. Had his spirit lost its power to impose itself on the slave? Was he beginning to collapse, and his mighty powers of concentration to get scattered?

"One day the *tulpa* leaped up and started dancing inside the cave in defiance of the ascetic, who had ordered it to bring him some water. Laughing arrogantly as it danced, it began dragging the ascetic by force, outside the cave, toward the abyss, as though it intended to destroy him. The ascetic grabbed hold of a rock to support himself. Gathering all his strength, he started upon the greatest and most difficult of all tasks—that of dissolving the *tulpa*. Very difficult, very dangerous; it's easier to create the *tulpa* than to decompose it.

"All that time, the *tulpa* had been absorbing all the ascetic's strength. Now that it had begun to soar, it didn't want to be dissolved. The struggle continued for three years. One morning during the third year the ascetic was found at the bottom of the abyss, dead.

The Chinese Buddhist turned about and stared at me maliciously.

"You understand?" he asked me.

"No," I answered again.

He laughed. "You Franks have also made a *tulpa* just like that," he said.

"What *tulpa*?"

"The machine. And it will eat you."

■ ■

All day long today, as I've been wandering through the dreadful and joyless streets of Manchester, the laughter of the malicious Chinese has been echoing in my ears.

Suddenly I could see a tragic meaning in Manchester, Liverpool, Birmingham, in all the industrial cities of the world and in this whole industrial age of ours. The machine is a *tulpa* of the human brain. Created in order to act as a faithful servant to man, it has gathered *élan* and is sending us to the abyss, in defiance of our orders to bring us water from the tap. How are we to be saved?

Only one solution is possible for us. By now this *tulpa* cannot be dissolved; that's vain romanticizing and nostalgia. Only one solution is possible: we must broaden and deepen our spirit enough so that it can impose its will upon its overgrown and menacing slave girl. The human spirit, a great modern philosopher has truly said, has remained as small as it was centuries ago, while the power which we have at our disposal has grown gigantic. Our slaves have become monstrous and all but omnipotent dragons; we the masters have remained wretched, ill-behaved, narrow-minded little people. After expending all our intellectual power, we now find ourselves at the mercy of the pitiless, brainless forces we have unleashed. The entire problem of our age centers about this mortal disharmony: the spirit has been weak, even while it has been shaking enormous forces from their sleep. These forces neither can nor will subside again into their old lethargy. Now, if the human spirit wants to save itself, it has to concentrate its own inner forces, and tame the wild beasts it has aroused.

I walked alone in Manchester with a rapid step, as though someone were chasing me. The mockery of the yellow monk, perhaps. I gazed in anguish inside the factories and behind the iron grilles, where the gigantic machines have been enclosed; I heard their groaning down in the underground tunnels. A strange, fierce joy stirred inside me. Today we find ourselves at precisely the critical point: the *tulpa* is dragging its master to the abyss, and the master is shouting as he clings to a rock.

What will come out of it? In every civilization one particular specialized capacity of the human being is overfed, and all the others are allowed to atrophy. If the world is to be saved, the future civilization will overfeed the specialized capacity of the spirit, which today is atrophied and deeply buried. The new civilization will be entirely different from the present one; and soon, for a few centuries, the balance will be restored.

Around noon I entered a museum to get cool, in the same way that we enter a forest when we're exhausted by the blazing heat. Once again I saw centuries of time and multifarious places looming before my eyes in fragments. Thousands of years, and the only traces left were one beautiful patterned vase, some mummies in their richly colored hieratic stillness, some pipes and pitchers from Peru, some female jewelry, some ferocious African masks, and some date leaves with old songs written on them in intricate black letters, which surely must tell of God, Women, and War, the three great primeval human concerns.

I stopped suddenly. Something you would never have expected to find in the steel heart of Manchester: a superb old Chinese statue made of wood, the Chinese goddess of mercy, Kuan Yin. She was sitting, a charming figure with folded legs, on a lion whose reins were being drawn by a slave. She smiled calmly, all sweetness and compassion, as though she knew very well what city she had been exiled to and how much they needed her here.

Serene and graceful, she was hiding in the smoky entrails of Manchester, waiting astride her tame lion for her turn to come—waiting like the seed buried in dung and mire for the inevitable time when she could bloom. And all at once all the agony I had experienced in Manchester found relief, as though this little goddess were our own soul and it was now riding her tame lion.

SHEFFIELD

Here, too, faces smeared with smoke; smudges of coal on naked, girlish legs; factory after factory, all looking alike; horrid brick apartment houses; tormented expressions. The workers grave, severe, their eyes blue steel. This was the first and last time I would see them. But it was all I could do to stop looking at them, and I felt pained as I turned away.

The same terrible tragedy erupts here as in the other cities, in the same contemporary setting: a drama written by some inhuman craftsman of genius. Certain apocalyptic signs, certain cries and silences and innuendoes, and the *hubris* that has reached its peak, give us the sense that we have come, with good augury, to the fifth act.

This atmosphere of tragic catharsis is salutary. It resounds with nerve-racking noise and outcries, and conveys secret hopes as well as nameless terror. You feel an overwhelming intoxication of a weird kind. The most insignificant event, the most fleeting human form produce in you a disproportionately intense excitement and emotion, as though in reality we were all one, and our end had arrived, and we were rushing pell-mell with a great sob in our throats and with shouts of "Farewell! Farewell!"

Nowhere is this atmosphere so heavily charged with messages as in the great industrial cities. Here tragic horror finds its most modern form. Whatever happens, however trivial it might seem to be, has an appreciable weight, and takes its place with a thud, for all time, on the scale of destiny.

On thousands of occasions, in a multitude of cities, I had seen the faces of young girls glued to the shopwindows, their eyes yearning. But that day in Sheffield the same event made me feel indescribably bitter and certain that we have reached the end. One poverty-stricken young girl, wasted away from hunger, had pressed her little face against the well-stocked window of a butcher shop. Desire shone in her eyes as she stared greedily at the meat. Through some mystic transsubstantiation, all this horrid meat might become yellow hair, fluffy curls on the nape of the neck, red lips . . . But where could this half-starved little girl find the money to undertake the divine trans-substantiation? And so the little girl withered and the meat rotted, and the union never took place.

I walked for hours in Sheffield, stumbling with mixed joy and terror from symbol to symbol. The workers, the stores, the women, the luxurious cars, the skinny, atrophied legs, the churches, the pubs, the radios, the way they were all wrapped in fog and seemed to be emerging at that very moment from the effervescent workings of some superhuman imagination. And you had a joyous sense of being yourself a part of the frosty mist, slightly denser than the rest of it, and of circulating within the same savage imagination.

In the heart of the frosty mist loomed the graceful, silent old cathedral. Old graves filled its grassy courtyards, and I wandered among them in the twilight, reading the half-faded epitaphs on the slabs. Occasionally some hyperbolic eulogy of the dead man would have survived, but with the name missing, consumed by time. Sometimes the name would have been preserved, but with the eulogy erased by time and people's footsteps.

In any of these oppressive, noisy cities, a walk in the en-closure of the medieval cathedral rests your eye and ear and brain. You find pleasure in the velvety green grass growing among the blackened tombstones. Two days be-fore, in the front courtyard of the old monastery at Chester,

I had seen a stone sunk in the grass but with big Greek letters still visible on it. "Faithful unto death," they read. A tremendous sweetness ascends from these plots of earth. Death assumes its most merciful guise in such cities as these: it's like the silence that falls after exhausting quarrels. Crowded close to each other, beyond speech and released from care, the former inhabitants of Sheffield are at last at rest. I trod lightly over them and whispered softly the old Saxon song of the dead:

> For you, before you were born, a house was built, before you emerged from your mother's belly. Low is its roof, low its door. The roof is built near your bosom. You will dwell in the cold earth, in the dark and blackness, where all things rot. You cannot escape from there. Death holds the keys. You will remain there with the worms. No friend will want to join you in that place. No one will ever open the door to ask how you are. For in a little while your visage will be horrid, and even the mother who bore you would shudder at the sight of you.

The sun had set now. The long road below sparkled like copper. I opened a little book I was holding and read some English verses, so as to end that day of prose with some poetry. There are electric things and telephones and cinemas, there are machines and railways and Parliaments and poison gas, but still no one has

> *built Jerusalem*
> *In England's green and pleasant land.*

A young man came and sat next to me in the church enclosure. He wore a green cape, the color of the beautiful English earth. We struck up a conversation about contemporary English poetry. He was himself a poet. He was pale, had long fingers, wore a shirt threadbare but spotless, and out of his sad, round face his eyes gleamed with a strange spark of fire.

"What becomes of your poets in the land of poetry, Greece?" he asked me. "Difficult times, laden with power, hope and terror. Laden with uncertainty. Have you seen what hatred has exploded among us? Never was poetry so indispensable as now."

"What becomes of poets in the land of poetry, England?" I asked him in my turn. And the beloved form of that sublime prince of lyricism, Keats, floated through my mind like a vapor.

He looked away at the setting sun, at the coppery road, and the black anthill hurriedly dispersing in the last rays of light. He smiled a melancholy smile.

"Only ten years ago," he said, "we all had only one concern: how to appear original, how to find a rare form of expression that no one had ever discovered before, and to open up a path uniquely our own. Barren individualism! We considered originality the highest virtue. No contact with other spirits; no traffic with our own epic age of greed.

"But day by day the danger to the world about us, and to our own inner lives as well, kept increasing. It increased so fast, and the tragic catastrophe swiftly approaching was sending out such an unbroken stream of secret messages— they weren't secret really, and now they're obvious—that eventually our poets emerged from their splendid isolation and began to mingle with the main currents. They gave up struggling for the most rare form of expression and began to seek the most responsible and most representative form, the one most universally human."

I was delighted with the lucid way that my chance companion on the churchyard bench had summed all this up.

He was another "brother," I sensed, in the throes of the same agonies.

"And in England what are these main currents?" I asked.

"Two currents—I think they're international—have begun to bring new life into our poetry. The aspiration for socialism and the neo-Christian revival. But both in a modernized form. The first group, those of them who are singing, aren't narrow Marxists of the old brand; they don't make the infantile oversimplifications that explain anything and everything in a convenient way. They want a wider and more human foundation for the new society. The same with the second group. They differ from the limited Christian bigots who have had similarly naïve explanations to offer and who have had a cowardly habit of transferring the struggle from earth to heaven. The members of this second group also have their eyes fixed on man's contemporary anguish, and they want to bring a bit of the kingdom of heaven down to earth."

Though he laughed sarcastically, his pale face looked contorted with grief.

"Will they succeed?" he murmured, as if carrying on a monologue. "Can Christ once more bring gentleness to the human heart? Is there anything we need more urgently? Will it be possible to satisfy the human mouth?"

Seeing that I remained silent, he grew more animated.

"If Christ should descend to earth again, this time not in sunlit Palestine with its blue lakes and gardens, but in the cold and dirt and smoke of Sheffield, what would He do? If He entered the factories, went down into the coal mines, saw the workers and then saw the bosses, what path would He mark out for our salvation?"

He looked at me with flaming eyes, waiting impatiently as though he expected me to have an answer. But I remained silent, because, for years now, I had ceased to be troubled by such problems.

"I'm writing a long ode now," he said, "a dialogue. Christ and a worker are talking. It's morning; the factory sirens whistling like demons. It's cold, snowing. Workingmen and women are rushing along, shivering, their eyes red, bodies misshapen by the work they do in the factories. My workman takes Christ by the hand and leads him around the factories, the mines, the seaports. Christ sighs. "Why all these doomed people? What have they done?" He asks. "I don't know," answers the worker. "You will tell me."

"Later he takes Him to his own hovel. The fire is out, and the place is filled with his hungry, weeping children. The workman shuts the door, grabs Christ by the arm, and shouts: 'How shall we act unto Caesar? What is his for us to render unto him? What is ours for us to take?'" The poet paused a moment, out of breath. His hands trembled nervously, violently.

"Well!" I asked. "And what does Christ answer?"

"I don't know," the young man said, knitting his brows. "I don't know yet, or, if you like, I no longer know." He lapsed into silence. The shadow of the church had fallen on us. Our faces were enveloped in darkness.

"Why do you turn backward?" I said. "Why do you ask the gods? Christ did His duty. He provided an answer for other ages, other problems. His answer created a great civilization. He did His duty. Now the agony wears a different face. The wheel has turned."

"I cannot . . ." murmured the poet with an angry frown.

"It doesn't matter," I said, "don't worry. Others will be able to. But all the same we must struggle as hard as we can, even if we never win. Let us shout, let us weep, let our hearts be torn. Even if our yearnings are impotent, they'll help the man of the future, who will be better than we are. This is our way to collaborate in our salvation. Do you understand?"

He got up abruptly. "Good night," he said. And I watched him striding through the courtyard on his slender legs, slightly stooped over, burying himself in the anonymous crowd. The flimsy green cape he was wearing billowed a few moments longer in the evening breeze. He looked to me a half-comic, half-tragic figure in this city of steel. That whimsical kind of human being, the Poet, who is driven by some prehuman, nightingalish pattern and will not leave off singing.

Surely in the famous steel city of Sheffield this young man, who looked so delicate and useless, must suffer a great deal from lack of communication and poverty. But if he could form a just estimate of himself, a worker in words, and of the others, workers in steel, he would forgive their jeers and accept his poverty with pride. For he would realize that the metal he forged was the mightier one.

As I saw him disappear into the unsmiling crowd, I got up and began walking over the old grass-covered graves, murmuring some noble lines of Moréas in a kind of farewell to him:

I who can lift Apollo on my ten fingertips have faced the
scorn of the plebs.
Justly I pay this tribute now and forever, as in the past, so
that order may reign on earth.

The following day, finished with the factories, I experienced a sudden surge of joy. In Sheffield too, hell had a drop of coolness at its heart. In the city's Art Gallery I saw a Chinese ivory statuette. It was the ancient sage, Lao-tse, wearing a cassock belted with a rope, his thick, well-groomed beard descending down over his broad belly, his hands clasped behind him. The hood of his costume was set back at a jaunty angle, and his whole head was thrown back. He was bursting into laughter.

According to tradition, he had been born an old man with white, white hair, but the more he advanced in age, the younger he grew. Isn't this the natural course of things for the perfect man? He got younger and younger, and his pupils were dumfounded. One day one of them decided to ask him about it.

"Master," he said to him, "when you were born, you had white, white hair. And now, the more time passes, the blacker your hair gets. Why?"

"Because I'm beginning to understand," Lao-tse responded with a broad smile on his lips.

The anxieties, the agonies, and the inconsistent impulses of youth had been transmuted into tranquillity, gentle irony, and pleasure in the spectacle. So now the ivory Lao-tse stands in his glass pagoda, gazing on Sheffield amid volleys of laughter.

■ THE ENGLISH GOD

PETERBOROUGH

After these modern industrial cities with their inhuman and satanic beauty—or ugliness, if you will—I slipped suddenly into a small, peaceful city from another century, the site of a lofty, proud cathedral: Peterborough. Of the old English cities, some came into being in the environs of an ancient fortress, others at the intersection of commercial roads or in harbors, and still others, finally, around a cathedral. War, commerce, religion—the three great mothers of civilization.

These little cathedral towns have an ineffable grace. On the Saturday evening when I arrived in Peterborough, men and women were moving slowly along an uphill road, as if in a liturgical procession. I followed them. Their day's work was over. Some were holding purses or little baskets for shopping. Others were sauntering at a leisurely gait with their wives and children. As I knew, there was a good chance I would find the shopping center branching out around the big cathedral, and at this hour of twilight, the kindly provincials would probably be ambling about in the square. The people trade and stroll and court each other in the shadow of the House of God. I went along with them, restraining my steps. I fell into their slow rhythm and followed with a sense of confidence. I felt that I was about to come face to face with the majestic medieval fortress of God, and to enjoy three very good things. I would see something beautiful; I would buy some fruit and refresh myself; and for the first and last time I would watch the women of Peterborough.

In these idyllic little towns, life has lost contact with the hustle and fury of the feverish modern period. They are backward and eternal. Such has been their life for thousands of years, and such it will remain after thousands of years to come. The fever lasts but a little while, however much it may offer in the way of excitement. Here in the provinces the people's faces are less marked by anxiety. Their spirits are somewhat dormant. Their bodies are not subjected to such harsh treatment and are better nourished. And the corpulence of old age accumulates swiftly and surely. You toss a stone into the water, and the circles grow calmer, the broader they grow. Peterborough lives in the broadest circle.

When we reached the crest of the hill, I raised my head and saw the celebrated Cathedral of the Apostles Peter, Paul, and Andrew looming up in the midst of dense greenery against the gold-red sky. All around it I could see the open-air market bursting with fruit—pears, apples, plums, bananas. I felt jubilant. That evening this was enough to satisfy both my body and my soul. I hurried ahead to buy some fruit and refresh my body so that it would not annoy my soul. Then I entered the utterly charming cloisters of the church.

How the Gothic cathedral differs in England from the ones we are familiar with on the continent of Europe! What a profound and direct relationship exists between the English cathedral and nature! The grass stretches out around it; trees and water and gardens embrace it. That it is a fortress of the military God you can see beyond any doubt; these English cathedrals are not palaces, pleasant and comfortable, nor are they lonely villas set in some wild solitude. Yet this military God loves greenery and is intensely sensitive to it. He is an English God.

As I toured the cathedrals that are scattered like fossilized mammoths through the quiet little English cities, I could sense how unerringly the architect's hand had been guided by love and understanding of earthly life. Love, understanding, and a sure, practical mind. The English cathedral does not have its force concentrated toward an arrowlike summit aspiring to reach the sky. It suggests neither ecstasy nor excessive asceticism nor contempt for life. Spreading over the grass as it does, with its ample doors and lacy carvings and smiling, winged youths, it seems to form a kind of continuation of the soul, a slight elevation that, instead of beckoning us upward, allows us to rise just far enough so that we can survey the surroundings and see how green and enchanting the earth is. To pray in such a temple becomes a way of expressing copious thanks to God for making the land so green. The mind is not exalted above the plane of earthly things. Rather it is invited to take up a firm abode on the earth's surface, to expand over it, and to cast strong, hungry roots into it.

Powerful enticements that could easily lead the spirit astray! For, when neglected, the spirit asks nothing better than to slip gently down the delightful slope of fleshly ways. And in time the monks were lured by the verdure and water and flowers surrounding them, by the comfortable cells and blazing hearths and good food, into the all-too-human path of sin. The old chroniclers have described for us the blissful life led by the monks who dwelt a few centuries ago in the holy shade of these cathedrals. They adored women, we are told. They got drunk and had women come in and sing and dance for them. In their carefree gaiety they forgot their austere God, and in their impatience they brought Paradise down to this world. Theirs was a brazen-faced, mundane joy, the traces of which were eventually to be annihilated by the flame of the Puritans and the icebergs of the Victorian era. God was transformed by the Puritans into a general, solemn and merciless; and by the Victorians, into a cold, forbidding, virtuous pastor.

Inside the lofty cathedral I sat down in one of the delicately carved pews and opened a copy of the lovable old poet Chaucer. I wanted to exhume from its pages that vanished creature, the monk of long ago. Gradually I found the figure emerging out of the clumsy but rich fourteenth-century English—an affable, well-fed, hearty friar of the Middle Ages, smelling of lard and incense and speaking in the honey-sweet tones of his choir voice. He had no love at all for the poor and the sick.

> *"Thy selve neighbour wol thee despise;*
> *If thou be poure, farwel thy reverence!"*

He enjoyed giving confession to the rich and above all to food merchants.

> *Ful swetely herde he confessioun,*
> *And plesaunt was his absolucioun;*
> *He was an esy man to yeve penaunce*
> *Ther as he wiste to han a good pitaunce.*

He went from door to door in the village, begging.

> *"Yeve us a busshel whete, malt, or reye,*
> *A goddes kechil, or a trip of chese, . . .*
> *A goddes halfpeny or a masse-peny,*
> *Or yeve us of your brawn, if ye have eny;*
> *A dagon of your blanket, leve dame,*
> *Our suster dere, lo! here I write your name."*

Thus he collected charity, loaded up, saddled his mule, and the moment he had left the village behind him, he erased all the names he had promised to commemorate, and set off for the next village.

In this particular village, the friar whom Chaucer describes so vividly had eagerly sought out his friend Thomas, whom he loved dearly because Thomas was rich and had a beautiful wife. Finding him sick in bed, the friar went over to embrace him.

> "God woot," quod he, "laboured have I ful sore,
> And specially for thy savacioun
> Have I seyd many a precious orisoun.
> And for our othere frendes, god hem blesse!
> I have today been at your chirche at messe, . . .
> And ther I saugh our dame; a! wher is she?"

At that moment the lady entered. The friar rose and greeted her with great politeness.

> The frere aryseth up ful curteisly,
> And hir embraceth in his armes narwe,
> And kiste hir swete, and chirketh as a sparwe.

In his psalming voice, he told her:

> "Thanked be god, that yow yaf soule and lyf,
> Yet saugh I nat this day so fair a wyf
> In al the chirche, god so save me!"

Then presently:

> "Now dame," quod he, "Je vous dy sanz doute,
> Have I nat of a capon but the livere,
> And of your softe breed nat but a shivere,

And after that a rosted pigges heed,
(But that I nolde no beest for me were deed),
Thanne hadde I with yow hoomly suffisaunce.
I am a man of litel sustenaunce.
My spirit hath his fostring in the Bible.
The body is ay so redy and penyble
To wake, that my stomak is destroyed."

When the wife had gone off to prepare him this frugal repast, the friar began terrifying poor Thomas, threatening him with hell-fire for giving contributions to other monks besides himself. He alone should have gotten the contributions, the friar complained. The miserable Thomas retorted with a complaint of his own:

"As help me Crist, as I, in fewe yeres,
Han spended, up-on dyvers maner freres,
Ful many a pound; yet fare I never the bet."

At that the friar flared up in anger:

The frere answerde, "O Thomas, dostow so?
What nedeth yow diverse freres seche?
What nedeth him that hath a parfit leche
To sechen othere leches in the toun?
Your inconstance is your confusioun.

.   .   .   .

'A! yif that covent half a quarter otes!'
'A! yif that covent four and twenty grotes!'
'A! yif that frere a peny, and lat him go!'
Nay, nay, Thomas! it may no-thing be so.
What is a ferthing worth parted in twelve?
Lo, ech thing that is oned in him-selve
Is more strong than whan it is to-scatered."

"Yif me thanne of thy gold, to make our cloistre," demanded the friar, and added one last threat:

> "And yet, god woot, unnethe the fundement
> Parfourned is, ne of our pavement
> Nis nat a tyle yet with-inne our wones;
> By god, we owen fourty pound for stones!
> Now help, Thomas, for him that harwed helle!
> For elles moste we our bokes selle.
> And if ye lakke our predicacioun,
> Than gooth the world al to destruccioun."

As I bent over Chaucer's archaic verse, I could see these prodigious cassocked figures issuing out of the depths of time. And I found it pleasant to roam thus in the ecclesiastical jungle of that age. In the medieval English monasteries the monks would often appear at the church services dead-drunk. They played cards and dice, loved horses, fought in tournaments and shed blood. They kept mistresses openly. They were rich and loved luxury and magnificence. What sumptuous grandeur when the splendid Archbishop of Canterbury, Thomas à Becket, went to France! What a royal cortege attended him! A throng of barons, two hundred knights, dogs, carriages, carts, an entire army of servants lavishly dressed and armed. Two hundred fifty young boys led the way, singing. Twelve men and twelve monkeys rode atop twelve gleaming horses. Behind followed knights in their gorgeous array, falconers and priests. And in the middle of this entourage sat the Archbishop Becket, the representative of the poor man of Nazareth, with his closest friends at his side, all decked out in velvet, gold, and precious stones.

The common people watched. They watched and did not forgive. In the wineshops and workshops and in the homes, workers and members of the bourgeoisie began reading the Bible with passion and putting their own interpretation upon it. Their anger accumulated as they compared the simple, humble life of Christ with the shameless and arrogant life led by these greedy bishops and abbots.

It was some time before they dared to raise their heads. The angelic pattern continued to hold them in awe and terror of its mysteries. They were afraid to flout the pattern lest at the same time they might blaspheme the terrifying content of the pattern. However, the churchmen grew more and more rash. Periodically monks and bishops would arrive from Rome, carrying papal letters with big red seals on which were carved in relief the crossed keys of Saint Peter. They brought indulgences from the Pope. "All those who have sinned," was the gist of the message they trumpeted, "let them come to pay, and we shall forgive them! So many pounds for murder, so many for theft, so many for adultery!" In their dread of hell many people opened their pouches and paid. They got their indulgences, hung them as a talisman around their necks and felt relief. But other people rebelled and sprang up in protest. "Sin," they cried, clutching the Bible in their hands, "sin can be quenched only when the heart is humbled and repents. It is not quenched by pounds. It is not God's will to let the rich pay and enter Paradise and to make the poor go to hell!" The peasants raised their sickles and pickaxes, and with their fellow workers, the craftsmen, launched a furious assault upon the Pope's emissaries and drove them away. But the wily, well-fed monks laughed, made themselves comfortable again, and kept on draining the milk of England.

A DRAGON: HENRY VIII

Until the tumbler overflowed . . . The throne was mounted by a dragon, a glutton, a woman-chaser, a cruel autocrat, who had no fear of the Pope. Henry VIII. A mighty, plethoric body, champion in archery and tennis, an untiring horseman: he was capable of wearing out ten horses in a day's hunt. Wrestling he loved so much that once he grabbed hold of Francis I, King of France, in front of a crowd, and tossed him playfully to the ground.

Henry VIII was one of the most brilliant monsters created by the lush, exotic climate of the Renaissance. A body with big primitive needs—eating, drinking, fighting, killing—and he satisfied them all liberally, undeterred by either society or Church. And his soul also had huge needs and curiosities: he yearned to be initiated into the divine mysteries and, in his leisure hours, to enjoy the delights of music and poetry. He was a theologian, loved literature, wrote poems, played the lyre and flute with great artistry and composed music for the songs and hymns he sang.

Though he had no fear of the Pope, he did fear hell. Throughout his entire life, his athletic body was consumed by the worm of "conscience." Tragic centaur that he was, he was half an emancipated Renaissance lover, while the other half of him was still sunk in the dark terrors of the Middle Ages.

He married six women. But he was not merely sensual. He was God-fearing as well, and he wanted to satisfy his passions in security, with the assent of God. When he saw the dark-blue eyes of Anne Boleyn, he went mad, and at once conceived a desire to be freed from his first wife, Catherine, the Spanish princess. However, the Pope refused to grant him permission to divorce Catherine. The God-fearing king fell into despair. Then one day his crafty counselors told him: "You don't need the Pope's permission. Summon the most famous theologians, ask them to give their opinions, and act as they judge fit." And the famous theologians of Oxford, Cambridge, the Sorbonne, and northern Italy, some of them induced by rich gifts and others by threats, provided him with the answer he sought. The people vainly protested on Catherine's behalf. Anne Boleyn was pregnant and the king was in a hurry. He no longer needed the Pope. He shook off the yoke and married the charming coquette with the dark-blue eyes. Cupid had waved his omnipotent little hand and in the act of pursuing an entirely different aim had propelled the English conscience to its salvation.

It wasn't only little Cupid that propelled England to find deliverance from the yoke of Rome. The national consciousness of the Englishman was stirring also. The rising bourgeois classes longed to rescue their country from religious and economic subjection to the papacy. They had lost confidence in the religious authority of another nation, which allied itself sometimes with France and sometimes with Spain. Nor could they any longer bear to see such great expanses of English land and so much of the nation's wealth in the hands of the monks. Besides, their spiritual consciences had been awakened. With the invention of printing, the Bible had begun circulating everywhere, and now everyone could read it—not in Latin, which they could not understand, but in their own language. And they could interpret it also with no need of depending on the priests because of the priests' knowledge of Latin.

And so the nation accepted the liberation from the papal yoke with relief. Fierce persecutions began. All the clerics who still remained faithful to the Popes were beheaded, burned, hanged in a bestial fury of religious intolerance. At that time England had twelve hundred monasteries, possessed of huge wealth; they had everything. This wealth was now divided between the king and the aristocracy, or else sold to the bourgeoisie and the peasants. The precious manuscripts were bought by grocers to be made into cornucopias and paper bags. The holy images and statues were burned, the frowned-on holy relics were thrown away. Within five years all the monastic property, movable and immovable, had been sold. Naturally the thousands of persons who benefited from the sale became the most implacable enemies of the Pope, being well aware that if his power returned to England they would lose all they had gained.

Henry did not become a follower of Luther, who was simultaneously preaching religious emancipation from the Pope. He remained faithful to the Catholic religion. All he wanted was to make it national and English, with himself as its leader. The older he grew, the more ferocious he became, and the more obsessed he was by strange fears. He hanged many Papists and Protestants: blood flowed around him. He lived in panic terror of going to hell. Yet all the same he had delivered the English conscience from a mighty yoke. Anne Boleyn's sweet eyes were only the delightful motive; the cause lay deeper. Inside himself for some time the Englishman had been groping for freedom.

When some one area of the human soul becomes illumined, the light spreads everywhere with irrepressible momentum. Now that the English people had become delivered from the Pope, they straightway felt a need for liberation from another yoke—the Latin language. Hitherto the priests had communicated with God in a language that the common people could not understand. Now that the people could remain alone before God without the mediation of the priests, they felt impelled to speak with Him in their own tongue, the simple language of the people. King Henry himself wrote the following in one of his letters:

> For us to use a foreign language we do not understand can neither please God nor bring salvation for man. He who does not understand the words he is speaking in his prayer to God is like the harp which

produces sounds but does not understand what value
they have. And the Christian is something more than
a musical instrument, and my subjects must be able
to pray like rational human beings in their own
mother tongue.

Then the famous Book of Common Prayer appeared, written in the language of the people, in a style simple and
austere, and brimming with primitive poetry. For the first
time the people could address their God in their own
language, aware of the full resonance of every word. Grave,
harsh English words; now the services assumed new meaning, every word laden with import.

Speaking your mother tongue may have an incalculable
influence on the illumination and liberation of your spirit.
For when you understand the precise meaning that the
words convey, you try to confine yourself to those which
fit. And in this way you delve more deeply into your own
spirit; and as you delve, you bring light there and give
meaning to your most secret desires, even the ones that are
the hardest to disentangle. What does "giving meaning"
to them imply? You elevate them out of the dark and
anonymous mass. You distinguish them from other wishes
associated with them. You give them substance so that
they can no longer be swallowed up in vagueness. You
save them. And in saving them, little by little you save and
free your own soul.

PURITANS

"Excessive and untimely violence to the heart darkens
and dulls the intellect." This sobering thought uttered by
Simeon the Theologian came to my mind one Sunday. In
the company of a friend from an old Puritan family I was
strolling around a church in a small English town. When

the church service came to an end, I stood off to one side, watching the men and women as they came out, each one clutching the prayer book. They held it as though it were a stone and they were about to hurl it in anger.

I shall never forget their cold, pitiless eyes, their tight-pressed lips, the dry, motionless exaltation on their faces—as though they were emerging from some terrible spectacle, or as though they had made a solemn vow to themselves, and seeing the world bubbling up before them like some satanic dream, they were stamping it down in disgust. Neither charm nor compassion nor Christian love. Once in Hebron, outside Jerusalem, I stood before a small mosque and watched the Moslems coming out from their prayers. Their faces too were affected, still burning from the prayer, and their eyes seemed blinded by the flame of their God. But their lips hung open, and they expressed fire and sensuality. These people here were coming away from their God in a frozen state.

"I feel terrified when I see them," I said to my friend. "What's the matter with them? What happened to them in church? Why have their faces frozen like this, as though they were epileptics?"

My friend dried his thin lips. "What can you understand, you children of the sun," he answered, "about the terrors of the North? You can change your religion as much as you like, you still have only one god: Apollo, the god of the sun. Not a fierce African sun, mind you, that dries up the waters and rots flesh, but a pleasant and moderate sun that loves the waters and the cool shade and human beings. But just hear what we've to say!"

He fixed his eyes on the thick fog that was descending over the grass. Separated by the sharp contours of the trees, it was hanging like rags of clouds about the pointed steeple and stone angels of the church. The whole building rose pitch-black and angry, and with its cloak of mist, it looked as though Jehovah had touched it and it were smoking.

"Just hear what we've to say," my Puritan friend repeated through his anaemic, unkissed lips. "My ancestors for generations have not smiled. My father was a pastor. When I was still a small boy I asked him one day why we never laughed at home. He looked at me in amazement. 'Have you read the Bible?' he asked me. 'Yes.' 'Does it mention anywhere that Christ ever laughed?' I was silent in shame. 'So you see? How then could we sinners laugh? But the Bible does report that Christ often wept. So we too ought to weep.' In your land of Greece has a father ever uttered such words to his son?"

"No, of course not," I replied, laughing. "Because the sun wouldn't let him. One of our saints—I can't remember which one—was once asked if he was in a hurry to leave the earth and enter Paradise. 'No,' the old ascetic said, 'I'm in no hurry. I've asked God to let me go to His Paradise by the longest way around.' He loved this earth so much that he'd asked God to let him stay as long as possible and enjoy the bliss here."

The Puritan shook his thin, pie-shaped head. "Our God," he said, "is molded out of darkness, rain, and cold. My Puritan ancestors used to gather on those endless winter nights and the one who knew how to read would read out of a thick book clamped with chains—the Bible. Everyone around would add his explanation of God's Word, piling up terror on terror. And it wasn't Christ's Word, but Jehovah's. He's the real God of the English."

By now the last members of the congregation had passed by and disappeared into the crooked lanes of the little town. Houses and shops all closed, a Puritanical deadness, our footsteps echoing on the pavement as though we were walking over tombs!

The quest for holiness, I was thinking, represents man's highest urge. But the only way to fulfill this highest urge is to ascend all the steps, including the lowest and most sinful. Whatever it is that makes plants and animals is certainly Nature. But the thing that struggles within us to conquer plants and animals is also Nature, is indeed her ultimate desire entrusted to her ultimate creature, man. This is man's real mission: to struggle to overcome the plants and animals inside himself.

"Life is a brief taste of honey," and the bee, or practical human being, has an idea that the honey in the flower was put there only for him to eat. While he eats it, it never occurs to him that his pollen-smeared wings are fertilizing the flower that had set him its honeyed trap. But when the superior human being sees the honey and falls into the trap, he does it with his eyes wide open. He gathers it, knowing all the time that this is not the purpose. He proceeds beyond the honey, all alone, into a state of extreme solitude. This rejection of the honey is called by many people purity.

My Puritan companion turned around to look at me in anxious excitement. Apparently he sensed that he had at his side a disbeliever from those far-off, sunny, diabolically beautiful countries where joy is not regarded as sinful, nor laughter an aberration from the lofty model of Christ. Involuntarily my friend felt scorn for these countries with their light morals, as he would call them. However far he had progressed beyond his ancestors, however much his brain had broadened, deep inside he still condemned laughter as shameless arrogance.

Once again he licked his tight lips. "What a terrible age it was!" he burst out, with an admiration he could not restrain. "In that period life had ineffable gravity. Men writhed in the palm of God. They knew that very few were going to be saved. All the others had been damned, thousands of years before they were born, to an eternity in hell. Neither good words nor good deeds nor pure thoughts could alter the divine verdict of damnation.

"Agony overpowered them, an unbearable terror. On Sunday when they used to meet in church and listen to God's words and threats, many would fall down in a faint. Not just the frail women, but big, strong men as well. They would return home speechless and pale, with downcast eyes. They would lean the Bible on their knees and slowly turn the pages, hanging in suspense upon each page, each paragraph. They learned the most fearful passages by heart so that they might whisper them softly as they walked through the streets, or when they found themselves in the presence of some temptation—food, women, gold—and wanted to exorcise it. My father, the pastor, told me that, before going to church, people often made their wills and bade farewell to their children and their wives because they didn't know if they would come out of the ordeal alive."

I remembered a shopwindow in London where I had seen a huge Bible, bound in thick boards like doors and black pigskin, with heavy chains and a rusty iron lock. Gothic letters, yellowed pages, soiled by the sweaty fingers that had leafed through it so feverishly. As though the Word of God were imprisoned in these chains to prevent it from getting loose and consuming the world. Didn't they have a similar practice in archaic periods and put chains and ropes about the statues of the gods to keep them from escaping?

"What a nightmare such a God must be!" I murmured. "What slavery!"

"What a yearning for salvation!" my friend cried. "Because never forget this: the religion of the genuine Englishman is neither a matter of feeling nor escapism. The problems that occupy his soul aren't theological or supernatural theories transcending the human condition.

There's only one question that arouses his passion, and he seeks the answer to this terrible question day and night, in agony. 'Do I belong to the Chosen Ones? Do I belong to the group that will conquer the earth in the name of the Lord?' This is the great, the terrible question."

I smiled involuntarily, but my friend looked at me sternly and I felt ashamed. "Pardon me," I said, "now I understand better. So then, the great, the unique question for the Englishman is this: 'Do I belong to the church that will conquer the earth in the name of the Lord?' "

"The conquest of the earth belongs to the Church of God. God invests His Church with the mission of governing the world. 'Therefore,' says the practical Englishman, 'I too must belong at all costs to the Chosen Ones.' Thus the Englishman combines perfectly the salvation of his soul with productive, practical energy."

My friend looked at me in amazement that such a patent truth should strike me as strange. "How else," he continued with some nervousness, "do you think man's soul can be saved? And how else can we understand that our soul has been saved except by looking at the results produced by our actions. Don't we judge the tree by the fruit? God blesses the labor of none but His Chosen Ones. So if an endeavor goes well, that's a sign that God is with it. Of course, we can't guess what the reason is. The will of God is an abyss. One's success has much more meaning than one thinks; it is Divine Grace. God intervenes incessantly in man's life, and whomever He loves He helps in his work. For to each individual and to each nation God has assigned a definite task for them to carry out on earth.

"In the Old Testament the Chosen Ones of God were the Hebrews. In the modern age, they are the English. Centuries ago our great religious poet, Milton, proclaimed it: 'God is decreeing to begin some new and great period in His Church, even to the reforming of the Reformation

itself. What does He then but reveal Himself to His servants, and as His manner is, first to His Englishmen?' Or, as
the famous lines run:

> And guardian angels sung the strain:
> 'Rule, Britannia! Britannia rule the waves!

"Is this faith justified? We have only to observe its results. Look at Puritanism and the English Renaissance.
What miracles! The salvation of the individual soul was
the beginning of the salvation of the world! How fruitful
the Messianic faith of our nation proved to be! No slack-
ing-off or faintheartedness. Every day, every night, a little
to save the world. And how? By conquering it, by pushing
it, either by kindness or by force, to take our road, which
was the road of God.

"The English saint is not someone who withdraws like a
coward from worldly contamination. He is someone who
plays the game up to the end. What game? The conquest
of peoples and places. Within his own individual orbit,
and in cooperation with the people of his race, he carries
out the mission of conquest entrusted to him by God.
The 'white man's burden'—the Englishman feels that the
whole responsibility for it rests on his shoulders."

Suddenly my friend became conscious of having talked
a great deal. Some Puritan missionary inside him, having
been roused from slumber, must have been preaching the
Word of God to the disbeliever.

"Forgive me," he said abashedly. "I've said too much.
But today is Sunday, and it's right for us to speak with our
friends about God and the salvation of the soul. Of course,
all I've said is at the opposite pole from the radiant visions
you have over there in the lands of the sun's dominion.
But here in the unsmiling North, such is the face of our

God—stern, fierce, harsh. We like it, though, because it's flesh of our flesh and fog of our fog."

JOHN WESLEY

Often I recalled what my Puritan friend had told me as I walked around the old English churches. Such was the Puritan religion: relentless and unsmiling. Their God was not the spotless Lamb sacrificing Himself for the salvation of mankind. Their God was the awe-inspiring general who ruthlessly gathers His Chosen Ones and conquers the world. So the fanatical Puritans fought like soldiers in the armies of God. They fought as warriors, as merchants, as workers, as sailors. And as their faith grew, England grew.

Time passed—not many years, to be sure, for even in the North, man's spirit cannot endure very long on such icy peaks as these. This accursed world has its good points too: food, drink, your friend's wife, sleep, dashing apparel, music. Cheerful human weaknesses, licit or otherwise, began to flaunt themselves and mocked at the exaggerated asceticism. An era of prosperity arrived, of the golden mean, of a general atmosphere of rationality. Religion and the common mind became reconciled once more. The superhuman torment and obsession with God ceased to be prescribed as the path leading to heaven. Puritan ecstasy begot epicurean reaction.

The human animal, pent up for long years, now broke its chains, streaming hungrily through all five of the body's cisterns. The eyes had longed to see bright spectacles and ladies beautifully dressed and beautifully undressed. The ears had longed to hear the sound of sweet songs and instruments, for the Puritans had forbidden games, dances, bells, celebrations, as well as wrestling and hunting. The nose wanted to smell some fragrance other than incense; the mouth to taste delicious food without fear of sinning; and the hands to touch and caress the world sensually. For years the human animal had fasted, and now it was starving. All barriers were overturned. Morality was ridiculed as an archaic fashion restricting the body from revealing all its charms. Hell shrank into a big bad wolf to frighten very little children or very little minds. Freed from his religious and supernatural fears, man found his real totem awakening inside him—the pig. And he rolled in the mud, squealing with delight.

At least the lords rolled in the mud. They got along well with the new religion and their new God. They had rich palaces, boundless forests for their hunts, the whole teeming earth and millions of slaves beyond the seas.

But the peasants, the workers, the poor people, who felt they were being wronged, suffered. In the religion that suited the lords they could find no consolation. To be able to bear the misery of their terrestrial life they required an entirely different kind of God—one who would give them definite assurances of justice after death and who would promise that all the lordly profligates and perfumed wastrels would be cast into hell while the hungry, ragged beggars of this world would enter Paradise.

So strong was their longing for reward and punishment that early in the eighteenth century they created their own prophet, John Wesley. As Professor of Greek Literature at Oxford, Wesley preached a new "Method of Life"—rigorous, ascetic, steeped in fasting and prayer, but in compassion as well. Since the rich princes and lords kept him from preaching in the churches, he preached in the open air—in the fields, along the riverbanks, in village squares. He founded Holy Clubs. For fifty years he rushed from village to village, square to square, in England, Ireland, Scotland, and North America, proclaiming the fiery new doctrines. Such a magnetic power glowed in his face that men and women often began to tremble upon seeing him, and sometimes to faint or fall down in ecstasy. And he himself would go without sleep in order to tame the unruly fires burning him and the passions of his flesh. He wrote and traveled here, there, and everywhere, organizing the faithful. He delivered some forty thousand sermons, and his followers, the Methodists, multiplied. A new flame had manifested itself in the faded, corrupt Anglican Church.

The Methodists spurned comfort and rediscovered the path leading to the heights of human existence—the path to God. The mistreated workers and peasants of England found relief from the misery of their life on earth by devoting themselves to the future life. They did not seek justice through revolutions or social reforms. Having rejected the good things of the earth, these religious rebels became patient and obedient citizens.

The Methodists made the most reckless choice that man in his pride can make. Scorning the kind of rationality that produces small but certain profits, they chose the chimera with its big, dangerous wings. They inverted the proverb "A bird in the hand is worth two in the bush." They stood Sancho's commonsense views upside down and dared, as all fierce and desperate men do, to risk their lives, heads or tails.

I shall never forget those hours—sometimes flooded with a gentle, northern sun, sometimes enveloped in fog—that I spent in the spacious paved courtyards among the graves surrounding the great cathedrals of England. I found deep happiness in meditating about the power that man possesses because of his capacity to transform the world through his own imagination. Above the first floor on the level of the earth, he erects a second floor that corresponds to his heart's desire. He holds the magical philosopher's stone, imagination, and all the base metals of God he turns to gold.

All these English graves in the churchyards, covering like shields the great warriors of the human chimera, were sending up the battle cry of the mountain Scots: "Fight with fury, accept death with joy." In the heroic medley that issues from English history, I could clearly distinguish the warlike groan of the eternal Don Quixote in man. And my heart was suffused with love and compassion and a pride transcending all ephemeral human endeavors. I remember in particular one twilight beneath the fortress-like Cathedral of Durham when two familiar voices swelled within my heart: the one, a female voice, questioning, and the other, the manly one, uttering the responses:

"How can we love God?"

"By loving human beings."

"How can we love human beings?"

"By struggling to bring them—by kindness or by force —along the right way."

"What is the right way?"

"The uphill way."

■ THE DIPLOMA
OF MAN

ETON

One fine summer day I threaded my path through the charming narrow lanes of Eton and entered the world-famous school where the English aristocracy is educated from the elementary level through high school. I wandered around worm-eaten old hallways and staircases. As I passed through the long, dark corridors I glanced at the cells where the boarding pupils stay, and I felt as if I were in a monastery. Except that here the public school requires the little monks to wear tail coats and top hats. These are their cassocks.

The walls of the classrooms and corridors had wooden paneling from floor to ceiling, and thousands of names, thickly clustered, had been carved on the wood, memorializing the students who had followed one another on these benches over the centuries. The air seemed to be thronged with thousands of souls; it was difficult to breathe. That magical condensation of the invisible human essence which one meets in landscapes or buildings or objects much frequented and much worshiped is almost visibly present in Eton, at least to any spirit strong enough to disengage itself from the strangling noose of logic. The air of Eton is dense with souls. Apparently the old tales telling how the soul, after abandoning the body, roams passionately around its favorite places are more than just tales. The soul does indeed get so attached to this world that it cannot bear to sever its ties again. Life is very fleeting, a brief taste of honey, and the soul cannot get its fill. So it returns, naked this time, the soul without the flesh, to whatever it loved and did not have time to enjoy, breathing over it like an erotic sigh. "And thus every soul an Aphrodite."

This distilled longing and nostalgia impinges on you as you inhale the air of Eton. Almost all the leaders of the English nation for centuries have spent their childhood and youth here, within these walls and in these fields and gardens. These enclosed courtyards and creaking, antique staircases and these jasmine vines over the arched doorways have remained throughout their whole lives the objects of a profound and incurable yearning.

When I left this holy cloister, I felt that one of my own wishes had fused forever with the air of the place: the wish that my own race might some day acquire an equally severe and equally happy school for leaders. Then the siege tactics of Alexander the Great might be imitated in action. When Alexander's army was unable to conquer a city, he would himself lunge into it, leaping off the ramparts into the very midst of the enemy. At that point, his whole army (his inferior self) would follow him, and the fortress would be overpowered.

And so, leaving a Greek wish sighing in this aristocratic English air, I went off to stroll about the green town. I passed by a garden where an inscription in Greek letters was written over the gate: ΕΞΩ ΔΕ ΟΙ ΚΥΝΕΣ ΚΑΙ ΟΙ ΦΟΝΕΙΣ ("Keep out the cynics and murderers"). In the adjacent royal city of Windsor that morning I had seen another inscription on a wall, the name of an Englishman and beneath it in Greek capitals: ΚΑΛΟΣ ΚΑΓΑΘΟΣ. And alongside, two reliefs from the Parthenon. Here in this famous little town where the English aristocracy is reared, you feel that the Greek spirit—luminous, bold, and balanced—is still marvelously active, even while exiled in the northern fog.

I crossed a little bridge over a river and arrived in an open space, where the older students, some wearing sky-blue caps, some white, were playing cricket. Beautiful, slender bodies, grace and strength, disciplined impulse, a delight to the eye and to the mind as well, for these bodies looked as though, with practice, they would become good conductors for the spirit to pass through.

An Eastern sage once saw some tightrope walkers executing some extremely dangerous feats of physical daring. And he burst into tears. "Why are you crying?" they asked him. "Because I'm thinking," replied the sage, "that if we could only train our souls the same way that we train our bodies, what wonders we could accomplish!" Here in Eton, however, the visitor cannot burst into tears. For neither will he see amazing tightrope feats, nor does the soul in these flexible bodies remain uncultivated. There is moderation, proportion, a parallel cultivation of body and mind on a human scale—Greek harmony. The two parallel and interconnected modes of education at Eton are classical instruction and sports. Not individual sports, such as the javelin, jumping, or discus throwing, but group sports: punt racing, cricket, tennis, football.

The group games serve a great moral purpose. They accustom you to subordinating your own individuality to a general activity, to feeling that you are a member of a group instead of merely an independent individual, to defending not only your own individual honor but the honor of the entire group to which you belong—school, university city, nation. Thus from step to step the game can raise you to the loftiest and most disinterested peaks of action. It also teaches this most important of lessons: the indispensability of leadership for victory. In participating in the group game you learn to submit yourself to the leader, you learn how to obey so that, when your own moment comes, if you wish, you may also know how to command.

Only thus can worthy leaders and eager followers be created—that is to say, a disciplined army able, materially and spiritually, to dominate the world.

In sports you do not train your body alone. It is your soul that you train above all. If Wellington remarked that the battle of Waterloo was won on the playing fields of Eton, he was entirely right. In these group sports you learn to be prepared, to exercise self-control, to await the appropriate moment, to sacrifice individual joys or preferences for the interests of the group. You learn how to adapt your own special capacities to the needs of the community and to use your strong points and weaknesses with a view to contributing as much as possible to the victory. This is the only way you can practice for the great game of public life later on.

In order to act on this high level you have to know yourself well, know the fellow next to you, know the whole group to which you belong. And besides, you have to know the opposing team. You must not scorn it; rather you must study it with impartiality and respect. You have to know its virtues and capacities in order to organize your own virtues and capacities accordingly, lest you lose the game. And there's one other thing more important than anything else, for it constitutes the most universally human and at the same time the most recondite purpose of the game. You have to know that the other side is ultimately not an opponent. It is working with you, because without it there would be no game. The purest moral lesson the game can teach is this: what matters supremely is not victory; it is how, by what methods, by what training and discipline, always maintaining strict fidelity to the rules of the game, you struggle for the victory.

Pondering thus as I watched the handsome blue-capped and white-capped Eton boys battling each other in the peaceful twilight, with their supple, alert bodies poised so delicately that they quivered like slender steel swords, I tried to analyze the fundamental laws of the training. I discovered four:

1. Training your body and soul as an individual, independently of the group.
2. Training your body and soul as an individual, within your own group.
3. Training your body and soul in relation to the opposing group.
4. The training of each team as a whole in relation to the other team as a whole.

Life is a game, like tennis or golf. You do not play by yourself. You play with others. You have a responsibility in relation to all your companions. All your companions have a responsibility in relation to you. Individual and group are one.

The game has rules. Whoever wants to play ought to know these rules and respect them. If he doesn't know the rules or doesn't want to respect them, he is not worthy of participating in the game. Within the circle marked out by the rules he is absolutely free; no one, not even the king, has the right to interfere. These laws may be antiquated or misguided or arbitrary. That doesn't matter. The important thing, in terms of the training of the human spirit, is to obey them. You must not be ashamed of having been beaten. You must be ashamed only when you have played badly and been beaten for that reason. Or—and this is worse—you must be ashamed when you have won by playing badly or dishonestly.

Fair play, this is the supreme duty. Playing the game well, whether it's football or war or a whole lifetime. This is the first and strictest command in the English Ten Commandments. "Be strong and play the man!" Do this duty of yours and don't worry about anything else. Success and failure are merely practical values, not spiritual ones. You have done your duty. What other reward do you want? If you expect any reward whatsoever, if you do not work in order to satisfy your own internal commands, but in order to be paid, then you are an employee. You are not a free combatant.

"He who does not find his compensation within himself is a slave. The desire to please others rouses the five poisons, the five senses of man." These noble words by the great Tibetan ascetic Milarepa would free the human heart and let it soar. They suit the green playing fields of Eton perfectly. Only a person who lives these words and puts them into action in his everyday life is a free man.

An English mother whose son was killed while fighting bravely in the last war had this simplest of English odes written on his tomb: "He played the game well."

Strong bodies, strong souls, love of danger, disciplined vitality, and an outlet for impulse. A friend of mine who had lived with English officers in India once told me the following story:

"We were sitting, a few young English officers and I, on the terrace of a Hindu village restaurant, overlooking a microscopic lake. It was noonday. The sun was blazing. The lake was full of crocodiles crowded close to each other. They were drugged by the burning heat and sluggish. Every now and then they would open their long jaws and yawn, and their pointed white teeth would flash.

"We'd drunk quite a bit of whiskey and were in high spirits. Suddenly one of us said: 'Who can jump from back to back over the crocodiles and get to the opposite bank?'

"'I can,' a lieutenant said calmly, and he went down the stairs.

"I caught my breath. 'We mustn't let him,' I shouted

anxiously. 'We mustn't let him attempt this mad act. Isn't he in danger?'

' 'Of course he's in danger," the officers answered as they filled their glasses.

"The young Englishman had already reached the lake. He raised his head, looked at us, waved his hand as though he were bidding us farewell, and all at once leapt onto the back of the first crocodile. From back to back, as lightly as a dancer, he stepped on the crocodiles, and sprang off on the opposite bank.

" 'Bravo!' his fellow officers called to him. 'Come on back now!'

"The young man came back, once again treading on the crocodiles with a light, sure step. He climbed the stairs of the restaurant and calmly sat down in his chair. They filled his glass with whiskey.

" 'Drink, and your heart'll go back to its normal place,' they said to him laughing, and changed the conversation."

My friend added: "I'm sure that when this young man returned from his tightrope walking over the crocodiles, he was no longer the same man. He had done a brave deed. He had faced danger and gambled his life. He had put his strength to the test and come out the winner. His spirit had been elevated a degree above the level where it had been before he'd done it."

A few days afterward, when I recounted this exploit to an English professor, he smiled. "Do you know why the English can perform such feats?" he asked me.

"Because they value human dignity more than life itself," I answered.

"No . . . They perform such feats because they have no imagination. Their soul is like a steel coil. They obey a sudden impulse. They spring up without stopping to reflect and to analyze the danger beforehand in their imagination. They plunge into it, following their instinct blindly and unerringly, and it just happens to be gallant. Cecil Rhodes, our great conqueror in South Africa, was right. He'd discovered the secret."

"What secret? What did he say?"

"The world belongs to the English," he said, "because they have no imagination."

OXFORD-CAMBRIDGE

I walked through the high, masterfully carved gate of the first college I came to at Oxford and found myself in a square medieval courtyard sown with old and tender grass. As I stood there, I had such an other-worldly sense of well-being, I was conscious of such a pleasant nostalgia for things past and such a potent desire for things to come, that my eyes felt dazed. Suddenly I became aware that this life of ours does have a deep meaning and wants nothing but rhythm—rhythm is what it lacks—in order to become rooted in the earth like a tree, with confidence and time to blossom and bear fruit.

A bitter longing was born in me, bitter because it was now too late for me to begin my life over again. It was a wish to escape from the vain and wretched meanderings in which we get lost, and to start life, having acquired from the beginning the broad, deep human rhythm that is imposed by this calm, graceful, and powerfully integrated courtyard with its age-old lawn. To begin life all over again; to love one's body and teach it to jump and swim and ride horseback! To be strong and preserve one's strength! To feel joy or pain and not to stoop to grimaces of joy or pain! To enrich one's mind as much as that conceited little advocate requires without letting it become overweening and get notions of running one's life! For what would life be worth then? To learn that there is a force in man which feels more profoundly than the heart, sees more clearly and further than the mind. It has no name and becomes manifest only in daring, nobility, purity, action. And you must let this force guide you and you must have absolute trust in it. And even if it casts you into death, do not ask why. If it does so, that means that so it has to be.

What then is rhythm? A central movement that governs our thought and action; an invisible "monarch" that commands—and all the elements, material and spiritual, that constitute the ephemeral confederacy of our existence, freely obey. Freely because they know that this command is their own deepest separate desire. He who has rhythm is liberated. Whatever he does is correct, that is to say, harmonized with his whole existence. It is involved in an unfaltering continuity with his own psychic past and is a fruitful seed of the future. He who has rhythm is not afraid of going astray or of transgressing any command. For with him the legislator is at work, and every act represents merely a confirmation and application of the law inside him.

Rhythm is a magnet in our vitals. It attracts all the sawdust of our flesh and spirit and suspends it in the air in a continuous line, like an impregnable, indissoluble bunch of grapes. Only rhythm is capable of conquering decomposition and death.

As I walked from college to college, the thought kept returning to me that this has been their great contribution: they have given rhythm to the English race. Out of all the virtues that can embellish man, these colleges isolated the ones that are distinctly English. They studied the English way of moving—slow and taciturn. They consolidated these ways with words and deeds, created a tradition, and so saved them from becoming dispersed once more. If they had included other virtues which were not genuinely English, the rhythm would have broken. Inconsistency would have been introduced and the tradition would have lost its power of continuity—that is to say, all its value.

Rhythm is a very delicate and very mysterious balance. If the Englishman should acquire French wit or Slavic propensities toward rebellion or the transcendental bliss of the Hindu, all his virtues would be threatened. Rhythm is like the face. Let one feature be changed, and the whole face becomes distorted. These colleges—and this is their great glory—kept the Englishman's face intact.

That is why I felt so much respect as I strolled here in Oxford through these workshops of English destiny. Everything took on a hidden meaning: square courtyards, Gothic gates and arches, half-eroded works in relief. Chimeras, lions, monsters of the Apocalypse, men with beards and others without beards, content with their lot and bending down in high good humor to watch the passing years through their stone eyes.

As sometimes happens, these colleges realized purposes far higher than those for which they were originally founded. They were founded for quite different reasons. At first they were educational monasteries to enable impecunious young men to study for theology or the priesthood. The Church, at that time omnipotent, paid for their sustenance and their teachers and supervised their religious education. Students and teachers also constituted a guild, which defended their rights against both the higher clergy and the rich townsfolk. They learned ecclesiastical law, Latin, theology, medicine, mathematics, and Aristotle's philosophy. They conversed passionately from morning till evening. They had a craze for sophistical disputation and intricate syllogisms. They drew their swords in every progressive movement, religious or social. Often the Pope would threaten them with excommunication, and the king would send his army to quiet these inflammable and dangerous innovators. At night they used to carouse in the wine cellars, fighting and killing each other or chasing after women.

In the middle of the thirteenth century, the first Franciscan friars landed in England. Poverty, chastity, obedience were the three great commands imposed upon them by their saintly founder, the Poverello of Assisi. The Franciscan flame was still in the stage of intense purity and energy. The admiration of the English people was aroused by these barefooted monks in their earth-colored cassocks, eating their crust of dry bread, sleeping in any shelter, and preaching the Word of God with unprecedented sweetness.

When the pious citizens of Southampton built them a stone monastery, the Franciscan abbot ordered them to tear it down at once. "We did not come here to erect walls," he said. And when a fastidious monk asked him for a pillow to sleep on, he answered him: "You don't need this little mound in order to raise your head toward God."

The Franciscans reached Oxford, and the students, impecunious and rebellious as they were, gave them an enthusiastic welcome. The friars themselves did not respect learning; it was Franciscan doctrine that the cultivation of the mind led to arrogance, insubordination, and hell. "Do not cut fruit from the tree of knowledge," they said; "you will be poisoned! Satan is the rebellious baron of the mind!" In time, however, they were forced to study theology, philosophy, and literature, so as to be able to answer the questions asked them by the faithful and to refute the attacks of their adversaries. And after a short while three great Franciscans were radiating light at Oxford: Roger Bacon, Duns Scotus, and Occam. Here at Oxford, in the heart of the Middle Ages, in the depths of the darkness, they were the first to light the way.

ROGER BACON

Roger Bacon, "the prince of thought in the Middle Ages," as Renan called him, was the greatest pride of Oxford. Physicist, chemist, mathematician, doctor, philosopher he was the first to teach the vanity of *a priori* dialectics, and he laid the foundations for empirical observation.

"Follow Nature if you want to subdue it," was the substance of what he told his contemporaries. "If you want to know that your reflection is something more than a vain plaything, verify it by experience and action. Reflection has no value unless it is confirmed by facts. In order to enter into the mysteries of nature, only one way exists: experimental science."

A solid English scientific attitude. But in the dark, scholastic thirteenth century, who was there to hearken to this founder of positivist science! He came too early. His contemporaries were destined to be born centuries after his death. Alone, without teachers and without pupils, he studied the laws of chemistry, delved into the study of physics, invented lenses for magnifying distant objects, and proved that the Julian calendar was not precise and had to be better adjusted to the solar year. He is also said to have invented gunpowder.

Naturally his colleagues cursed him and accused him of being a heretic as well as a magician. They drove him out, but he returned. They did not allow him to keep anything in his possession. He wrote the Pope, beseeching to be allowed ink and paper, nothing more, ink and paper in order to write.

With fiery passion Bacon preached his faith in scientific research and in facts, and he ruthlessly satirized the empty sophistical syllogisms of his day. "Experiment! Experiment!" he cried. But the students, poring over their scholastic translations of Aristotle, remained submerged in dialectical acrobatics. If he could, Bacon said, he would burn all the translations of Aristotle. He would burn them so that the students might open their own eyes and see the world. Over and over again he returned to his bold assault on what he called "the four chief obstacles in grasping the truth": vanity, trust in popular opinion, submission to the views of the authorities, and habit. If these four foes could be conquered, he said, the world would unveil itself before the students' gaze.

In intrepid defiance of his persecutors Bacon gathered the young men in Oxford and tried to infuse his spirit into them. He had an unshakable faith in the omnipotence of the mind when it operated not up in the clouds but well tied to solid earth. He prophesied many of the conquests that the mind has made in modern times. Thus he predicted a day when there would be boats sailing with motors, without oars or oarsmen, without sails; and when there would be cars moving "with fantastic rapidity," without being drawn by any animal. He foresaw flying machines: a man would sit in the middle, he said, "revolving some engine by which artificial wings would be made to beat the air like a flying bird." If the human mind only followed nature, it could achieve all things.

A strictly English method of pursuing knowledge and coping with reality: by obeying reality, with eyes wide open.

But anyone who sees much further than others is considered a menace or else mentally unbalanced. All the established people, all those in official places, fall upon him and try to stifle his voice. Forerunners are hunted and tormented. Often they tremble, and well might wish that the fertilizing word hadn't descended on them and consumed their vitality. When the second-century mystic, the unfortunate Maximilla, felt this seed inside her, she heard it cry out: "Why do you hunt me like a wolf preying upon the sheep. I am no wolf. I am the Word, the Spirit and Power!"

In a Moslem cemetery in Constantinople stands the tomb of a dervish. The marble tombstone has a round hole in the middle, and out of this there sprouts a most beautiful Apollonian laurel rooted in the heart of the dervish. The laurel has grown and blossomed and borne fruit out of the human vitals it has consumed. This is the way that the fertilizing word is nourished in the bosom of the forerunners.

Bacon endured tremendous suffering. He paid dearly for his outstanding gifts. He was severely persecuted, he was imprisoned for fourteen years, and at his death, he made this bitter judgment: "I repent of having said so much in my struggle against ignorance."

THOMAS WYCLIFFE

A century after the first martyr, Bacon, another voice made itself heard on this same hallowed soil of Oxford: the voice of Thomas Wycliffe. A religious voice this was, audacious and proud. It declaimed against intermediaries between God and man, and demanded the deliverance of conscience from the clutches of the popish Church.

Because of him, I had gone to Balliol College as to a shrine. Wycliffe was a professor of theology there when he raised the banner of freedom. I entered the big courtyard with its green lawn, looked around the cells and dark medieval corridors, and sat down on a stone in the sun. What a joy it is to be in solitude and in despair, like a tranquil fugitive, in a huge, sunny courtyard; and to feel that some grand shade, risen out of the depths of time, is lightly treading the grass, about to merge with your own shade!

The shade appeared, looking thin and sickly, just as Wycliffe was during his lifetime, when he was consumed by prayer and fasting. But the sacred fire shone in its eyes, and an unsacred arrogance. Wycliffe wrote a book called *On Divine Dominion*, and this the shade held tightly in its bony, crooked fingers. The Byzantine frescoes depict the Pantocrator in exactly the same way: clasping a heavy Bible in his arm with a gesture of such violence that he seems to be gathering momentum in order to fling it at men.

And I could hear the withering tones of Wycliffe's voice as he hissed out his message, telling men that they had no need of middlemen or dragomans in order to communicate with God. Telling them that God was the master of the world, and that He had turned over part of His dominion to the temporal rulers, and not given it all to the Pope; that the royal right therefore was no less sacred than the papal right; that, moreover, each and every Christian had received a part of God's dominion as a gift from Him, so that all men were representatives of God on earth.

I bent forward to hear Wycliffe's voice; I was pleased, because it was a voice I liked. These words do not age, do not fade, for the rhythm moving them is immortal. It is the rhythm of man's struggle through all the centuries for freedom.

As soon as the voice of this new trail blazer was lifted, the well-fed abbots and bishops and the licentious lords organized themselves to suffocate it. They dragged the new grand martyr to the courts. The priests rushed at him with the intention of pulverizing him, but the people of London intervened in anger and saved him. Wycliffe's sardonic voice had awakened in the untamed vitals of the Saxon the familiar and well-loved reverberations of liberty.

At that point the bishops demanded that the Pope excommunicate him. The fearless prophet only laughed in mockery. No one could be excommunicated by the Pope, he said, unless he had first been excommunicated in his own conscience, which alone could condemn or sanction. And he proclaimed that he would turn to the people, speak to them, and let them judge! He would write in their own language, in their everyday speech, so that they could understand him.

Wycliffe was the first to use the colloquial English language in writing. Until then, no one had condescended to write in it. He launched the full force of his irony and invective against the sale of indulgences. He condemned the bishops and the Pope for hoarding riches by deceiving the people; he excoriated them for the immoral, unChristian lives they led.

The people followed him wherever he went, wild with enthusiasm. They had no need of bishops and abbots, or of the Pope, the fiery apostle of human liberty told them. They would be able to read and understand the Bible for themselves without these intermediaries, once Wycliffe had translated it into the popular language. No priest need stand between God and the human conscience.

He was expelled from Oxford. Taking refuge in a small village, he settled down there and translated the Bible into the spoken tongue and handed it over to the people. An awesome weapon. For the first time the common man could hear the Word of God in his own tongue and understand it without the intervention of the prelates. For the first time he could speak to God and know what he was saying. Gathered in someone's house around the lighted fire, peasants and workmen and craftsmen began to read the Bible. A new world opened before them. Their spirits were pervaded with a deep joy and pride, as though they had for the first time found courage to enter the palace of heaven and to stand before God, dressed in their own coarse peasants' garments.

The Pope was enraged. He summoned the rebel to apologize, and the latter responded ironically:

> I am always happy when I am given the opportunity to expound my opinions in front of whosoever it be; above all, before the Bishop of Rome. For I am certain that if my faith is orthodox, he will condemn it; and if it be heretical, he will defend it!

Wycliffe founded bands of poor priests, and he sent them all over England to disseminate his ideas. He didn't allow them to possess anything—not even a little tray to hold alms. Just one kind of alms were they allowed to accept, a bit of food, and that only when they were hungry. Barefoot, wearing long, reddish cassocks, they roved from village to village, preaching independence from the Church, equality, poverty. They filled the people with zeal. Women were carried away and began preaching too. The poor, the illiterate, the despised, and all those who could no longer bear the wealth and immorality of the higher clergy listened with ardent excitement and satisfaction to the fiery message of salvation.

The proud prophet was by now exhausted from the toil and persecution, which he had willingly endured, confident in the ultimate triumph of the truth. In his debilitated state he became afflicted with paralysis and died. Even after his death the papacy pursued him. Fifty years later the Pope ordered his bones to be disinterred and burned on a pyre.

Nevertheless, the liberating movement kept spreading and awakening the masses, though the Church vented its wrath and the fires were kindled on all sides to burn anyone caught reading the Bible in the popular tongue. For a century the followers of Wycliffe continued to grow in strength and numbers. In 1414 they just barely failed to conquer England. But the revolution was drowned in blood. And one of the leaders, Lord Cobham, was hung over a slow fire, bound with chains, until he turned to charcoal.

"Whenever it happens," said Saint Augustine, "that I am more moved by the singing than by the thing that is sung, I admit that I have grievously sinned." I felt that I had sinned, letting myself revel with such delight in these past ages and forgetting the agony of the present hour. The chimes of the great clock in the courtyard roused me with their solemn, deliberate tones, like the voice of a well-loved father scolding. It was noontime and I had a pleasant sensation of hunger. As I went out into the street I felt that I was being suddenly whisked from the Middle Ages to the immediate living moment.

The medieval streets of Oxford glistened in streams of sunlight, gay, crowded with young people. Handsome, sunburned young men with slender bodies, small, delicately molded heads, elastic step, and clear confident eyes. These young men gave the impression of never having wrestled with great spiritual problems. They had never gone off the beaten track, up higher roads or down lower ones, than the ordinary man. They knew perfectly well what they wanted, because what they wanted was not murky or indefinite. And they had the happiness of being able to achieve it each day, because it did not exceed the ordinary powers of a human being. Spiritual ease, moral conviction, bodily joy. As you walk the streets of Oxford, you feel contented—the way you might if you watched well-bred horses, all aglow, as they emerged neighing from the sea. One calls to mind the proud words that the poet of the English race put into the mouth of Mother England, glorying in her children:

Flesh of the flesh that I bred, bone of the bone that I bare;
Stark as your sons shall be—stern as your fathers were.
Deeper than speech our love, stronger than life our tether,
But we do not fall on the neck nor kiss when we come
   together.

. . . .

Go to your work and be strong, halting not in your ways,
Baulking the end half-won for an instant dole of praise.
Stand to your work and be wise—certain of sword and pen,
Who are neither children nor Gods, but men in a world
   of men.

Splendid products of Oxford and Cambridge, where the
body and the spirit are cultivated in harmony, where the
human being is not maimed either by overstrenuous
physical training or by exaggerated mental tension.
Measure, harmony: Greek youths with narrow brows, eager, athletic bodies, and a springlike spirit.

These two nurseries of human beings, Oxford and Cambridge, friendly rivals that they are, sometimes indulge
in mutual bantering. One day a charming and cultured
graduate of Cambridge, who had a job in the Foreign Office, gave me the following description of the difference
between the two universities: "A graduate of Oxford walks
as though he is saying, 'The whole world belongs to me.'
A graduate of Cambridge walks as though he is saying, 'It
doesn't matter to me whom the world belongs to.'" He
laughed and added: "I'm a graduate of Cambridge."

In the colleges of Oxford and Cambridge the main ob-
ject is not the loading of the brain with learning or knowledge. The students do not emerge from here as specialists
—doctors, lawyers, theologians, physicists, or even athletes.
Too much emphasis is not accorded to any kind of spe-

cialization, either physical or intellectual. These are the places where the most select young people of Great Britain come after they have finished high school. They stay here two or three years to acquire the "harmony," the balanced physical, spiritual, psychic training of the perfect man, no more; and then, if they want, they can continue special studies elsewhere, in universities, law schools, or polytechnic schools, or hospitals. At Oxford or Cambridge one does not receive a diploma for specialized study. One receives the Diploma of Man.

The youth in primitive tribes, as a preliminary to achieving the status of grown men, leave their villages for a few months and bury themselves in the forests. There they lead a life of cenobitic rigor, subjecting themselves to harsh trials. They are bidding farewell to their childhood and making themselves ready for the difficult time of adulthood. They fast, learn to resist hunger, thirst, fatigue. They train their bodies in war and swimming and hunting of wild game. At night they beat great drums, light fires and dance. No one is allowed to approach them, neither child nor man nor woman. All by themselves they train body and soul to play the part of a man well.

The English youth's sojourn in Oxford or Cambridge resembles this; he comes in order to fit himself for entrance into manhood. In these modernized monastic communities, he experiences the tradition of his race, strengthening the most fundamental English virtues: discipline, self-possession, determination, the longing for action. He mingles with other young men. They play together on the same team, work together on opposing teams, and forge dreams of future collaboration. They talk with each other and try to convert abstract meanings into precise meanings, so that later on they can more easily transform them into action.

And simultaneously they sift the knowledge that is indispensable for the ennoblement and cultivation of the white man—above all, ancient Greek poetry and philosophy, which up to the present day still constitute the highest intellectual triumph of the white race. As Mosley says, "How is it possible to be a gentleman and not know Greek?"

Oxford and Cambridge, the two great workshops where the leaders of Great Britain are hammered out. Everywhere throughout the entire British Empire you can meet graduates of Cambridge and Oxford, model human beings. Their influence on the English race has been enormous. They saved England from the grossest materialism, from the barren sophistries of scholasticism, and from subjection to narrow-minded leaders. For here it is character and not the specialist that is created. The real Englishman does not ask you, "What do you know?" The only question he asks you is, "What are you?"

These colleges, as we saw, had been built for moneyless young men who wanted to study theology, but beginning at the time of the Renaissance they began to aspire to something more. The indigent candidates for the priesthood were relegated to the side, and henceforth the colleges came to be reserved for the aristocrats, who entered them in order to cultivate body and spirit for broader ideals and to prepare themselves for the task of expanding and governing the Empire. Then in time the bourgeoisie gained wealth and ascended through the ever-open doors into the aristocracy. They too began sending their sons to Oxford and Cambridge. A few more generations passed, and from the middle of the nineteenth century on, still humbler social classes rose in the scale, acquired power, and once again impecunious young men who were outstanding in their studies could take their places in their old colleges. Blood crossed and became renewed. Opportunities were given to the working classes to participate, through their best sons, in the governing of the nation. After the last World War the democratic and popular strata began entering the universities in still greater numbers.

In a country house during the summer I had met the wise historian and superb human being, H. A. L. Fisher. As Minister of Education under Lloyd George he had proposed a law enabling chosen young men of the people to study in the colleges of Oxford and Cambridge with all expenses paid. He was proud of this law and expected it to bear rich fruit.

"These young men of the poor classes," he once said to me, "by receiving the best English education in this way, are destined to govern the British Empire eventually, along with the aristocracy and the middle class. We are giving strong members of the working class new opportunity to assume national responsibilities and to put their capacities at the service of England."

He watched me as if divining what I was thinking. Then he added with a smile: "Don't be surprised. Our two highest schools will always preserve their aristocratic essence. They will not become democratic. On the contrary, in harmony with the solid English tradition, they are transforming the common people into aristocrats. Every Englishman—this is his nature—wants to become an aristocrat, that is, to perform such services for the community that the always-open doors of the English aristocracy will welcome him. And there is no more direct or more essentially English path for that ascent than Cambridge and Oxford."

GENTLEMAN AND ROBOT

One day in Cambridge, in a grassy courtyard of one of the colleges, I met an old professor who was taking a stroll around the lawn. I struck up a conversation with him.

"Haven't the students changed their psychology at all

since the World War?" I asked. This indiscreet question put an abrupt end to the old professor's morning stroll. He shook his yellowy-white head.

"England has changed," he answered after a brief silence. "England has changed. How could her children fail to change? Especially at their youthful and most critical and sensitive age. Most of our postwar students no longer have the old moral certainty or the conviction that English supremacy is unchallengeable. Many are beginning to hesitate. Still more have become indifferent and cynical. They scorn conventions and cannot understand, however much we old people rail at them, that the conventions are not something merely external, superficial, unimportant. Essence and convention are one; the convention is the visible aspect of the essence. But do you think they listen to us? And that is why today you can see well-bred gentlemen sitting at table in the evening without wearing dinner jackets."

The old man had caught fire. I liked him. His old gods were in danger. The hitherto inviolate fortress of English custom had crashed. The essence implicit in the conventions no longer commanded faith, and another essence had not yet been discovered which could be crystallized into new conventions.

The old man continued, his lifeless voice growing animated: "Before the war, our students were conservative. They carried on the tradition and obeyed it of their own free will. They were persisting in the path that their ancestors had forged for them. They thought that this English way would go on forever and that it would bring everything to a triumphant conclusion. Indeed in my own youth there were many imperialists who had espoused zealous, grandiloquent doctrines. They all had firm English foundations to base their thought and actions on. But now—" he raised his frail arms up toward the Cambridge sky in a gesture of bewilderment—"Now," he went on, and his voice faltered slightly, "many of them are pacifists or socialists. Some of them in fact aren't ashamed to say that Great Britain has grown old . . ."

"Do nations grow old too?" I asked naïvely. He was a professor of history and would know.

A sudden anxiety flitted through his blue eyes as he looked at me. The old historian did not answer immediately. He seemed to be debating with himself. For a moment the blue eyes lit up, then grew dark, as though little flashes of lightning had shot through his mind, lighting up and fading. His blood was seething. But he calmed his agitation after a bit and replied:

"Something has changed in England. We seem to find ourselves at a sharp and dangerous turning point. A few years ago we were the first in trade and industry and ships. We had all the seas of the world in our power and a quarter of the land. We had an unshakable faith in the supremacy of our race. We had a conviction that our tradition was infallible. We were sure of ourselves externally, sure internally as well. Fortresses. We walked slowly and steadily.

"Now since the war the rhythm of the world has altered. It's no longer remotely slow or sure. It's bafflingly hasty and unsure. So England is compelled to change her rhythm too, her natural gait. We are no longer, I admit, first in trade or in industry. Our military organization has found itself confronted by opposing organizations that are awe-inspiring, more youthful, and more flexible. We too must change our rhythm, so as not to be left behind. That's all."

"That's all?" I asked.

The old professor became stubborn. "That's all," he answered in a pique. "That's all; nothing more! We've got to readjust. England has never been governed by hard-and-fast theoretical rules. She has always spread her sails or drawn them in according as the winds blew. England is an organism that has always been accustomed to adapting itself to new necessities, and she's been ready to do it at every moment. So why have our young people become discouraged and cowardly? Why do they want peace at the very moment when we need imperialistic zeal to hold on to what our fathers left us? I don't understand! I don't understand!"

Again he raised his thin arms to the Cambridge sky in bewilderment. And I could see the two generations standing face to face, the one shouting and scolding and giving orders, and the other laughing and transgressing them.

In other eras the fatal distance between father and son was not so great. No gulf yawned between them. Quietly and automatically the young man continued in the footsteps of the old, and his life progressed slowly and surely. Today the rhythm has grown wild. The father watches the son with terror and does not recognize him. Life is in a hurry and no one knows why or in what direction it is going.

I said goodbye to the old professor and returned to the pulsing streets to watch the fleeting life of the moment. Men and women were rushing by anxiously. Their eyes had a strange glitter, like the reflection of a fire. Sunburned students passed along singing. Well-built girls on bicycles pumped their sturdy shins up and down and their silk stockings shone like steel.

A good race, a difficult moment. The spirit is aware of it and is getting ready. Will it do any good? We are about to see. The newspapers are blaring terrifying premonitions of war. The distant thunder of the approaching storm makes itself heard. There is no sun by day. There are no stars by night. The inner sky has turned black.

In this deep green, enchanting Cambridge I suddenly remembered a gruesome dream I had once had in Russia. I seemed to be lying on my back in the very heart of some big city. And as I looked up at the sky, I saw, like a kite held in an invisible hand, a corpse stretched out prone, grazing the roof tops. It was greenish yellow, had no lips, and its teeth were enormous. And now with my eyes open I could see the sky shrouded by that repulsive kite, grazing the houses and the tops of people's heads.

For centuries now there have been popular prophecies warning of a day to come when the calf will float in blood. This day has arrived.

Impatient and anxious, I walked along with needlelike sensations in my lips, as though I were feeling the first electric sparks of the storm. Kingdoms, I reflected, do not fall because of the power of the enemy, however formidable that may be. They fall because of their own weaknesses and lack of faith. "The enemy is within." When the worm of doubt burrows into a kingdom and begins consuming it, a peculiar scent arises. It is the scent, we said, that is smelled by the hungry corsairs before they surge forth. I wandered in turmoil from college to college, circling around the grassy courtyards. As I passed through those gates, which had been passed through so many thousands of times, I had a fearful question burning on my lips.

Here, in Cambridge and Oxford, England has created a marvelous human type: the Gentleman. Nobility, lordliness, dignity—virtues with ancient roots, blooming in a choice and delicate way. The Gentleman is the prize product of a very old nurture.

How, then, will England be able to face a different hu-

man type, mechanized, more up-to-date, created by nations with such demonic astuteness, such system, and such
determination? Two human prototypes are getting ready
and are on the eve of engaging each other in battle.
Which will be victorious?

■ THE GENTLEMAN

■ THE INDIAN HERO Yudhistra fought and conquered all men. And when he died, he went to heaven. All his friends had abandoned him. There was only one companion still faithful to him: his dog—faithful even unto death.

The gates of heaven opened, and God came out. "Enter, Yudhistra," He bade him. "Here is your home."

"I will not enter without my dog!" Yudhistra exclaimed.

"Dogs are not allowed to enter heaven!" God answered, knitting his eyebrows.

"Then I'll go away!" said Yudhistra, and he turned his back on heaven.

This Yudhistra might have been a Japanese samurai or an English gentleman. Heroism and tenderness, a perfectly polite demonstration of force. "The good warrior," the old samurai used to say, "can never be crude." Faith, gallantry, kindness. Never to betray a friend, be it only a dog—even in order to enter the eternal kingdom!

The ancient Greeks had created their own human prototype: the *kalos kagathos*. A harmony of body and soul. "A coordinated training of all the senses." The perfect human being is neither the great but withered wise man, nor the inhuman ascetic, nor the disfigured athlete. Balance—here lies the Greek secret of perfection.

The Romans created the proud *civis Romanus*—order, discipline, coarsely integrated power, bereft of flexibility and grace. Responsibility—the intrepid Roman citizen felt the entire Empire resting on his own shoulders!

The Italian Renaissance created the flexible, delightful, charming sinner, *Il cortegiano*, free of any strict morals. Life was a short-lived feast where the unknown host had laid rich banquets for us, bidding us to eat and drink, and setting us next to fair ladies and telling us: "Kiss them! Only eat and kiss with grace and nobility, like aristocrats!"

Spain created the fierce *hidalgo*, who saw the honor of the whole visible and invisible world dangling on the tip of his own sword. Life was no feast. For the men it was a military encampment and for the women a nunnery. God, King, Honor—the three great values; but above all honor.

France created the *honnête homme*, exuding social finesse and grace. Life was a compromise and a coexistence. Social conscience must set the pace for individual conscience. Virtues and vices must be measured so as not to annoy anyone. And indeed, if possible, they must be agreeable for human intercourse. Man was a social animal, decked out in wigs and laces.

And England created the Gentleman.

The ingredients of the gentleman changed according to each epoch. If we follow the various meanings of the gentleman from the fourteenth century on, we can see, as in a small faithful mirror, the characteristic ideal of the developed English mentality.

In the Middle Ages the gentleman was the noble knight with his coat of arms and his sword. His sword was double-edged, for he was duty-bound to strike the rich man who tormented and wronged the poor man as well as the strong man who oppressed the weak man. The gentleman was in the service of a militant God. He went to the Crusades as hero and saint.

In England, however, the gentleman never attained the

ecstatic whimsicality of a Don Quixote. Here the gentleman was a rational person, practical, bereft of great imagination. His manners were simple and his attire modest.
He saw human beings clearly as human beings and windmills as windmills. He never confused cloud and stone,
desire and reality. He was hero and saint—but in the current human proportions.

In time, the military facets of the gentleman atrophied
and his everyday social virtues multiplied. He had begun
to crystallize and survive in English society as a rich, peace-
loving bourgeois, no longer as a feudal warrior. It was no
longer indispensable for a nobleman to have a coat of arms
and a sword in order to be called a gentleman. Good manners sufficed, as well as self-respect and respect for other
people and the refusal to stoop to falsehood or any base
act.

Old-fashioned chivalry blended with the new humanism.
There was a slight translation of values, and with them
the human model changed. But as always happens with
English institutions, the new reality did not absolutely reject
tradition, and the new gentleman preserved many of his
old characteristics: his faithfulness and devotion to his
ruler, the King; his profound way of life based on personal honor; respect for women; a fine but simple manner
of dressing; and the determined cultivation and care of his
own body.

Henceforth, nobleman and gentleman were no longer
synonymous. You might be a prince, yet not be a gentleman. The former was a chance circumstance, a gift
that came by birth. The latter was a personal feat, your
own triumph alone. Once a mother begged King James II
to make her worthless son a gentleman, and the King answered: "I could make your son a baron or a marquess, but
not even Almighty God could make him a gentleman."

From the middle of the sixteenth century on, the word

"gentleman" had already begun to mirror the new social ideals. A scribbler of the period made bold to remark: "The unworthy son of a prince is no gentleman. The worthy son of a peasant is a gentleman."

But the wheel kept rolling. Time passed. The ideal human type changed. Puritanism descended on England. Now the indispensable ingredients of the gentleman became dour honesty, ascetic morality, a frowning manner, hair shaven to the roots, dark, somber clothes, a Bible in the pocket. "Merry England" became sulky, and the gentleman with her.

Once again, time passed, and the appearance of the land changed with it. The Stuarts reascended the throne. The face of England grew lighter and more pleasant. Once again the English people could let their virtues smile. Once more, they treated the body lovingly, bathed and dressed it in brightly colored clothes and plumes and ruffles and laces. Discreetly, without creating any scandal, they allowed their bodies to enjoy large or small transgressions of morality.

In the nineteenth century, during the austere Victorian era, the meaning of "gentleman" assumed the stable form it still has to this very day. The ideal was constantly becoming more democratic, without losing its aristocratic essence. Now the gentleman became the person who harmoniously cultivated his own personal and social idiosyncrasies, who controlled his passions, who never spoke about himself or slandered others—the master of his own nerves, the "captain of his own soul."

He kept all the virtues of the preceding types of gentleman, but with more flexibility and discretion. He promised less than he had decided to do. He never flaunted his passions in any obvious way and had perfect control over them, both the good ones and the bad ones. To a high degree, he possessed that great English virtue, self-control.

In his everyday life he was cordial and hospitable, but

never familiar. And he spent his money as generously and regally as he could, because avarice (and even economy) were characteristics he thought unworthy of the gentleman.

*Whoever is well born or by nature inclining to the good,
Even if his mother be an Ethiopian, is a noble man!*

Here the word "noble," as Menander used it, is translated in English as "gentleman."

"How can we define the gentleman?" I once asked one of the most perfect gentlemen of contemporary England, Sir Sidney Waterloo.

"The gentleman," he answered me, "is he who feels himself at ease in the presence of everyone and everything, and who makes everyone and everything else feel at ease in his presence."

A correct definition, but how could it possibly include the whole indescribable atmosphere—the invisible, quivering tilting of the scale between ego-worship and nobility, between sensitivity and psychological control, between passion and discipline—out of which the gentleman is molded.

We catch an inkling of him from uncalculated, apparently insignificant details: a movement of the hand, a tone of voice, a kind of gait, a style of dressing, eating, amusement; . . . the cold invincible intensity with which he loves the countryside, sports, women, horses, *The Times*.

In a Latin schoolbook from the tenth century, we read the following dialogue:

"Did they whip you today?"
"No, for I behaved well."
"Whom of your schoolmates did they whip?"
"Why do you ask? I can't betray them!"

This little English boy of the tenth century was a gentleman!

WEEKEND

Saturday and Sunday. Sunk in a deep comfortable armchair, in a state of enchantment, I watched the tongues of fire licking upward, whistling through the broad marble fireplace. Serenity, pleasant air, the ecstasy of being in some other world, three hours away from London, in the green heart of the countryside.

How well these country manor houses fit in with the natural surroundings of England! Nobility, comfort, a profound connection and continuity of the green lawns. Time stops pleasantly here, in archaic immobility. Beyond the green fence with its flowing vines, nothing exists—neither factories, nor big cities, nor the savage modern rhythm. We find ourselves in a microscopic fragrant island, on some green sphere in the middle of some Pacific Ocean. Only in Japan had I reveled in a similar miracle, where, on opening a little gate at the back of my house in a noisy city, instantaneously I found myself transported to utter solitude.

An aristocratic old hall, the walls laden with gilded books, the ancestors with their curly wigs, refined smiles, thick rings, staring out of their heavy gold frames. Precious works of art everywhere—Chinese clay horses, Japanese Buddhas, Gothic Madonnas, African masks, Mexican vases, young Greek maidens from Tanagra. These smiling ancestors, perched motionless very high up on the walls, seem to have returned in order to pillage the world.

The charming lady of the house had snow-white hair, a youthful face, rosy cheeks, like one of those marchionesses of the good old days, who used to wear powdered wigs. She was an author of children's tales. I had read one of her books that I had liked and I told her so.

She laughed. "There are few outstanding women in English history," she remarked. "Havelock Ellis had the patience to count them—to the ruination of us women! In the entire history of England, he found nine hundred seventy-five outstanding men and only fifty-five women! I am certainly not the fifty-sixth!"

She looked out the big window at the two solitary, silver-leaved firs rising in the middle of the garden. "It doesn't matter . . ." after a brief melancholy silence. "I write because I don't have any children. I never created any actual living people, so I make imaginary ones, as though I were still a little girl, dressing up my dolls in all sorts of clothes . . ."

A slight air of grief percolated through the pleasant atmosphere. The white-haired dowager watched the flames consuming the big logs in the fireplace, gently licking them away.

All of a sudden I recalled a German girl, thirty years old, ugly, unlucky, unmarried, exuding desire. One day she climbed on her bicycle and went over to visit a friend of mine staying outside Berlin. She was holding a heavy volume of Kant, when she went into my friend's room.

"I've come to have you explain a page I can't understand," she said.

They sat down next to each other. The girl opened the book. Their knees were touching. My friend began explaining the complicated abstract meanings. The girl bent over listening. But suddenly she closed the book abruptly and sprang up. "I want to have a child!" she said.

Now the lady began talking to me about the English novel.

"The Saxon elements in us push us towards the novel, the Norman elements towards drama. The Saxons loved the realistic representation of life. They observed and respected details, gathered patiently and understandingly and with deep affection, all the little everyday things, juxtaposing them one next to the other. And gradually out of these stones the construction rose. The Normans reveled in military conflict, quick formulation, a brilliant condensation of life into its most fundamental dramatic elements. The former is a peasant, the latter a warrior."

I was aware of all this, but I enjoyed hearing it from the mouth of an actual living English person. This was a fine hour before the fireplace in the English countryside. By now the sun had turned and the rosy twilight was seeping in through the big glass doors. The wigged ancestors came to life in the half-light.

"To our Saxon and Norman elements," the silvery voice continued, "another element was suddenly added—the Dutch. The effect of eighteenth-century Dutch civilization on us was great. Our small neighbor with her definite, neat mentality was the first to create a bourgeois civilization: commerce, a merchant fleet, middle-class architecture, comfortable homes, private gardens, simple solid clothes. And as painters: portraits, landscapes, everyday family scenes—small portable images for the walls of the middle class, no longer the magnificent spectacles and frescoes for churches, palaces, chambers. She made life smaller, more tidy. She made beauty accessible, cutting pleasure down to human proportions. Do you understand me?"

"Perfectly!" I answered. "She turned gold coins into pennies!"

"Yes." The lady's answer showed some annoyance. "But not in the humiliating sense you perhaps intend. You Greeks scorn quantity perhaps more than you ought to. Your only feeling is for quality. Your great desire is to concentrate as much beauty as possible into the smallest possible area. Here, look at this girl from Tanagra—"

She got up to take from a shelf a small clay compatriot

of mine and laid it in my hands. The face of the Tanagra maiden sparkled in the twilight reflection. My fists filled with beauty. With the tips of my fingers, in silence, I caressed the clay girl.

"You see?" the English lady continued. "Her tiny body has concentrated all the beauty not only of woman but of life as a whole."

"This is the golden coin," I said.

"Yes, but when the Dutch people turned it into pennies, as you say, they gave it back to us intact. Nothing was lost— Why are you smiling?"

"For me," I remarked, "art is a great secret, a rare precious metal— But let's not talk of that. I know it's impossible for you to agree. Let's get back to the English novel."

I got up and set the little maiden of Tanagra back on her shelf. The tips of my fingers felt hot.

"Well?" I asked.

"The English novel," the beautiful old lady resumed, "tries to make the beauty of everyday life accessible to everyone, by mirroring English society. A faithful mirror. In it we can observe our own faces. Bend over and you will see them."

"I have bent," I answered, "and I have seen three or four faces. The face of Wells, round, optimistic, with his darting blue eyes and his broad mouth, naïvely preaching scientific panaceas to save the world. And after him, the long satanic face of Bernard Shaw, mercilessly sarcastic and laughing, his voice hissing, antipathetic, prophesying the imminent doom of this world, where no one believes in anything any more and everyone makes love with everyone else just because they have nothing better to do—out of pettiness, vanity, boredom.

"And then I saw the pleasant face of Galsworthy condemning our modern life as inhuman and monstrous; acutely describing the injustice of our age, its imbecility and falsity. And last of all, the serene, ecstatic face of Arnold Bennett, neither preaching, nor judging, nor condemning, never troubled by social or metaphysical problems, forever opening his blue eyes to welcome the spectacle of life. Hungrily, sensually, he observed this strange flamboyant procession. And he smiled, without love or hatred. Which of all these faces should I believe?"

"All of them," the old lady smiled. "Our era is a kaleidoscopic image made up of many disparate views. Each of these is a piece—the cheek, the eyebrow, the mouth—of the hidden comprehensive view. Reality streams on, flowing in all directions. And it still has not become solidified.

"That is what I like about it. It is full of contradictions, unforeseen elements, spasms of creativity. Old and new coexist and intertwine, and we rejoice in the sensation that (thank God!) logic does not rule the world.

"Here, take a look at these children's books I'm so interested in. Alongside our childish books with their simple little songs and animals, plants and birds, we also have our modern books full of cars, motors, airplanes, sports, practical, useful instructions. Read these if you want to shudder—shudder or rejoice, I don't know which . . .

"Children from three to six are taught how to travel by train, how to buy a ticket, how to pack their baggage, how to look out the window at the landscape—all useful, practical, devoid of poetry. For slightly older children, there are books aimed at initiating them into the various everyday professions: policemen, mailmen, shepherds, farmers, engineers. Huge propaganda is directed towards the children about the professions that England stands in main need of: pilots, radio technicians, mechanics, sailors, cinema technicians, reporters.

"Children's books no longer describe novelistic adventures, no longer cultivate the imagination. A prosaic tide has risen to oppress our age. The spirit of the child has become confined. Poetry has dried up inside him. The world has lost its wings. The flamboyant peacock has molted and ended up an ungraceful, domesticated chicken.

"Poetry has vanished, disappeared . . . And even love has become a hurried, practical, brief sport. In my time, when we were young children, 2 and 2 used to make 22. Nowadays, 2 and 2 make 4. This is a big loss, don't you think?"

"A big loss"—I laughed—"but also a big gain."

"What gain?"

"We have gotten rid of our utterly faded poetic wings. Life is left naked, plucked, you might say, shivering. Life has lost its feathers and feels cold. That's all right. Let it freeze. Only in this way will it be able to understand the practical value of the great wings of imagination."

"Would that were so," the old dowager said, shaking her head dubiously. "But I believe I won't be in time to enjoy these new wings. Now, the only thing I can see is the old beloved wings molting away. Also, you should open the books that are being written for girls, and once again, you'll shudder—or more likely as I see, feel happy. What are our girls learning nowadays? How to become independent of the family and the husband, how to struggle and earn their own bread.

"Economic, spiritual, moral independence. They say girls have the right to follow the path they have chosen for themselves, ignoring whatever their former 'tyrants' may have to say—father, brother, husband. All the downy softness of the woman vanishes in this way. If we acquire the same virtues and the same vices as the men; if we become men disguised in skirts, we are lost. I am observing these modern girls, the new married couples. Womanly modesty, devotion, sweetness no longer exist. The family no longer exists.

"Like bankrupt shops, we find ourselves breaking up.

We are selling out, selling out at all costs old virtues, anxieties, hopes. I often feel I can hear the auction gavel banging on the rostrum. What do you say? Isn't this decomposition?"

"To be sure," I answered. "But it is indispensable for the coming synthesis. The desires of the children show the way. No books are more prophetic than the ones children like. We must make up our minds to this and not look back to the past, outdated order. We must try to pass through this sacred and indispensable phase of decomposition at top speed. There is no other way."

"Is there no other way?" the dowager asked, her cheeks flushing red.

But at that very moment, the other weekend guests arrived. A young diplomat with his wife; two bony girls, tennis experts; a pleasant, slender old man, one of the wisest politicians in England.

At once the atmosphere changed. The close warm connection between the old woman and myself was disturbed. It vanished as though suddenly some static had come between us.

A large group of people is a difficult chemical interaction and rarely can it attain a psychic or spiritual union. Every single visible human body is encircled by its own quivering, invisible, powerful stellar body, full of mysterious likes and dislikes.

The atmosphere changed. The old lady rose to welcome her guests. Laughter, voices, flowers, boxes of chocolates. The pipes lit up. The men gathered, looking for a subject which they could all stand around to discuss. The wise old man hit on it and began talking about eternal Greece. His eyes caught fire. At some point, while he was still a student at Cambridge, he had written an essay on Demosthenes, and now he was carrying on a passionate discussion about that narrow-minded, grand patriot who up till the last breath of his life had fought for one idea alone. In vain, Alexander the Great had expanded Greece to the edge of the world. And Demosthenes, stubbornly stuck on the rock of the Acropolis, kept blaring: "No!"

The two bony girls paced back and forth as though in a cage.

"Have you read Demosthenes?" I asked them with provincial naïveté just to see their reaction.

They both burst out laughing.

There was a gulf between us and I felt an unexpected bitterness, as though I had been left behind and the young people had passed me by. I felt ashamed of having read Demosthenes once upon a time.

But in the meantime, over by the fireplace, the old dowager had begun telling literary anecdotes. I drew close.

"We're talking about Bernard Shaw." She smiled at me. "Our modern Mephistopheles whom you have no love for. One day I invited him to dinner. Of course, I gave very strict orders to the cook to prepare all the foods without meat. In those days, I had a splendid Negro cook.

"Well, she boiled and baked the vegetables and concocted as many combinations as she could. She tried and tried them all, but the foods still seemed horribly untasty to her. In her despair, she grabbed some meat ever so fast, chopped it up, added some butter, made a sauce and poured it over all the vegetables.

"Bernard Shaw arrived. We were sitting around the table, laughing, eating the hors d'oeuvres. And then the trays appeared, and what should we see—God forbid!— but meat. Bernard Shaw sprang up. Without saying a word, he grabbed his hat and left."

"And Lawrence?" I asked him. "Did you know him?"

"Which Lawrence? David, the novelist? Always full of suspicion, charming, but insufferable."

"No," I answered. "The other one, the desert one."

"A great man"—the lady laughed—"a fearless, restless, spirit. But an underhanded rogue. One day he came to my home and I happened to be out. The maid was sitting in the living room reading. Lawrence thought it was some lady friend of mine, and he lost no time. 'Only you are capable of understanding me,' he told her. 'I will open my heart to you!' This phrase he used to repeat to everyone and above all, to all the ladies."

"And did you know Cecil Rhodes?"

"My dear friend, Sir John, knew him well," she answered, showing me to the pleasant old man sitting over by the fireplace, his palms extended toward the fire.

Sir John turned around.

"A great daydreamer," he said, "and a great conqueror. He had a mysterious magic power. No human will could resist him. Harsh, abrupt, frugal in his diet like a Spartan, he used to dream of conquering the world. For twenty-four years, he gave his entire fortune to a secret society that he himself had founded with one single, extraordinarily simple aim: that this society should impose the supremacy of Great Britain over the whole world!

"A Don Quixote, but one who exploited the most modern weapon to make his chimera a reality—money. He made an enormous fortune, conquered an entire kingdom, Rhodesia, aggrandizing not only England but the English spirit as well. He climbed all the steps, from the fiercest egoism to the most altruistic madness. At first he used to squander all his demonic energy to aggrandize his own ego; then, later on, to aggrandize England, and finally to give all humanity a rhythm of peaceful mature action, self-confidence and moral perfection."

Sir John smiled. "I loved him very much," he said. "But in his presence, I used to feel as a wingless chicken would feel in the presence of a male peacock unfurling its tail."

I watched the fire in the fireplace, thinking of what a joy it must be to belong to a race capable of begetting such spirits . . .

Sir John shook his head. "I have known several great spirits in my life," he said. "Another two: Lord Rosebery and Lloyd George. Lord Rosebery was short, with plump hands, beautiful blue eyes, a superb warm voice. He could not sleep, so he used to read all night long. He had a vast memory and knew everything about the seventeenth, eighteenth and nineteenth centuries. Sometimes in the depths of the night, he used to ride his favorite horse and race like mad through the dark forest, in order to get tired and go back to his bed, perhaps to sleep. "Three things I have made my aim in life," he often used to tell me. "To win the Derby, to become Prime Minister, and to marry the richest bride in England."

Sir John laughed.

"And he succeeded in all three," he said. "He was happiest about the first."

"And Lloyd George?" I asked.

"A magician. The most vital, refreshing, charming human being I have ever met in my life. Eternally young. Much younger than the young people. I love him so much I can't even talk about him."

And he turned back to the fire, spreading his palms toward it.

After dinner, the men stayed behind in the dining room to drink the last of the wine and converse more freely and gaily. The ladies with their bare shoulders and long silk trains withdrew to the living room to wait for the men.

Tonight, it so happened, the stories were not at all gay. The telephones and radios and newspapers had been spreading dire forebodings through the air. Would there or would there not be a war? Would the world be destroyed or not?

Sir John had drunk a bit more wine and had begun talking away in a calm pleasant voice, slightly hoarse.

"We are moving back into Chaos," he was saying. "At the present time, there are three great forces at work in England: the aristocracy, the bureaucracy, and the working class. The first of these is breaking down all the time. During the past fifty years, so many bureaucrats have entered the aristocracy that the old-time chivalrous, proud spirit is on the defensive. Money has become all-powerful and the aristocracy is beginning to lose the game. How many of its ancestral castles have been sold or turned into sanitariums, schools, museums, insane asylum or habitations for merchants and industrialists—or else ended up as ruins?

"The aristocrats are being shoved more and more off to one side. England is ruled by others nowadays. Fortunately, England has had time to create a human type, the gentleman—a person with power, who knows how to control and use it without barbaric means. And mark my words: When the internal and the external wars are all over and humanity has fallen back exhausted on the ruins it has heaped upon itself, then, I hope, this human value 'made in England' will leave its stamp on the world. Without it, I fear the Chaos can never become Cosmos."

"So, will there be a war then?" our host queried, filling our glasses with port.

"There certainly will be," answered Sir John. "Otherwise, tension like this cannot find a release. It will happen. The diplomats will patch it up again. It will happen again, and once again they'll patch it up and once again it will happen. These are the tremendous spasms of birth. The earth has a belly-ache and suffers. Pregnancy in the woman lasts nine months. But when the whole earth is giving birth, the pangs may last for centuries."

"Are you going to leave us to ourselves much longer?"

The door had opened halfway and the tiny, snow-white head and tightly corseted bosom of the mistress of the house emerged:

"How much longer are you going to leave us all alone?"

The men drained the dregs of their glasses and got up. They snuffed out the white candles and lights still burning and went into the living room. One of the girls was holding *The Times* open, trying to solve the daily chess problem, printed in black castles, black pawns, kings and queens.

"Come and help me, Sir John," she called. "I can't manage it."

And the old philosopher sat down, took out *The Times* and plunged into the game.

FRIEDRICH NIETZSCHE

August 25: a great, enormously bitter date in the diary of my heart. Wherever I happen to be, I dedicate this day in its entirety to a person I have deeply loved in the course of my life—Nietzsche. On this day, thirty-nine years ago, he died. And now, very early in the morning as I was strolling in a park along the banks of the Thames, his shade came back through the damp English air, beckoning over the dark-green grass.

Never before has the presence of this proud European been so imperative, he who had outgrown the borders of his own country and been so scornful of his Philistine compatriots. For no one ever sensed so nobly and passionately the necessity of metamorphosing our bellicose human instincts and setting them in a realm transcending nations.

We sat down on a humble little bench beneath an autumn-yellow chestnut tree. I didn't dare turn my face directly toward him for fear he might get angry and go away.

The present moment the world is undergoing is a heavy one, laden down with all the gifts of evil. Nietzsche, who sowed the dangerous seed of the Superman, beyond good and evil—beyond morals, philanthropy, peace—in what way and with what Dionysiac awe would he look upon the red ears of corn that have sprouted up now?

The seed you sowed was nourished with your own blood and tears until it became an independent hungry organism and left you, and you can no longer summon it back. For there is no doubt that only now, when it is too late, you become aware that this seed is not your own. A far crueler power has entrusted it to your vitals, far more inhuman than even your own most cruel and inhuman fantasies.

We are mere feminine hearts, and the male who sows the seed is some awesome and invisible dragon.

And often, in order that the mystery increase, the fiercest seed may choose the tamest and most sensitive hearts for refuge.

Such was your heart, Grand Martyr and Father of the Superman.

On all the uphill paths of your sublime martyrdom, I could see the drops of your blood still warm. In the village where you were born, one rainy morning I wandered in the fog all alone through the narrow grassy lanes, in search of you.

And afterward, in the little neighboring town with its great Gothic cathedral, I searched for your mother's home, where you often used to rush at your most feverish moments to find peace and become her child again.

And then, the heavenly paths along the shores of Genoa, where you so delighted in the sea, the pleasant sky, the humble people and the light air.

You lived in a way so gentle, frugal, smiling that the

simple neighborhood women called you a saint. And do you remember how you made plans for starting a simple, peaceful way of life?

> Let me be independent, yet not allow my independence to bother anyone. Let me have a sweet-tongued hidden pride. Let me sleep lightly, drink no drinks, prepare my own humble food by myself. Let me have no great friends. Let me see no women, read no newspapers, covet no honors. Let me associate only with the most chosen people. And if I do not find the chosen ones, then the simple people!

One January in the winter sun of the Engadine, between Sils-Maria and Silvaplana, I was looking with deep emotion for the pyramid-shaped rock where the vision of the Eternal Recurrence had first struck you, and you had burst into a lamentation:

> However bitter and unbearable my life may be, may it be blessed and may it come and come again, returning unnumbered times!

For you had tasted that keenest joy the hero feels, which petty spirits think a martyrdom: to see the abyss before you, to move ahead and not accept retreat.

The mountains all around smoked blue in the sun. Far off in the distance I heard a sound and saw a mass of snow melting, crashing down. And I recalled what your friend had written you: "Within your books, I seem to hear the distant sound of crashing waters."

And on entering Sils-Maria, just as I was crossing the little bridge with its poor cemetery nearby, I turned to my right, shuddering with joy. For just as you had felt Zarathustra suddenly by your side, I too looked down at my shadow and saw the "one become two and you walking by my side." Once again today, Grand Martyr, all your labor is flooding my mind.

At the time you were still a fiery young man questioning all the heroes in order to choose a trainer for your own heart—to tame and ease it from the violence of love—and one day you met Schopenhauer, the Brahman of the North.

You sat at his feet and discovered his heroic, despairing vision of life: that the world is our own creation; that everything we discern, both visible and invisible, is an erring dream. One Will alone exists, blind, without beginning or end, without purpose, indifferent, neither logical nor illogical—alogical—and enormous. Squeezed in place and time, it is shattered into innumerable forms. It annihilates them, creates new ones and in turn crushes these too and so on for all time. In this way, the self-convulsion of the Will becomes an insufferable, indestructible pain. There is no progress. Destiny is not governed by logic. Abstract conceptions and religious morality are base consolations for stupid men and cowards. The strong and knowledgeable man calmly faces the aimless phantasmagoria of the world. He can revel in dissolving and decomposing the multi-colored, ephemeral cloak of magic.

At this point, whatever Nietzsche had divined became organized into a strict, tightly integrated theory, elevated into a heroic vision. The poet, philosopher, and warrior combating inside Nietzsche's heart became reconciled. For a period of time, the young ascetic could rejoice in solitude, music, long walks.

When a storm broke out over the mountain one day, he wrote:

What do I care for moral precepts: "Do this; don't do that!" How different from lightning, thunderstorms, hail! Free powers, free of moralizings. How happy and strong these forces are, undisturbed by Thought!"

For a moment, he waxed enthusiastic over the growing strength of his native land. But soon Schopenhauer brought him back to Buddhistic impassivity: "The visions of man are vain reflections passing over the dark sea."

Nietzsche's spirit flooded with heroic bitterness, brightened only by his love of art. Then one day, in the flower of his youth, he came face to face with a fateful person (after Schopenhauer his second guide), the man who gave him the keenest joy in his life: Wagner.

A great moment. Nietzsche twenty-five years old, fiery, taciturn, with calm, agreeable manners and deep-set, violent eyes—and Wagner, fifty-six years old, at the peak of his powers, full of dreams and energy, a natural force exploding over the heads of the young men:

"Come!" he bade them. "I am the heir of Luther, Kant, Schopenhauer, Beethoven. Help me. I want a theater where I will be able to create freely. Give it to me! I want a people who are capable of understanding me. You must become my people! Help me. You are duty-bound! And I will make you glorious!"

Art was the sole salvation, Wagner said. All those who had ceased believing in the old lies, all those who believed in art alone, could still find consolation and refuge. Only through art would society attain its supreme balance. "Art," Wagner wrote King Louis, "by presenting life as a game, transforms its most terrifying facets into beautiful images, thus elevating and consoling us."

Nietzsche listened. He made flesh and blood of the master's words and fought by his side. He looked into the pre-Socratic philosophers and abruptly a grand heroic period burst open before him, full of sudden flashes, terrifying legends, tragic thoughts, strong spirits shrouding the abyss with laughing myths so as to overcome it. Greece ceased being as the masters had painted her so idyllically for us— balanced, carefree, facing life and death with simple- minded, smiling serenity. This serenity came afterward and remained as the fruit of a flaming tree when that tree had already begun to wither. Before this serenity, Chaos had roared in Greece's vitals, great bitterness, manly will. An unbridled god, Dionysus, had led the frenzied dances with the men and women on the mountainsides and in the caves. All Greece was dancing like a maenad.

In a fever of tragic philosophizing, Nietzsche strove to piece his vision together. Apollo and Dionysus were the sacred couple who gave birth to tragedy. Apollo dreamed and saw the harmony and beauty of the world in serene forms. Fortified within his own individuality, even in the midst of the stormy sea of phenomena, he was able to stand calm and confident, motionless, reveling in the tempest of the dream. His glance was bathed in light. And even when he was overwhelmed by fury or grief, he never destroyed the godlike equilibrium of beauty.

Dionysus crushed the individuality, hurled phenomena into the sea, following their terrifying gyrations. Men and beasts became brothers. Death itself became one of the masks of life. The multicolored veil of deception was rent, and standing shoulder to shoulder we could touch the truth that we are all one, we are all God.

At first the Greeks, safe in their Apollonian fortress, tried to erect a barrier against these uncontrollable Dionysiac forces rushing into Greece from all the roads of the main- land and the sea. But they could not tame Dionysus alto- gether. The two gods waged battle. Neither one could put the other down. They became reconciled and created tragedy.

The Dionysiac orgies were freed of their bestiality and

could now shine resplendent under the pleasant controlled dream. But the hero of tragedy always was one and one alone: Dionysus. All the heroes and heroines of tragedy were but masks of the god—smiles and tears sparkling calmly in the grace of Apollo.

But Greek tragedy suddenly vanished. Logical analysis killed it. With his dialectic, Socrates annihilated the Apollonian reflectiveness and the Dionysiac intoxication. With Euripides, tragedy turned to human passion, rhetoric, and sophistical preaching to propagandize new ideas. It lost its tragic essence and died.

But the Dionysiac intoxication survived and became immortalized in the mysteries and the great moments of human ecstasy. Would it then ever be capable of donning the godlike flesh of Art again? Or would Socraticism—that is, science—hold Dionysus in chains forever? Or perhaps, now with Kant, after human logic had acknowledged its own limitations, a new civilization would emerge and have as its symbol Socrates teaching music at last?

Until the present time, the ideal of our civilization has been the Alexandrian philosopher, who was essentially a librarian and printer, running his eyes over dusty books and spelling misprints . . . But the crown had begun to topple off the head of science. The Dionysiac spirit was becoming increasingly aroused. German music from Bach to Wagner was hailing its arrival. A new "tragic civilization" was dawning. Tragedy was reborn.

The deceptive world and dark wasteland of Schopenhauer became utterly metamorphosed! A tremendous whirlwind stirred all the dead, unmoving elements in the storm of German music:

Yes, my friends, have faith with me in Dionysian life and in the rebirth of tragedy. The time of the

Socratic man is past; crown yourselves with ivy, take the thyrsus in your hand, and marvel not if tigers and panthers lie down fawning at your feet. Dare now to be tragic men, for ye shall be redeemed! Ye shall accompany the Dionysian festive procession from India to Greece! Arm yourselves for hard strife, but have faith in the wonders of your god!

—*The Birth of Tragedy*,
(Fadiman translation)

Such were the cosmic ideas supported by Nietzsche in Wagner's work. The new tragic civilization would arise from Germany. The new Aeschylus stood before us, living, struggling, creating, seeking our help. But these prophecies found no reverberation. The philosophers scorned them. The young men were not moved. Nietzsche grew bitter. Doubts were born in him. He began to query whether it was possible for modern man to become refined. He fell ill, and at the university his students began abandoning him.

An agonized spasm. The poet in him hid the abyss with the flowers of art. But the philosopher in him sought at all costs to learn, scorning all consolation, even this art itself. The former created and found relief. The latter analyzed, decomposed, grew desperate. The critical mind crushed the idols.

What was the value of Wagner's art, he asked. It was devoid of form, devoid of faith—panting, rhetorical, bereft of any divine intoxication or nobility—exactly like the art of Euripides, good only for hysterical women, theater people and sick men. Nietzsche's demigod ended up now as a "man of the theater!" He had tricked him and failed to keep his word. Now he was working on Christian themes in the writing of *Parsifal*. The hero was vanquished and

collapsed at the foot of the Cross. The man who had promised us to create new myths and yoke leopardine logic to
his Dionysiac chariot!

Now Nietzsche began proclaiming that art concealed
the horrible truth, covering it with pretty images, so becoming a consolation for cowards. We must find the truth
even if the world goes to the dogs!

This was Nietzsche's new outcry, in opposition to his
own earlier belief. The critic in him had conquered the
poet. The truth had conquered beauty. And now even
Schopenhauer no longer satisfied the raging needs of his
mind. Life was not merely the will to live. It was something
more intense: the will to dominate. Life was not satisfied
to preserve itself alone. It wanted to expand and conquer.

Art was no longer the purpose of life. It was now but a
slight relief in the process of the struggle. Above poetry
stood knowledge. Greater than Aeschylus was Socrates.
Higher than the most brilliant, fruitful falsehood stood
the truth, even if it were mortal.

He writhed, wandering ill from place to place. The heat
paralyzed him. The wind enervated him. The snow hurt
his eyes. He could not sleep, and he took drugs. He lived
like a pauper, deprived of comfort, in unheated rooms.
But he used to say proudly that the sick man had no right
to curse life. From the depths of his pain, his hymn to joy
and health rose clear, unyielding.

He felt a great seed growing in him, consuming his vitals.
One day as he was walking in the Engadine, he stopped
short in sudden terror. Time, he reflected, was infinite. Matter was limited. So, of necessity, the moment must recur
when all these combinations of matter would be reborn in
the same, identical form. After innumerable millennia, a
man like me, I myself, would stand again on this same rock
and would rediscover this same idea. And not only once.
This has happened unnumbered times and would happen

again unnumbered times. Therefore there was no hope for the future to be better. There was no salvation. Always identically the same, we would turn and turn in the wheel of time. And thus even the most ephemeral things became eternal, and our most insignificant act assumed incalculable significance henceforth.

Nietzsche plunged into an agonized ecstasy. And so his pain was without end and the pain of the world incurable. But ascetic and proud, he accepted his martyrdom with joy.

A new work must be created to preach the New Testament to humanity. In what form? As a philosophical system? No . . . his thought must pour forth lyrically. As epic? Prophecies? And then, suddenly, the form of Zarathustra flashed through his brain. In this state of joy and agony he was found by Lou Salome.

Grand Martyr, this fiery Slavic woman with the penetrating, excited, curious mind bent over in silence to hear you. You gave her your spirit lavishly and she drained it, smiling hungrily. How many years had it been since you had opened your heart so trustingly, reveling in the turbulent, fruitful emotions inspired in us by women? How long had it been since you had felt your heart soften and melt underneath your heavy military panoply? That evening as you entered your ascetic cell, for the first time in the atmosphere of your own life you breathed the scent of woman.

This delightful stirring sensation followed you into the mountains where you had taken refuge. And you waited for the woman's letter in a state of deep emotion, O ascetic one. Then one day she sent you eight lines of verse, and your heart pounded like a twenty-year-old boy's as you shouted them out beneath the peaceful fir tree:

> *With all my strength I clasp thee close;*
> *Oh, send thy flame upon me like a lover,*
> *And 'mid the battle's rage and throes,*

Let me thy being's inmost self discover!
To think, to live till Time alone shall drown me,
With all thy floods my measure fill!
And if thou hast now left no bliss to crown me,
Lead on! thou hast thy sorrow still!

And immediately after this, the mortal days of parting. The woman was frightened of you as though you were some nighttime forest, and in its darkness she could not see the little god smiling at her with his finger on his mouth. And your martyrdom began all over again—illness, isolation, silence.

You felt like a tree breaking beneath the weight of its own fruit, and you longed for hands to come and harvest you. You were standing by the side of the road, facing the cities of man below, but no one came.

Ah, you thought to yourself, solitude and separation from the person you love. No, may you never ever relive those hours! You had to open a door of salvation within this closed circle of Eternal Recurrence!

He wrote *Zarathustra*. A new hope flashed through his mind, a new seed: the Superman. This was the purpose of the earth; this bore salvation. This was the answer to the old question, Could modern man become refined?

Yes, he could! And not as Wagner was now preaching in his new work, through Christ, but through man himself, through the virtues and struggles of a new aristocracy. Man could give birth to Superman. This was the purpose of life, the source of energy, the Saviour. Eternal Recurrence overwhelmed Nietzsche. The Superman was the new chimera which would exorcise the horror of life. No longer Art, but Action.

Eternal Recurrence was bereft of hope. The Superman was a great hope. How could these two clashing visions be harmonized?

From that point on, Nietzsche's spirit beat its wings along the brink of madness. Zarathustra remained a mere outcry. And Nietzsche abandoned this tragic poem in a crippled state, striving scientifically now to prove that the essence of life was the will to dominate.

Europe was disintegrating and had to be subjected to the strict diet of leaders. Nowadays the prevailing morality was the work of slaves, a conspiracy organized by the weak people and the masses against the strong man and the shepherd. The slaves, out of self-interest and craftiness, had revised values. They were proclaiming that the strong man, the creator, was evil. The sick and the idiots were good. They could not bear pain. They had become philanthropic Christians and socialists. Only the Superman, cruel to himself, was capable of forging new dictates, of giving new aims to the masses.

What were these aims? What should be the organization of the Chosen Ones and the crowd? What was the role of war in this new tragic period of Europe? These were the problems disturbing Nietzsche during his last years of light. But he could not answer. In the presence of the terrifying rising flood, his heart turned coward. Impotent and agonized, his brain began slipping downhill.

He plunged into his old Dionysian songs and with tremendously bitter foreboding, sang his own swan song:

The sun sinks.
Not much longer thirsteth thou,
O burnt-up heart!
Promise is in the air,
From unknown mouths I feel a breath.
   The great coolness comes . . .

The air is strange and pure.
See how the night

Leers at me with eyes askance,
Like a seducer. . . .
Be strong, my brave heart,
And ask not "Why?"

The day of my life!
The sun sinks . . .

In a short time, darkness was to settle over his mind, last-ing eleven years, until his death. At times he used to take a book in his hands and ask his sister: "Didn't I use to write fine books too?" And when they showed him a picture of Wagner, he said: "This man I loved very much!"

I turned around. The shade was still sitting next to me on the bench in this English park, misty and shrunken. Two airplanes roared away overhead. The shade did not raise its eyes to stare, but looked instead at the fallen yellow leaves of the chestnut tree, trembling and shivering.

A young newsboy rushed by, shouting the latest tidings of war. In Moscow, the German-Soviet treaty had been signed, and the little light still left in heaven vanished.

Genghis Khan wore an iron ring on which two words were engraved: *Rasti-Rusti* ("Might-Right"). Our age wears this ring too. Who proclaimed the essence of life to be the desire to expand and dominate? Who said that only might deserves rights? Who prophesied the Superman? Well, now the Superman has arrived, and its wrinkled prophet is trying to hide himself beneath an autumn tree.

Today for the first time, after all these years when I have celebrated memorial services for this martyr-prophet in solitude, I have felt such tragic compassion for him. For it is the first time I have seen so crystal-clearly that we are all reeds on the lips of some invisible shepherd, playing what-ever tune he blows us.

I looked at his deep-sunk eyes, his precipitous forehead and drooping mustaches. "The Superman has come," I murmured to him. "Is this what you wanted?"

He drew himself up still tighter, like a hunted animal hiding itself or like a wild beast poised to spring. And from the other bank, his voice echoed proud and determined: "This is what I wanted!"

I sensed his heart twitching to confess. "You sowed the seed and now you see the harvest: Do you like it?"

And from the other bank, a desperate, rending cry resounded: "Yes, I like it!"

When I left my park bench, alone now, a bomber plane was flying over the city. The airplane Leonardo had imagined as a kind of artificial bird carrying snow down from the high mountain-tops in the summer to scatter it over the cities and cool them, was now passing by laden with bombs . . .

My mind was still on that peaceful prophet of war and I said to myself: Just in the same way, our own thoughts fly out of the human mind like larks at daybreak; but the moment the harsh morning air strikes them, they are transformed into fierce carnivorous birds. The unhappy father shouts: "I didn't want this!"; but the birds pass over his head shrieking and mocking him.

▌ WAKE UP,
   JOHN BULL!

▌ ONE DAY in Mani, where we were coal-mining, a worker I dearly loved, the most unspoiled Greek spirit I ever met, Giorghos Zorbas, was telling me how the last World War came about:

"Listen here, boss," he called to me. "Listen and learn how and where this damned thing started off. A few under-age boys had read a few patriotic books and turned patriots. Then they read socialist books and turned socialist. Then they read anarchist books and became anarchists and decided to kill. But whom? This they didn't know yet.

"One of these underage boys (Princip was his name) went to Sarajevo. You know Sarajevo?"

"No!" I answered him.

"I know it. A beautiful Turkish city, damn it! Well, he went to Sarajevo and sat down in a café. The waiter rushed up. 'What do you want, sir?'

" 'I'd like to ask your advice. Whom do you think I should kill? I say the Governor . . . or the Bishop . . . I don't know. Tell me.'

" 'Well, my boy, wouldn't you do better to kill the Crown Prince? He'll be coming this morning.'

" 'All right then, the Crown Prince!'

"He took up his post. The carriage passed. Princip threw a bomb at it. The bomb went off all right, but it killed two other people. Princip asked a professor nearby: 'Was that the Crown Prince?'

" 'No,' a deacon answered. 'It was somebody else!'

"Then the Crown Prince went to the Cathedral to make a doxology for having been saved. He made the doxology, came out of the church, said he was going home because he was hungry—it was noontime, you see. There were two roads.

" 'Right or left?' the chauffeur asked.

" 'Right,' the Crown Prince answered.

"The chauffeur failed to hear him. 'To the right?' he asked again, stopping the car. He stopped and some demon brought him face to face with Princip. So Princip brought out his revolver. Bang-bang! Down went the Crown Princess Sophia. 'Sophia,' cried the Crown Prince, 'you must live for our children's sake!' Bang-bang! Off went another bullet, and the Crown Prince fell. They were picked up and carted off to the cemetery. The father of the Crown Prince heard of it—his father or his uncle, I can't remember which—and got angry and drew his sword. Then another relative of the deceased drew his sword too. Everyone began drawing swords. And that's how the European War, as you call it, came about, damn it all!"

This is how the past war has become distorted in the popular imagination. Now once again we are facing difficult days. As I roam the streets of London, I am trying to guess how these present days will become distorted in the people's imagination and how the new legend will be created.

I am standing with the crowd in narrow Downing Street, where the Cabinet is meeting. And I am waiting, surrounded by men and women holding babies in their arms. They are speaking softly or they are silent, with their eyes glued on the closed door. War? Or peace? . . . The English people, calm, confident, are standing waiting.

The German-Soviet treaty has been signed. Russia has

stirred, emerging far off to the north, sniffing the air. Germany has sent her ultimatum to Poland. France has answered that she is standing by Poland's side, fully armed. The Home Fleet is at war stations.

The English ministers have gathered to weigh the "Yes" and the "No," justly, without haste. Reality seems to be standing outside the door of 10 Downing Street, waiting with us for their decision.

In the course of accompanying his prince to the court of Charles II of England, Count Megalotti correctly psychoanalyzed the English people: "The English take a long time to make a decision," he wrote. "But once they have made it, their decision is unbudgeable and they keep to it stubbornly."

I am happy to have this chance of seeing a great people at such a critical moment of their lives. What will come of this awesome collaboration and clash of historical Necessity, blind imbecilic Coincidence and the Human Will? Peace? Or war? . . . Honor hangs in the balance. Life is in danger. In what direction will England's fate tend?

The masses rise and fall silently. The roads are flooded. Nelson's Column cuts the fog vertically, decisively. At its peak, he stands motionless, wearing his three-cornered hat —he whose last words were: "I have done my duty!"

The ministries are emptying. Big carts are hurriedly carrying away the most precious of their archives. From the British Museum, the rarest treasures are being moved— statues, paintings, books, manuscripts. There are thick layers covering the costly windows where the noblest labors of man have been concentrated. From the National Gallery, other trucks are moving the superb paintings to safe, secret basements. My lips tightly pressed, I am mentally bidding farewell to the heavenly masterpieces perhaps about to die. All the superhuman things created by the miraculous, earth-born human hand are now in danger from man himself.

Everywhere, pavements and parks are being dug up, troglodyte trenches for men to save themselves from other men. We are retrogressing thousands of years. All the walls are plastered with instructions in big letters on how to protect oneself from bombs and poison gas. The children (the great hope) are being moved quickly to the countryside. The tragic gas masks (far more tragic than the masks of ancient tragedy) are making their appearance, fierce, mysterious, monstrous, filling the air with terror.

Banks, shops, ministries, churches are dressing themselves in thick defensive armor—thousands of tightly stacked sacks of sand. In Hyde Park, in among the golden autumnal trees, huge antiaircraft guns have been set up. I am cocking my ears, expecting the first siren, the first whir of the enemy airplanes high over our heads, the first cry of terror.

The policemen smile unruffled, as they break up the groups collecting on the streets. Every morning, Chamberlain with his legendary umbrella, carries on his customary walk through St. James Park with the same firm calm tread, the same English (slightly delayed) rhythm. He is England's great policeman. And they say his umbrella is no common umbrella, but a lightning conductor receiving and conducting the lightning bolt without danger. How long can this last?

The women kneel in the churches, praying for peace. I see them by the big tombstones of Westminster, where England's greatest sons lie at rest. They are pale, with their hands twined and their lips moving like two poplar leaves in the springtime.

How are we capable of knowing what is good and what is bad? Are we capable of feeling anything that goes beyond the threshold of our own bodies? Our world ends where our own five senses end, where our own bodies end. Outside this leather sack of blood, tears, sweat, urine, we cannot distinguish anything. So what right do we have to dare give God advice and submit petitions to Him on how to govern the universe?

I went back to the British Museum to look at my beloved barbarous statue, the tutelary deity of London, Hoa-Haka-Naka-Ya. Today his eyes seemed darker, his forehead narrower and his mouth broader. Perhaps he was the god of war?

I watched the people's faces, eyes, gestures. I remembered a saying of Lady Asquith: "The Englishman is the least vain and the most proud person in the world." Dignity, confidence in his own power, few words, few gestures, confidence in the leaders whom he himself has chosen, ready to execute even the heaviest duty silently, stubbornly. I envy these manly virtues and only wish that our race had them too—self-control, discipline, equanimity in the midst of the most terrifying tempest that has ever arisen in the history of England, and the conviction that victory is the offspring of struggle and patience.

This morning an Englishman remarked to me: "We don't want war. We don't want peace. We want what our leaders want." A perfect organism. All the members—hands, feet, stomach, heart—waiting for the signal to be given by the head, because they feel that this head constitutes the entire body.

The slightly antiquated, yet perfect organism of the British Empire with its reliable impulse is well aware that it is in danger. "At the highnoon of danger." Heads or tails, it is now about to play its fate all the way.

Never has it been in such danger. As we have seen, up

until the time of the destruction of the Spanish Armada, England was essentially one with the Continent. It had not been able, nor had it wanted, to remain isolated, surrounded and fortified by the sea. It was not yet an island.

After the Armada's downfall and after she too had armed a mighty fleet and rejected the unsound attempts to unite with France, England flashed resplendent and alone on the ocean, a perfect island surrounded and guarded by invincible merchantmen and warships. In a peaceful, secure way she could now concern herself exclusively with her own overseas colonies, indifferent to the provincial quarrels of continental Europe; she was an imperial island!

But at the beginning of the twentieth century, a new awesome weapon entered man's bloodthirsty, acquisitive hands—the airplane. This new satanic machine flew over the sea, and with its diabolical speed, joined all the countries of the earth. From the moment of the airplane's invention, England once again ceased to be an island. Once again, by fate she became one with the Continent. Her fortunes fused with the fortunes of the mainland.

A grand moment. A change of weapon has often been the reason for the downfall of nations unprepared and for the disappearance of great empires. Bronze was conquered by iron, infantry by cavalry, the spear by the bow, the bow by the gun and the cannon . . . At the present moment, Victory whose wings man has never been able to cut, is flying perhaps in the direction of the airplane.

Yet another dangerously vulnerable point: the standard of living in England is higher than that of all the other peoples of the world. Other nations live more frugally, work at cheaper rates, have inexhaustible deposits and most important of all, are aware of their still unspent impetus to acquire power. They are still on the way up, on the offensive.

The English no longer have any appetite to make any

offensive, or attack. For what purpose? What do they lack? Other nations lack many things. They do have an appetite for attacking and seizing, and they do attack. They have not yet reached their peak. The English have arrived. Their old offensive slogan: "Action over all!" has now become the slogan of indigent nations ready for the offensive. For the English it was only natural to accept a new defensive slogan, Baldwin's motto, "Above all else, security!" To keep and secure what they have, and not let anyone else take it away from them.

An enormous change. A critical moment. The English are aware of this with all its tragic overtones. They are ready. Their virtues are great, indeed unique in the world. But happiness and prosperity have slightly tempered these virtues. Happiness and prosperity have always been dangerous to individuals and nations.

Now the danger has emerged. The English people have seen it. They are biting their lips, clenching their fists. They sense that the moment has come for them to play their fate all the way, head or tails. "Wake up, John Bull!" They too have seized the new weapon. They too have boarded the airplanes and are prepared.

They are slightly behind time, but this is their rhythm. During the first days of my stay in England, I learned one of their extraordinarily characteristic proverbs: "Don't cross the bridge before you get there!" Only when you arrive face to face with the problem, try to solve it. The Englishman feels the need of seeing reality from close up, of touching it and letting it touch him, of searching for its whole outline like a blind man groping, and so to see where he can profitably proceed. And only then does he proceed.

A shortsighted, but sure method. If he started making theories and taking decisions from afar, he would be in danger of going astray, misled by his own likes and dislikes. He might fail to recognize one of the great elements of reality that often plays the main role: the unpredictable. Englishmen are like insects, those wasps who love the sand and, in order to paralyze their foe, must come in immediate close contact with it, finding the vulnerable vital part where they will sink their stingers. And this they find infallibly by clinging to the foe, one on top of the other.

I was wandering through the streets, impatiently inhaling the atmosphere of danger.

The Cretan shepherds believe there is a worm, the oxfly worm, which sits on the head of a ram and enables it to catch wind of the greatest danger: Death. Sometimes at critical moments, human beings can also feel this prophetic worm trembling atop their heads: the Prince-Worm-of-Death.

With this terrifying worm in my mind, I have been busily wandering through the streets since daybreak. I have been noting the people, the houses and shopwindows and parks with all their details, as though bidding them farewell forever.

Around twilight I reached Hyde Park. Superb autumn trees, all golden, full of sparrows and the setting sun. Girls running beneath the trees, many of them dressed like men, chasing after the young soldiers or playing with them. They too seemed to have the oxfly worm set between their taut breasts so that they wanted to console the young men about to die.

Standing in front of the antiaircraft guns, a pastor dressed all in white was surrounded by soldiers in elegant khaki, holding light sticks. He was performing a service in the open air. And the guns were turned with gaping mouths toward the sky. A tiny old Chinese man with mauve silk trousers and a long green overcoat, an elegant green silk umbrella and miniature embroidered slippers, glided back and forth noiselessly with an apathetic, almost wooden face, indifferently watching the guns, the girls, the yellowing trees . . . like Buddha.

ROBIN HOOD

Up on one of the big terraces of the British Parliament, Sir John had invited about fifty men and women to tea. A peaceful early evening. Down below, the Thames flowed past, mute and dim. Here the voices of the newspaper vendors could not penetrate. These last days, they have been bringing bad tidings to people. The autumn is here. The crops are ripe. This is the critical moment: harvest, vintage, war.

Yesterday from all over Great Britain the representatives of the nation arrived in their frock coats and high, shiny hats. They have entered this enormous Gothic parliament, so like a cathedral, in order to make a decision that will determine the fate of the world. Serious, formal, buried in their black suits, they seem to be on their way to a marriage or a funeral.

A weighty moment. All that the Englishman loves and honors most in this world—Freedom—is now threatened, and he is hastening to protect it, as though some great English divinity were in danger.

The Frenchman, they say, loves liberty as he loves his mistress, and the German as his grandmother. The Englishman loves it as his lawful wife. Just as Saint Francis wed himself to Poverty and Dante to Poetry, so the Englishman weds Freedom!

In order to acquire it, he struggled for centuries, sometimes against kings and feudal lords, sometimes against the Pope and the priests. From their dark forests and fierce coasts, these harsh Anglo-Saxons had brought with them the longing for freedom. They had also brought their national hero, Robin Hood.

This medieval English hero is not the ruler astride his horse, setting out on distant crusades, nor the crafty parasite tricking everyone and by his cleverness escaping from every hazard, nor the saint on fire in his solitude, indifferent to the things of this world. Robin Hood was a sinner and a thief, who roamed through the thick forests as an outlaw, inciting rebellion against the recognized authorities.

Robin Hood fought the judge of the locality and the bishop. He robbed the rich and shared the booty with the poor. Fearless, generous, gay, kindhearted, extremely cruel. He killed the judge, the mayor, the guards of the town and a throng of forest wardens eager to capture him. They often used to thrash him soundly, but he always sprang back undaunted, full of life, as though he had nine lives and could begin all over again.

His power surged. Every moment he was seeking an excuse to spend his excess strength. One night he dreamed that an acquaintance of his was beating him up. He leaped up from his sleep in a rage, rushed to meet his friend, lunged at him and began beating him up—to wash away the disgrace!

At the same time, Robin Hood was also a gentleman. Once he was walking with two companions and he met an enemy of his, a forest warden who was all alone. "Go on with you," Robin Hood called to him. "It's a shame for us to attack you. There are three of us and one of you."

Songs were composed about him, and from village to village, at the great festivals, the minstrels used to sing his manly deeds and torments. And even up to the sixteenth century, the peasants used to hold festivities and leave their work in order to celebrate their national hero.

One day the bishop went to a village to perform the

liturgy. He found the door of the church barred. He called angrily to have them bring him the keys and ring the church bells.

But the wardens rushed up and informed him: "My lord, the present day is a great holiday for us. We cannot listen to you today."

"What holiday?" the bishop asked in amazement.

"Robin Hood's. All the villagers have gone to cut branches for Robin Hood. Don't bother to wait."

Robin Hood was the popular personification of the Anglo-Saxon. He took to the woods and fought for freedom. His home was a fortress. His soul was a fortress. He did not allow anyone to enter except when he himself wanted.

He wanted his own home to be far from his neighbor's house—not because he hated his neighbor, but because he wanted to be free in the broadest possible area—and to leave the other man free.

He was an individualist not because he wanted to be different from the others—on the contrary, he enjoyed being like the other members of his race—but he wanted to follow the tradition as a free man, and as a free man, to co-operate with the community when he himself so wished (and he always did so wish). For him, freedom was no abstract conception. It was something tangible, his own property, his flesh-born desire, his wife, to whom he owed marital fidelity just as she too was duty-bound to be faithful to him.

The English people loved their king, because he kept their freedom safe, holding the balance between the nobles and the people, bridling the nobles and not allowing the people to release their savage impulses.

But the day came when an unworthy king betrayed this lofty mission of his and set about trampling down their freedom—John Lackland. A clever fine diplomat, but hypocritical, greedy, cowardly. "However foul with stench Hell may be," the saying went, "when this man dies, he'll make it reek still worse!" All social classes loathed him and united against him—nobles, bourgeoisie, common people alike. The nobles (and this was unprecedented in English history) refused to escort him to his wars. The King was beaten by the French and returned to his throne in deep disgrace. At the same moment, the Pope excommunicated him. King John had humiliated the name of England.

The nobles conspired and swore an oath to limit the arbitrary acts of the base King, and they forced him to sign the Charter for freedom. The King learned of the conspiracy, enlisted mercenaries and tried to fight the nobles. But it was too late. The entire nation had united against him. London was the first to give the signal. The ruling power became paralyzed. The people armed. The cowardly, crafty King saw the danger and was forced to give in. And on June 15, 1215, he summoned the nobles and higher clergy to a meadow near Windsor and willy-nilly signed the famous constitutional Magna Carta, to the effect that there were laws of the state and rights belonging to the commonwealth. The King had to respect these. If he did not respect them, his subjects would no longer be obliged to obey the King. On the contrary, they had the right to make a revolution.

> Scutage or aid shall be levied on our kingdom only by the common council of our kingdom [namely by the synod of bishops and nobles].

> No freeman shall be captured or imprisoned or disseised or outlawed or exiled or in any way de-

stroyed, nor will we go against him or send against him, except by the lawful judgment of his peers or by the law of the land.

Besides these two epochal pronouncements, there was another provision that there would be twenty-four nobles and the mayor of London to supervise the working of Magna Carta and to pass judgment on every complaint against the King. If the King refused to follow the opinion of this supreme council of twenty-five, the nobles would have the right to raise arms against him.

A tremendously important victory. The King was no longer unchallenged master. Above him there was now a council to judge him. From that point on, Magna Carta remained the foundation stone of every English liberty.

The King signed it, "gnashing his teeth," as the chroniclers relate. "He rolled his eyes till they bulged. He bit pieces of wood and made furious gestures." He writhed on the ground, shouting: "They've set five-and-twenty super-kings upon my neck!"

From the moment he signed it, he had one and only one thing in his mind: how to violate his promise and get rid of the Charter. He asked the Pope, with whom he was now reconciled, to annul it. The Pope did so, at the same time excommunicating the citizens of London.

But the Pope's prestige had begun to be shaken in freedom-loving England. The church bells rang. The churches opened, and no one was upset by the excommunication and threats of the Pope.

Fortunately, one day (sixteen months after the signing of the Charter) the King consumed a surfeit of peaches and apple cider and died. And English liberties were saved.

I was sitting there on the terrace of Westminster watching the Thames flow, misty and dense like time, carrying with it to the sea the shadowed image of the tall, lacy Parliament. The sun began to set in the sky, and the stone lace lit up aslant. A heraldic device wove in and out from one corner to the other, inscribed in French with the Norman motto: *"Dieu et mon droit!"*

What a struggle, I was thinking. What a feat of cleverness and care, as well as of blind pushing necessity, for the English people to create this tall, lacy edifice of Parliamentarianism! All classes collaborated in its construction —King, nobles, bourgeoisie, common people—but without any architect, except for the great formal architect of England, Time. Everything happened out of necessity, chance and the three clashing but essentially complementary desires: the King's desire to impose his will more easily; the nobles' desire not to lose their privileges; and the desire of the bourgeoisie and the common people to acquire new privileges.

In order to have the consent of the whole nation for all great questions, the King used to summon not only the council of nobles, but also another more democratic representative body, composed of two knights from each county and two citizens from each major city. The means of communication were still primitive, and it was difficult for the King himself to come in contact with all his subjects. So he used to summon near him representatives from all the land, a miniature England, and with these men he used to communicate.

These representatives had no right to intervene in discussions of the Supreme Council. They listened in silence. If they wished to make any comments, whether in agreement or disagreement, they announced it to the royal appointee, the Speaker, and he would express their point of view to the Council. But in short order, the representatives of the nation met and held their discussions in a special chamber, by themselves—at first, secretly, like conspirators.

Thus clearly from the fourteenth century on, the House of Lords and the House of Commons became crystallized. But in England, there was no unbridgeable opposition between the nobles and the bourgeoisie. The lower clergy and the lower nobles mingled with the bourgeoisie. These classes became united, acquired a common psychology and common interests. The noble-born head of a family might attend the House of Lords. But his sons might be members of the House of Commons. There was no abrupt separation between the middle classes and the aristocracy and therefore neither incurable hatred nor war between them. They communicated easily with each other and often to the disadvantage of the King.

In time, the Houses became omnipotent. They seized and manipulated, sometimes by violence and sometimes peacefully and deliberately, the three greatest royal prerogatives of the day: the right to impose taxes, to legislate laws, and to control the external politics of the government.

At a time when unbridled absolutism reigned in other nations and the people followed like sheep, the English were choosing representatives, holding their own opinions, not having to pay taxes unless they themselves voted for them. They did not recognize any principles unless they themselves chose them. Even in the thirteenth century, the Archbishop of Canterbury wrote the Pope: "In this kingdom of England, all the interested parties are in the habit of having an opinion on every single thing that is decided!"

The most solid social and political structures erected by man on the face of this earth never had abstract principles as their foundations. Their foundations were based on long-drawn-out experimentation, purposeful adaptation, submission to the rhythm of necessity.

England is founded on broad strong foundations. Her

whole social and political system is like an alluvium of time. Each year, each century (without great revolutionary or psychological upheavals) rebellion, uncertainty, chaos diminished and England was created.

WAR

All of Sir John's guests had arrived by now. They had scattered to the little tables with their colorful Scottish tablecloths and were drinking their tea there. Soft-spoken chatter, discreet laughter, perfumed women, and from down below the sound of cars and trams and the dense human masses surrounding the House, like bees around the queen bee.

Sir John moved to and fro over this Westminster terrace, playing the role of host tonight with unmatchable politeness, speaking cheerfully to everyone, saying a kind word to each person and smiling, vaguely uneasy and sad. A murmur arose from the low conversations of the men and the silvery laughter of the women.

I looked at all these forms around me—serene, controlled, smiling. And they were all aware that it was a critical moment their race was about to undergo and that, every second, the big hand of the clock on the Parliament tower above us was impelling England's Destiny to take a decisive step.

"What will England do?" I asked the man next to me, a charming professor, humorous and intellectually refreshing, who had been to Greece once and when he spoke of it, his eyes sparkled full of sun.

"The clever old fox?" he laughed. "What she's always done. She'll follow her own interests."

"And at the present moment, what are her interests?"

"War!" he whispered with a solemn air.

We both fell silent. This terrifying, bloodstained word seemed to have fallen between us like a corpse.

"Are you afraid?" my friend asked me, watching my eyes darken.

"The human mind is not easily frightened," I rejoined. "It knows and looks Necessity straight in the eye and is not afraid of it. But my heart felt afraid."

"I was afraid too," my friend admitted, "because I know what war means. . . . But it is necessary."

We fell silent again, staring at the waters along the shores flowing muddy toward the sea. A damp, lukewarm twilight. The giant city roared like the sea. The Parliament towers were still shining in the rays of the sun.

I looked around me at this superb region of Westminster, the heart of London, with its present-day intensely fast pulse beat. I let my eyes amble slowly, mournfully, over the Gothic arches, lacy carvings, medieval courtyards. And suddenly I was terrified—feeling as though I were bidding them farewell forever.

I turned to my friend. "Is this then England's interest?" I asked.

The professor smiled. "You find that strange?" he asked. "But you know that Englishmen in general—and still more, official England—have no love for ideological programs and abstract principles. For Englishmen, the 'truth' does not belong to learned circles. It belongs to the active circles. We consider the truth to be whatever proves fruitful in practice. And what do we mean by 'fruitful'? Whatever is good for the community. That is why foreigners are bewildered when they see England changing friends and enemies, eternally ready for new combinations and eagerly transforming yesterday's enemy into her friend. 'Inconsistency!' they cry. 'She doesn't know what she wants. She's a crafty fox. She's betraying us!'

"No, it is not inconsistency! England knows very well what she wants. Throughout all these apparently crooked twistings, she is following unerringly one straight line and one only: the interests of England. But since reality keeps changing, England's position also changes with it, following its curve and adapting itself. Can you understand me, you descendant of Themistocles?"

"It seems to me," I laughed, "I'm more a descendant of the Byzantine ascetics. That is why I feel so bewildered. Surely, it must sometimes happen that the individual morality of the English does not coincide with the official morality of England. What happens then?"

"At that point, the Englishman plays a slightly woebegone role," the professor rejoined. "Or else, he is inconceivably unhappy, trying desperately to persuade the others (and above all, himself) that his nation's policy is moral; that it is dictated by the loftier interests of humanity; and that it is in harmony with the Ten Commandments. For essentially, the Englishman is still a Puritan, constantly tormented, consciously or unconsciously, by the specter of hell.

"And then, we have these agonized attempts to reconcile the irreconcilable. But many Englishmen, the most sensitive or the most violent of them, are aroused and raise a hue and cry, denouncing the immorality. And that is why our government is always trying its utmost to cover with a mask of morality even the most immoral activities it is obliged (to its great sorrow, never forget that) to perform on behalf of England's common interests! For our government suffers too, and it too is composed of Englishmen—namely, Puritans. It too is afraid of the voice inside it. It too is afraid of public opinion. And so, in all sincerity it calls upon morality. And that is why we are called hypocrites. But even if we were still more immoral, we still would not be hypocrites! Do you get my meaning?"

"I understand very well," I said, "and I like this psychoanalysis. But in this present war, now—if the war does happen?"

"Now, if I may say so, the English will be happy. Not happy—because they don't want war at all. They will just feel deeply calm. Calm because in this present struggle, they feel that they are in the right; that they are defending England's interests and at the same time, the interests of the whole world. Individual and official morality are following the same line. Englishman and England are identified. In making this war, they feel sure that they are carrying out the supreme moral duty which is to the interest both of England and of humanity. And this gives them incredible power.

"That is why I am sure that if there is a war, England will amaze the world with her power of resistance, her determination and her strength."

Sir John approached. "You're discussing very serious matters, I see," he said, smiling. "I was watching your faces from over there. What were you talking about, if I may ask?"

"About England, Sir John," I answered. "And about the war."

Sir John shook his head. "We need another Lloyd George," he said. "Or him himself. He never ages."

A latecomer, a lady, emerged through the arched stone gate with its lacy carvings. Sir John hastened to welcome her.

My friend remarked: "Sir John isn't absolutely right, I think. For England is one of the few nations that has no absolute need of great men. She herself as a whole is a great person. She, her instinct, her demonic spirit if you will, governs and guides even the most mediocre leaders. A leader with a hyperbolically great personality, even if he could exist in England, would be dangerous—because he might, perhaps, be capable of leading us astray. Whereas a good middling sort of man can more easily and surely become the tool of the infallible will of the community. He continues the tradition more faithfully. He walks steadily."

As my friend talked, I stared over the way at Westminster Cathedral, pink in the last rays of the sun. It was sparkling more ethereally, as though some enormous many-petalled rose had risen from the dirt.

All the architectural styles of England are reconciled in this building, one after the other, from the thirteenth century on. An organic continuity, faithful and obedient to tradition, a steady, harmonized crystallization in stone of passing time.

"What are you staring at?" my companion asked me.

"England!" And I pointed to the Cathedral of Westminster across the way, in the last rays of the setting sun.

■ THE DAY,
THE GIANT DAY

■ ON THE THIRD of September around noon I was walking through London, wandering around Gordon Square. A gentle, peaceful day . . . Greek sun . . . pleasantly warm. The trees sparkled, full of light, slightly yellowed. The grass in the park had just been mowed, and the air smelled of grass and earth—a scent consoling and refreshing to my innermost being. A Gothic gray stone church rose suddenly by my side. Simple, slender, proud, like a high, high stone arrow charging through the sky, pointed as a lightning conductor.

I stood there admiring my favorite style, which for me has given religious architecture its most perfect form. No longer the equilibrated square logic of Greek style, imposing human order on superhuman mystery, balancing desire, inaugurating man's logical communication with God. It was something passionate and impulsive, some God-given dissension stirring man suddenly and making him rush outward to the blue solitude to try and capture that great anthropophagous thunderbolt called "God." This is the way prayer ought to be, I was thinking to myself. Such a form befits the spirit of any genuine person. For the whole body to swallow human joys and bitternesses and desires and to cast them like an arrow to some unattainable chimerical, inhuman height. Impulsiveness and pride, a cry vanishing in the midst of light, a spear standing isolated, waiting.

At that very moment, the first air-raid sirens could be heard screeching throughout London. For days on end now, all over this boundless city, huge wall posters had been warning her unfortunate inhabitants, teaching them to distinguish the various danger signals: the sirens announcing the approach of the enemy airplanes; the bells announcing the poison gases and weapons of biological warfare taught to man by the barbarous modern scientists in order to devastate whole cities.

All at once, the air filled with an invisible terrifying presence. Instantaneously, I looked around me. For a moment the passers-by stopped, turned to marble. They cocked their ears. Their faces had grown slightly livid. Doors opened. Men and women emerged, looked up at the sky and slammed their doors again. Others ran back to their homes to get their masks. Black hands painted on the walls near Gordon Square all pointed in the same direction, and underneath them, the word "Shelter."

A splendid moment of calm, mute panic. A young man in arm with a young girl, turned around, glanced at her with a smile to give her courage. A policeman was standing calm at the crossroads extending his hand and pointing the way. The passers-by obeyed this mute movement and ran toward the shelter with as much dignity as they could muster.

It was the first sensation, the first "visitation" made by these modern metal angels of the Apocalypse. We had five minutes at our disposal and I didn't want to lose them. A wild inhuman curiosity held me there immobile. This was the first cry, I said to myself, the first death rattle of industrial civilization. The signal for catastrophe was being given. The human brain, creator of all this magic and miracles, devoid of moral conviction and human kindness is thumping its tail now like a scorpion full of poison to sink into its own bosom.

Never before, I was thinking, had I experienced a moment so critical on an international scale.

"Move along! Move along!" the policeman shouted at me. "Where is your mask?"

He shoved me, making me follow the other passers-by. From black hand to black hand we reached the shelter—the Gothic church.

I raised my head and looked a moment at the proud arrow in the sky. All the stones were topped with a pointed spire. A fine tombstone, I said to myself, and I like it; let's go down.

We entered the arched doorway. The pastor welcomed us, smiling wanly. We descended a narrow stone staircase and then another, and entered the domed underground passages. There were two or three images hanging on the walls. The Virgin holding her infant; farther along, a rosy-cheeked jovial Christ . . . There were pews to the right and left, and we sat down. In the corner, a makeshift first-aid station: cotton, gauze, bottles, little phials.

Two or three young men in front of me held their masks in their hands. A lady with pretensions to elegance had made a silk bag for her mask to match the color of her jacket. Another girl was tightly, mutely, gripping the hand of a young man in khaki.

"They're newlyweds," I heard someone whispering next to me. "They're spending their honeymoon like this!"

A plump little woman took out an apple and began gobbling it ever so fast, as though she were afraid of not having time to finish it.

A rosy-cheeked housewife, dressed all in white, with a red cross sewn on her sleeve, emerged from the corner to hand us some cotton. "For your ears," she said.

The pastor stood there between the two rows of pews, mumbling a few words about God and Divine Providence and Paradise. Then he brought out a phonograph, set it on the table and took out a few records. "What music do you prefer?" he asked us.

Most of them chose some light sentimental song, a sort of "Tipperary." The music started up. Through our clogged ears, sweet sentimental notes on love and parting reached our souls, as though wafted from some other shore.

A man next to me asked me where I was from. We spoke loudly about Greece and her steel blue sea . . . He also knew the classic verse of Homer and began reciting it to me proudly, with his Erasmian accent: *"Meenin aeide, Thea . . ."*

Then silence. They handed us white candles. The electric lights went out. There were about fifty of us, men and women. Five or six got scared in the dark and lit their candles. Inevitably, the spectacle became macabre. An old man took out his newspaper and began reading. But his eyes were motionless. All those who had masks put them on. The women took safety pins out of their little purses and tenderly and firmly fitted the masks on the awkward men near them—like mothers, up to the last moment, faithfully performing their duty as women.

"Each of you should have your name written on a piece of paper and keep it in your pocket!" the pastor announced, still standing there between the pews. "Your name and address."

"Why?" a girl asked. But no one answered her. And she blushed at not having understood for a moment. "All right," she called back, taking a piece of paper out of her pocket and writing.

The pastor opened his little Bible and began reading in silence. I watched his face in the pure light of the candles . . . well fed, well shaved, his snow-white collar and his clean bald spot shining like precious silky ivory.

I was sorry not to have my pocket Dante there with me, to read those last songs from Purgatory I love so much.

Well, it doesn't matter, I thought; it's enough that I recall their essence, their springtime tenderness—Lucia among the flowers and the white, white legs of the women dancing over the green grass. And if it is here that my perambulation through this world must end, then it is well ended. I felt my entire being flooded with harmony.

Five or six minutes passed. Most of us had taken the cotton out of our ears now. We were all trying to hear what was going on up there on ground level . . . Nothing . . . Calm . . . We seemed to be in a tomb. . . .

Suddenly the door opened. A short, plump, blond man appeared, his face beaming happily. "Raiders passed!" he cried. "The airplanes are gone!"

Resurrected, we rose and rushed out quickly *"a rivedere le stelle,"* our lips still dry and our necks slightly stiff.

CONVERSATION WITH A YOUNG MAN

It is difficult for modern man to exist without being forced by internal or external pressure to submit to some camp. To the right or the left, if he is a vital man; to the middle ground if he is a gentlemanly, old-fashioned soul still hoping that by logic and current morality, everything can be arranged. But nowadays, everything "is steered by thunder." All goodhearted, peace-loving spirits that cannot bear blood, injustice, disaster (however many of these spirits do still exist) will not be able to survive long in this new high temperature of the earth.

And any human being who still insists on serving the "spirit," if he wants to be saved, must see what his duty is, with clarity and bravery. He must see what mission he can have among the behemoths, and he must take his position in this present-day upheaval and creation of the world.

We have entered on a period which will perhaps last one or two centuries, wherein, time and time again, war will follow peace. Values will be altered. Archaic virtues atrophied in the course of civilization will be revived: hero-worship, demonic activity, the passionate longing for danger.

In all genuinely alive nations, the young people have never had so primitive and mysterious a paroxysm as today. They are convulsed by the "magical" slogans of the masses; by a sort of conjuring that appeals not to pure logic or the free spirit, but to far deeper, less enlightened forces of growth that reside no longer deep in the human heart and head, but in the viscera.

Are not these forces, so scorned and feared by our delicate, worn-out intellectuals, what have always renewed the earth?

To be able to judge correctly and broadly and transcend our modern greedy, inevitably shortsighted passions, we must go as far beyond the tiny aperture of our own time as we can and look beyond.

We must not feel terror. We must have faith in this clay that goes by the name of man, who cannot easily be dissolved to dust.

How can we define the duty of men of the spirit in this present international mobilization of matter and psyche?

I recall a brief conversation I had with a young man in London one day in September. He had heard the sirens screeching after the first enemy planes had been spotted, and he had cut short a lyrical poem he had been writing for some mistress who had left him. He was in despair and he thought the whole universe was in despair as well.

"The spirit's done for!" he said in a whining voice. "The barbarians have come. What's to become of us? Where will we turn for refuge, we people of the spirit?" He thought we were of the same breed. And he believed the world was done for because his mistress had left him. Woman, the sole idea he believed in, the sole hope the poor fool had based his whole life on.

"Get thee to a monastery!" I said, laughing at him.

"How can you laugh?" he complained to me, pursing his anemic lips.

"I was remembering when I was a small boy in Crete," I told him, "and a kind, soft-spoken old man always used to come out wearing a green shawl with red checks. He was a musician and gave guitar lessons. He was thin, sickly, and he wore elastic-sided shoes. His name was Myrtaios. The way he used to shiver, winter and summer alike, as he walked through the market place with the people shouting wildly at him, he was both comic and lovable. The Cretans loved him and made fun of him. He always kept a long book, like an account book, under his arm, and because of that the merchants in the bazaar started calling every intellectual Myrtaios. When they saw some young man bending over his little books, refusing to play or laugh or run after the girls, they would jeer at him: 'Hey there, poor old Myrtaios.' That's how almost all the intellectuals of our time strike me—they're all Myrtaioses."

"And what about me?" the young man asked in a melancholy way.

"In a few days," I answered, "I mean to go to Scotland, and I'll bring you a shawl. If I find one, green with red squares."

"You have no sensitivity. And I who was about to read you my last ballad I was writing when the first sirens—"

"Unless it has the rhythm of these modern sirens" I interrupted, "don't read it to me. By now I'm fed up with reading about love affairs and sighs and delicate secret desires. Our age is epic, and you can't understand it. It's epic and full of action."

"And what about art and poetry?"

"Just as in every other period, our age too has spirits that are past, present, and future.

"First, in this present age of terrifying activity, the only man who deserves to be a poet is someone who holds within him a great deal of the future. Prophetic poetry, the poet's effort to conceive a civilization so created as to eliminate crime and bloodshed, his effort to forge new human types, whereby he helps fluid reality to enter the ideal patterns which he himself has desired and forged.

"Second, there are the spirits that bear within them a great deal of the present. These spirits, if they have any inclination toward poetry at all, simply try to reproduce through disorganized verse and disorganized thought the contemporary decomposition of the world.

"But the most vigorous of these modernized spirits scorn art, considering it (except for purposes of propaganda) a superfluous, incomprehensible luxury. The vital spirits plunge into action. They scorn the spirit. They have witnessed the bankruptcy of the old generation, with its fake stage-scenery liberties and its tricky morality and its saltimbankish acrobatics and with the amoral outlook lauded by the so-called theoretical mind. They have witnessed all this and felt disgust at it and set about destroying this web of camouflaged slavery, prosperity, deceit. They are on the offensive. The best of the young people in the world nowadays are not writing. They are acting, facing death heroically, driven by a God-given madness. The trap door has opened and the chthonian powers have sprung back up out of the ancient sacred darkness of the subconscious, ready for the attack.

"Thirdly and finally, there are the non-up-to-date spirits, the backward ones, usually very polite, sensitive and slightly absurd. They do not act. At the very most they react. And if they do have a poetic disposition, usually their songs reveal sensitivity and nobility, impeccable form, passionate, erotic nostalgia. But they have ceased being bearers of life. Perhaps later on, if they happen to be superb poets, they may find some response in other 'similar' eras. But at the present moment, their existence has left behind it only empty skulls.

"Not even God Himself (by which I mean the supreme human desire of the present time) wants them! 'O Lord, . . . For the grave cannot praise thee, death can *not* celebrate thee: they that go down into the pit cannot hope for thy truth. The living, the living, he shall praise thee, . . .' [Isaiah, 38: 16-19.] This is an age-old voice. The only thing that ages and changes is the ideal, but the voice remains the same—for it is the voice of that poor wretch, man, longing to escape from his wretchedness!"

"We are at the end of a civilization," screeched the young man. "We are the children of our own age, without faith, or fancy, or grand words. We hold the mirror, reflecting this decomposition, as you put it. We are doing our duty!"

"Perhaps," I answered, "but now of late, I'm beginning to suspect (for nowadays, the wheel of Fate turns so rapidly) that these young people no longer mirror their own age, but an age that is already transcended. We seem to be now transcending this stage of decomposition. An amazing new synthesis is crystallizing along the horizon. And these up-to-date young people as you call them (who in my opinion are already out of date!) are not yet capable of seeing this synthesis. They hold up their mirror and sing of decomposition, because they still can see only their own decomposed spirit.

"Big words, big deeds, a violent wind, impassioned and therefore romantic, characterize the newborn yearning of the spirit.

"We find ourselves at the entrance to the beginning. Our age is no longer a declining one, as you like to believe in order to justify your own existence. It is a high point of tremendous forces, perhaps barbarous, but that is the way civilizations always begin. The rhythm of our age has been elevated to a heroic rhythm, impelling us toward great risks, toward assuming cosmic responsibilities. It isn't for anemic, sensitive intellectuals (the Myrtaioses), for those old men (even if they're only twenty) with their soft, ink-stained hands and their sunless flesh."

In spite of myself I had caught fire. I stopped short, feeling abashed, because I had just noticed that my young friend's fingers were blotted with ink, just seen his slender sunless neck.

"Well?" he said through tight-pressed lips, "you've finished?"

"Excuse me," I said. "You've come to my home and I've been acting like a boor."

I called Rosalind, the maid at the boardinghouse, and told her to bring him some tea and butter and biscuits and marmalade to sweeten him up.

"My mind was somewhere else," I said. "I was thinking of other things, hard, bitter things, but they concern me alone. Forgive me." My friend left and I went out into the streets to catch my breath.

At the present time I was thinking to myself, events are maturing far more quickly than human beings. In our age it's difficult for a young man to find the time to concentrate, to disburden his spirit, to find his own rhythm, to follow it and in following it so to mature. Today the young people are forced to follow international events that unfold and change at a tremendously rapid pace. They find no consistency, and they leap from one thing to another, from one psychological situation to the next. They themselves lose every form of consistency. A natural maturing process becomes an unattainable feat and our young intellectuals today, even the most select of them, decay before they mature. That's why they have such incoherence and bitterness inside them, and they strive in vain to cover it up with cynicism, indifference, sensuality.

I must have been walking through the streets for some time, plunged in thought, for suddenly I became aware that night had fallen, pitch black—no light. The giant city was like a terrifying, murky forest teeming with baleful noise. The windows were barred, blue or black curtains hiding the minimal light inside. The streets had become fierce, returning to their medieval darkness. Underneath the trees shadows flitted and stumbled. The buses and cars had a very dim little green light like a glowworm scattering a handful of darkness with its tremulous little rays. Young men and women rested here and there on the corners, beneath the trees, embracing one another, enveloped by the darkness blessing their own private adventures. They were kissing. Like the wolf, Love too rejoices in the storm.

I raised my eyes to the sky and sprang up happily. For the first time during all these black nights of danger, I could see the stars over London. For the first time during these nights in the giant city, I remembered that the stars exist—calm, cold, cruel, indifferent to the destinies of poor wretched man.

▪ SHAKESPEARE

▪ THESE ARE DIFFICULT MOMENTS we are passing through, and we feel the need of regulating our hopes and fears, of bending over Destiny's ledgers, which now stand open, and of ascertaining the state of Great Britain's account.

Without my consciously reflecting about it, some obscure but infallible instinct in my own soul made me rush to Stratford. I wanted to approach the supreme spirit born of this race and from that point to turn my gaze outward.

A serene landscape, gracious and genteel. The inhabitants move about like dwarfs under his giant shadow. The River Avon flows blue-green, filled with white swans, which sometimes float and preen their backs in the peaceful water, and sometimes, getting bored, suddenly spread their wings and fly about, making a big stir till they return with their feet pressed tight against their bellies.

On the banks of the river stands the Gothic Cathedral of the Holy Trinity, damp and dark among the towering trees and old grass-grown graves. The most immortal mortal ever shaped on English soil rests in the depths of this church: William Shakespeare. "In Judgment a Nestor, in Genius a Socrates, in Art a Virgil: the earth covers him, the people weep for him, Olympus holds him."

At a crossroad, among ruined houses with broken windowpanes, another church, an abandoned one, rises like the skeleton of some benign, vegetarian monster. Its bones are washed and sun themselves crystal clean, now freed of all excess ornament. Only in the rear, up over the choir, the Second Coming is still visible on the aged wall, pale, faded, fantastic. The face of Christ is obliterated and the Apostles have been worn away by the rains. The just and the unjust have vanished, and all that is left is a far-off, uncertain green.

Pretty wooden houses, blackened by time and damp; spick-and-span streets; people whose faces sparkle from the reflection of the poet; a park of roses and apple trees laden with apples. I had walked out from Stratford, taking the road toward Shottery. Everything was deep-green and gay, and I was in haste to reach the house of Anne Hathaway, Shakespeare's humble and most certainly unhappy wife. Rarely have I seen so enchanting and green a road. The sun was shining that day, the vegetation fragrant, the insects buzzing back and forth, bearing love to the marriage-ripe flowers.

This must have been the road taken by Shakespeare as a beardless young man when he came to kiss Anne in their secret trysts. By then his father had met reverses in his business, had spent his wife's dowry, and was in debt. And he had taken his son out of school, so that he could have him as an assistant in his own work.

They say this son was a dreadful drunkard and often used to come back staggering to his father's house. Sometimes, they say, his legs refused to carry him and he couldn't get back, so he'd stay out till dawn in the fields beneath a flowering apple tree. Love, wine, youth; his blood was on fire. He may already have begun to compose verses, for another tradition tells us that at one point he'd entered a butcher-shop as hired help and before slaughtering a calf, he delivered it a whole funeral oration in rhyme.

He must have dearly loved to chase after the young girls in his village. He was a child of his time, overflowing with the heady sap of Renaissance paganism. Catholicism had degenerated into an empty formalism, no longer capable of binding the people's souls to an effective discipline. And Puritanism had not yet cast its mournful shroud over England.

Shakespeare's tender, sensual spirit was in fact born into the climate most propitious for its complete fulfillment. An insatiable, exuberant, pleasure-loving era, rife with antinomies: barbarism and gentleness, refinement and filth, extravagant waste and unimaginable poverty. Shakespeare's two favorite books were Foxe's *Book of Martyrs* and Boccaccio's *Decameron*. An insatiable era, unwilling to forgo any form of joy or baseness or bitterness. It could encompass and love opposite things, without fear of madness or chaos.

A springtime moment of history, a torrid wind, as in the budding time of trees. The sap surged up, defying restraint, and burst through the outworn barriers of morality. The churches on Sunday glittered with the costly and colorful clothes worn by both men and women, and reverberated with their gay chatter and laughter. Lovers talked things out during the service and the young gallants paid a special tax for the racket made by their spurs on the stone slabs of the church. One old religious writer of the sixteenth century wrote in a querulous tone: "In my own youth, of a Sunday, the people had no mind to interrupt their games and dances, and often the person in charge of the service was forced to halt until the flutes and voices of the merry-makers ceased. Sometimes dancers would even enter the church in all their masquerading folderol, and with little bells on their legs . . ."

There was a superabundant force. Hearts swelled. Boundaries vanished. A yearning to live, eat, dress, speak and think according to your own personal individuality, just as you pleased, without asking anybody's leave. "Wild English beasts," Benvenuto Cellini called them. In Cellini's eyes they ate and drank like dragons, were hot-blooded, and when overcome by anger, they would fall like bulls on their adversaries, reckless of danger or shame or sin.

They told coarse, brazen stories. They cursed abundantly and good-humoredly. They had no excessive sensitivities. Their nerves were made of hemp. They could stomach the goriest and most horrendous spectacles. They gambled their own and other people's lives and paid no heed. For pastime they set bears and bulls to fighting, and dogs to tearing each other to shreds. And Queen Elizabeth herself did not hesitate to strike and pinch her ladies or to spit on her courtiers and slap them.

They had inordinate passions and they gloried in them. The wild beast inside them had been let loose and was free. It had not yet been put in an iron cage by Cromwell or castrated by that virtuous housewife of the nineteenth century, Queen Victoria. An unrestrained, Dionysian intoxication possessed these carnivorous bodies, dominating their brains and souls as well. Their hearts overflowed. They created great things in the realms of poetry and of action. They dispatched ships that discovered strange new lands with exotic birds and fruit and unfamiliar habits and customs. The earth's sphere was expanding and becoming more bountiful. The sciences, with the dew of youth upon them and youth's unqualifying absoluteness, optimistically proclaimed the omnipotence of the human mind. The earth was no longer motionless at the center of the universe. With Galileo it had begun to move. People were commencing to guess the infiniteness and mysteriousness of the starry heavens. The printing presses were working day and night. Ideas were traveling in their immortal new garb, the book—traveling and entering even the most distant houses and workshops, and setting spirits astir.

Life was becoming more commodious, the beds softer, the food less simple and more tasty, the carriages more comfortable; and Greek mythology arrived to adorn the royal palaces and the chambers of the ruling class, adding a smile and a touch of nobility to the stern, rough masks of Fate that had come down from the Middle Ages.

Plutarch and Boccaccio and the Oriental tales enriched and embellished the imagination. The medieval people of the North surged ahead with *élan*, and became rejuvenated. Crimes, wars, love, heroism, adventure had a certain candor and innocence which are encountered only in strong young organisms with childish, greedy hands, avid to pluck and taste all the fruit from the tree of life.

Such were the spirits and the bodies of the people attending the theaters. And the spectacles had to fit their ebullient life. Great passions, great heroes, much blood, and at the same time the heavy melancholy of youth, erotic tenderness, friendship's pathos, and exaggerated confidence in the earth and soul and fate of man.

All of their dramatic poets—except for Beaumont and Fletcher—were torn from the entrails of the people. They were Bohemians, poor folk, topers, quarrelers, woman lovers. They learned life and its robust, succulent language not in dictionaries and old chronicles, but in taverns and brothels and market places and harbors and prisons and in war. They did not live a quiet, respectable sort of life, or sit for regular hours at their desks to write about human passions. They lived all the human passions, and kneeling down in taverns or in their own hovels they invented comic scenes and tragedies, dashed them off at top speed, and then hastily produced them in their primitive theaters on the banks of the Thames.

And what theaters! Barbarous, devoid of scenic illusion and of all stage tricks, because these people with their child-like imaginations had the power (just like the child who

makes a horse out of the pole he is riding) to transform a
paper branch into a whole forest, a lantern into a Vene-
tian festival, and a couple of soldiers into two raging armies.

Dramatic poets, theaters, spectacles, spectators—what a
harmony! In creative epochs everything seems to be born
all at once by the simplest of motions, perfect from the
start, without trial and error or second thoughts or hesita-
tions. And as though they made up one body and one soul,
all the Elizabethan spectators were ready for such spectacles. Some would sit on the benches, some stretched out on
the ground, most of them would stand upright. And when
it rained, they used to get soaked, but they did not mind!
Their eyes were glued to the stage. Their imaginations had
caught fire. Now they lived and moved and lost themselves
in ferocity or tenderness within the vision of the tragedy.
And sometimes they would get so carried away that they
rushed out and beat up the poor actor, identifying him
with the criminal character he was playing.

They drank beer, ate walnuts and chestnuts, and relieved
themselves in a big basin in the corner of the pit. The
theater was reeking. Immersed in the spectacle, they smote
down the barriers between spirit and spirit, and became
one with the heroes. They shattered the boundaries de-
marcating truth from falsehood and entered into the
magical reality. Everything became a tangible truth. Pole
and horse became identical, and all the spectators began
howling and crying or bursting into laughter.

Cosmic moments when the whole human being, from
head to toe, from beast to angel, was creating and rejoicing.
This period of the English Renaissance reminds me of those
geological eras when a high temperature prevailed and
when brontosaurs and dinosaurs and behemoths were born
in such wild and disorderly profusion. The creative force
was still unspent, had no moderation or rules. It loved
monsters and played without restraint.

I was sitting on a bench in the warm, fragrant little garden of Anne Hathaway, thinking to myself that William Shakespeare was just such a behemoth when he came here at night amid the intertwining verdure to kiss Anne. She was eight years older than he. He married her when he was eighteen years old, and had three children by her: Susanna, Hamnet, and Judith. Then he left her and went to London, plunging into great inner adventures and bitter love affairs. And he forgot his wife. We never hear of her again. Only, thirty-five years later, in his will, her amazing husband mentioned her for a passing moment: "I leave my wife, Anne Hathaway, my second-best bed."

II. By now the sun had set. I bade farewell to the garden, which had so often seen a youth leaping over its gate in just this way as he left at dawn, his hair dripping dew. How the morning star must have sparkled upon him! How the lark in his own heart must have warbled! These were his very first exquisite, simple delights with woman. Those early mornings his future verses, still unborn, must have been kicking inside his vitals:

> Lo! here the gentle lark, weary of rest,
> From his moist cabinet mounts up on high,
> And wakes the morning, from whose silver breast
> The sun ariseth in his majesty;
> Who doth the world so gloriously behold,
> That cedar-tops and hills seem burnish'd gold.

Women must still have seemed to this youth like a garden full of white roses, larks, and freshness—a Paradise.

> Haply I think on thee, and then my state,
> Like to the lark at break of day arising
> From sullen earth, sings hymns at Heaven's gate

A few years later the young Shakespeare came to know women better—better or worse?—and he adorned her with other attributes, calling her in various sonnets "tyrannous" "false-speaking," "cruel," "disdainful," "forsworn," "black as hell," "dark as night," and saying of her:

If eyes, corrupt by overpartial looks,
Be anchored in the bay where all men ride,

. . . .

Why should my heart think that a several plot
Which my heart knows the wide world's common place?

These epithets are exaggerations too, just as the extravagant paeans had been. Poor woman is a sickly, most agreeable, weak creature. But this is what it means to be in love: that one cannot find the golden mean. You listen to the lovesick Shakespeare, so often betrayed, and involuntarily you remember another luckless, love-stricken man at the other end of the world, in the Indies, who also cried out, with the same lack of moderation, that fire never has its fill of wood, nor the ocean of rivers, nor Hades of the dead, nor the female of males.

What suffering Shakespeare must have endured in order to be able to describe with such clairvoyance (or such passionate injustice) the sick, wounded, downy animal, woman!

> *When my love swears that she is made of truth,*
> *I do believe her, though I know she lies*

Or elsewhere:

> *How sweet and lovely dost thou make the shame*
> *Which, like a canker in the fragrant rose,*
> *Doth spot the beauty of thy budding name!*

Man too was a sick and wounded hairy beast. And Shakespeare was deeply aware of what a sweet and painful martyrdom it is to humiliate yourself for a woman. Why be ashamed?

"Love is too young to know what conscience is"

Open-hearted, delicate-fibered, not very determined, sensual, the "Sweet Swan of Avon" swam through all his life in the muddy waters of love without muddying his own wings. "Love is my sin," he says in one of his sonnets that are so bitter and revealing. It was in the shape of Aphrodite that love manifested itself to Shakespeare in his first song, *Venus and Adonis*—an Aphrodite like a voracious flame darting and eating and eating without fill.

She red and hot as coals of glowing fire

I took the road back to Stratford. The shining apples on the laden apple trees looked like young girls' bosoms. The pear trees, stretched out one after the other against the walls as though they were crucified, rustled in the breeze, and hanging on them were heavy, honey-sweet pears. Small, well-tended gardens; rich country houses with straw roofs; pink-cheeked English girls, girls who stand like pillars, upholding the English home. Stones, trees, plots of earth, the sparkle on ordinary human faces—you get the impression that a never-setting sun caresses everything here, from Shottery to Stratford.

When I reached the idyllic river, a swan was tearing angrily through the waters, in a hurry to reach a group of swans that had outdistanced him. His wings were fluffed out, all curly. His breast protruded truculently, and all of him was bounding with his driving impulse to race and pass the others. In the sky, an airplane loomed up roaring, passed over the swans who didn't even turn to see it, and disappeared in a rosy cloud, in the direction of London.

I passed by the simple, comfortable theater which was built in recent years for playing the works of the great brother of the swans. And then I reached the house where I was staying as a guest—the home of Shakespeare's beloved daughter, who was "more clever than woman," Susanna.

An aristocratic house, with thatched roof, thick black beams, and crystal windows patterned by ironwork. In the kitchen the enormous long table of thick oak cut from a single plank, dark and shiny like old amber, was still standing. The great fireplace was lighted. All around, copper cooking utensils were hanging. Through the panes you could see the garden sparkling outside, planted with all the flowers mentioned in the Shakespearean tragedies. And upstairs, many rooms, with costly porcelain and Susanna's heavy, delicately carved bedstead; and precious glass in all the windows, mauve, sky-blue, and green.

Every morning I used to walk in the garden with its laden apple trees and pear trees and the great old mulberry tree planted, they say, by Shakespeare himself. A crafty little figure of Pan laughed at one end of the garden, and at the other, amidst the honeysuckle and the bushy white roses, stood a grief-worn Gothic virgin of stone.

Unforgettable, sun-bathed September days. An enclosed paradise, over which the airplanes of the modern hell kept flashing. It was disgraceful, in the midst of the war that had broken out, and at the very moment when so many millions of human creatures had been cast—using Shakespeare's own image—in the role of food for cannon, to be going about your peaceful stroll through a warm garden, with a book in your hands. Disgraceful—but this book happened to be Shakespeare.

If the human beings created by God were to vanish

and those created by Shakespeare were to sally forth from his densely printed pages, the world would turn out for the better, I think. The men, all the men, even the greatest, who surround us in real life, and the women, even the most innocent and tender ones (if such women do exist), even the most ruthless and dishonorable ones, are such miserable creatures! The flesh-and-blood people of real life cannot attain extremes of good and evil. They do not dare to live their destiny wholeheartedly. They are afraid of doing evil all the way. They are afraid of doing good all the way. They stop in the middle, as though the coiled spring had not been properly wound up to the end —the spring that the puppetmaker inserted deep inside them. They spread over all the continents and grab them. They have all the oceans at their disposal and innumerable flocks of animals, trees, ideas and gods. And yet they do not dare. They get no farther than the middle ground.

But this master of Stratford, who enclosed a tiny space in boards and installed rags and painted paper sitting inside it, put some fifteen thousand words together and managed to create human beings. He wound their springs well, screwed and unscrewed their brains to perfection, trod on their bellies and hearts, and from their mouths spouted the wildest or the tenderest of words: such words as God had never been able to put into the mouths of His human beings. What lover created by God ever sang like Romeo? Who of God's subjects ever blasphemed like Lear? Who ever sighed like Hamlet?

Turn around, look about you; bend and see your own spirit! What a wretched pace is yours, what cowardice! What prim, calculating self-interest! A single gram of gold indissolubly fused with the ton of rusted iron that envelops it. With the woman you love, one tender word becomes encircled by a host of dark, unspoken threats. You sacrifice your life for an idea, and feel inwardly delighted when your palm touches the rich usurer's reward. In your hands you hold eternally a scale short in weight. And all your life long you struggle to make profits by cheating love and the Idea. The roots of even your purest act are caked with mire.

And on the other hand the most dishonorable of your acts is steeped in secret tears. You steal, you commit adultery, you kill, you tell lies, and involuntarily, without knowing it, you blush inwardly or outwardly. You are still miserable.

But here in Shakespeare's workshop, the essence of pain and joy, love and horror, has been isolated, and every foreign element winnowed out. It has become an infinitely rarefied poison or honey, a quintessence.

If matter did not offer such great resistance, if the spirit could guide its body without the body's weight diminishing the impulse of the spirit, then the creation of Nature might possibly match the creation of Art. But we circulate in a heavy, leaden atmosphere. In order to raise our arms and conquer the force that drags us downward, we have to mobilize our spirit in its entirety. And in order to lift a thought to a higher plane, we must organize our lives and struggle with innumerable armies that are mortal enemies of thought.

The nature of the spirit is to fly in a buoyant, etherlike element, like a swallow. Yet within the body, even while floating, it has to live in a grief-filled and inimical world, like a flying fish. Only once in a while, when it can no longer bear it, does the spirit fly high to its own particular buoyant element—Art—to find relief.

Shakespeare's creatures breathe this weightless ether eternally, insatiably. Our minds take a proud delight in watching the limits to which human joy and terror can reach. This is not a struggle between blind forces. Here, Destiny is not outside man, a heavy wheel, eyeless and deaf, turning and killing. There is collaboration between man and Fate. The giant dark monster would never awake unless it was gently tickled in its sleep by some daredevil butterfly made rash by pride and passion—the human soul.

In the world created by Shakespeare, there is human responsibility. All the disasters erupting and crushing the hero in that enclosed epitome of the cosmos—the tragedy—bear his own face. He, the hero, begot them, for in transgressing the mysterious rhythm controlling the world, he dared to go off the track. Egoism, weakness, exorbitant power, blind passion, the hero's unlimited ambition—these are the seeds, and they burgeon into catastrophe.

There seem to be certain laws which have to do with morality and harmony, and woe to any mortal who transgresses them! Apparently there is a power outside and inside man which has one aim and only one: to rise. Where? Up toward what? No one knows. We can only occasionally, by eavesdropping on our own blood, guess its rhythm. And when some act, some human being, some thought happens across its path, hindering its ascent, the spirit is overcome by anger. It surges out, strikes blindly, destroying many men, good men and bad, and tearing its own flesh. It tears its own flesh as though this were the evil, this the impediment that lies across the path leading upward. The flesh of its own flesh. Rhythm and transgression of rhythm, as though both were parts of its nature. That is why this tremendous power lacks the capacity to eradicate dishonor, crime, passion, vulgarity, without inflicting grievous wounds upon itself.

The human soul becomes a terrifying spectacle (and there is no spectacle more terrifying) when, in the course of some great upheaval, Fate itself becomes covered with blood. Suddenly the weeping we see is no longer that of a human being in his recognizable, individual shape; it is that of some invisible, overwhelmingly depressing presence, far superior to man. All we can do is to let the tears fall on our own cheeks, hot and thick.

To produce this magical identification that is more true than the truth, Shakespeare did not fashion his heroes out of abstract conceptions or inhuman monsters. His heroes are made of the same essence as ourselves. Only they dare to go to the very edge of the precipice, whereas we do not dare. They are whole and we are fragments. All of us, if given the opportunity, could become caricatures of Macbeth, Coriolanus, Othello, and we might be eager to, but we are so chary of danger and so ridiculous that the blind ascending power refuses to grapple with us, and leaves us in the tepid mud to limp through life, limp through love, limp through desire.

But when some unimpaired spirit—the unimpaired one, of which we are the fragments—arises and stands before the ascending power, the threshing ground of earthly clay trembles and the tragedy explodes. And we follow the hero's frightful adventure, gaping and trembling because we sense dimly that it could be, and should be, our own adventure too.

Trembling, yes, but feeling a savage pride as well. For, since we live deep in the dark, unexamined subterranean areas of the brain, we know that though the hero may die, may be reduced to bloodstained mire beneath some invisible heel, there is something within him that will not die—or, rather, the hero's death will give him a new and indestructible life. If the hero did not die, if everything came to him easily, if life continued its rhythm unhindered and for that reason without passion, this mysterious essence which does not die with the hero would be in danger.

And that is why we feel an unforeseen relief at the end of the tragedy. A strange reconciliation with the power that kills. Mere reconciliation? Possibly gratitude also, I think. For, as we see the noble hero destroyed beneath the weight of the entire universe, this power gives us our first opportunity to surmise that the human soul must be something awe-inspiring; and that within this human soul there is some other force still more awe-inspiring (sheer quality) that scorns, even to the point of death, blind pretensions, bestial quantity.

III. As I wandered through Susanna's garden with the big book of her father's plays, I let my soul take wing and buzz like an earnest, hungry bee seeking a drop of honey in the poisonous heart of each tragedy. For this drop of honey, I felt sure, was the essence of the tragedy.

Some dire disaster strikes a great spirit and crushes it. What was the origin of this disaster? Whence did it come? Who brought it? Who is responsible?

If it were only external blind Fate, if it were just the human soul on one side against all the weight of matter on the other, there would be horror but at the same time an unquestionable consolation. For we would be watching the marvelous spectacle of a conscious human being with his own minuscule gallant light struggling against the imbecility and omnipotence of boundless, dark, amoral, blind necessity.

We would say: "I've done my duty. I am pure. I have been shattered, but I have no responsibility. For one thing only do I accept guilt: for having a conscience, for being man, who alone dares to transgress the dictate. I ate of the Tree of Knowledge, departed from the paradise of vegetable beatitude, and essayed with my own strength the dangerous adventure of freedom. I do not want to return to Paradise either by Christ's road or by Buddha's. I want to go onward, to reach the farthest point. If the conscience is a Luciferian rebel, then let's arouse all the souls and let's move ahead together along the upward path of

freedom. Let's take the responsibility! This is the genuinely human way, and I like it. I transgressed the dictate.
Let me pay for it. But my conscience remains pure."

If the tragic clash were limited to this duel between Spirit
and Fate, the tragedy would surely communicate terror to
us, but it would not succeed in cleaving our hearts asun-
der. The heart would face such catastrophe and horror unimpaired and with a single unified sentiment. But Shakespeare carries the tragic horror a step further. He adds a
second floor to the tragedy. In the Shakespearean tragedies, the conflict explodes not only between Spirit and
Fate, but inside the very heart of the hero. The hero then
has to fight on two fronts: against the dark external forces
and against that part of his own spirit which is treacher-
ously collaborating with the external besiegers and trying
to open the gates of the fortress for them.

The tragic horror is thus augmented; the conflict acquires
depth, passion, the dimension of responsibility. No longer
is it a case of mere blind necessity killing the pure and
guiltless hero. The hero himself is to blame. The catastrophe
is not entirely unjust. The disaster that has overtaken the
hero had its roots in his own foibles and egoisms and unfathomable passions. Now it is not simply a clash between
spiritual and physical forces. Simultaneously involved in
the clash are forces that are moral as well as spiritual.

Human destiny is not determined in advance. We cannot say, by way of self-justification, that whatever we do,
however pure and careful and enlightened we are, there
is no salvation, for Fate will intervene to annihilate us
anyhow. Necessity is not omnipotent in Shakespearean
tragedy. In the human spirit there is a small spark of freedom. A little gate to escape by. Therefore we do have responsibility.

But the way that the external and internal forces have
become allied and intermingled with each other, they

have become invincible. We lose the power to strive against them. A dark, irresistible current sweeps us along. We want one thing and do another. Our benign intentions may beget disasters in the course of being executed. Our evil intentions may work out in such a way as to bring justice and happiness. Between our intention and the result, some great mystic power interposes itself, and guides our course; and everything turns out exactly right.

What is this power? What aims does it pursue? In what direction is it moving, impelling us to go along with it? Sometimes it rushes out in fury to exterminate the evil, as though that were its chief adversary. Sometimes it gleefully destroys all that is best in this world. If it were devoid of moral desires, why should it fight so ardently against shortcomings, dishonor, deceit? And if it were entirely moral in its desires, why should it kill great spirits with such malice and unerring aim?

Ponderous questions, and Shakespeare could not answer them. He was neither a philosopher nor a religious pioneer, to give answers to such questions as these. He was a poet. He advanced beyond all other poets and then stood still at the edge of the abyss. There, mute and utterly alone, he felt dark, bloodstained wings seeking him out. Blood and tears fell on his cheeks. Were they his own? Or those of the whole world? He could not distinguish. He had the most sublime experience the human being can have: the feeling of awe. Of looking at the abominable darkness surrounding us outside and within, and not saying: "This is it; this is not it. I want this; I do not want this." But remaining silent, with unsleeping eyes and lips tight sealed, and from head to toe feeling the tragic quiver.

These were my thoughts as for days on end I walked in the garden beneath the fruit-laden apple trees, breathing in the heavy air of war. I read and reread, darting from

Julius Caesar, Hamlet, or *Macbeth* to the comedies and *The Tempest.* I was struggling to find, so I thought, the essence of the tragedy, and to discover in addition what this northern dramatist had taken from the ancients and what new tingling sensation he had introduced. . . .

But the thing that most deeply interested me in Shakespeare's work was something else, only I didn't yet have the courage to face it. Fate, the human spirit, struggle, death, immortality—all those frightful enigmas that the mind could mull over for thousands of years, or else dismiss with some hasty, ready-made solution to end the torment and keep from going to pieces. But the mind is forever shifting position and getting further along, and the solution also shifts and advances with it, going further and further all the time.

In trying to put my finger on the secret consolation tragedy gives us, I felt I was trying at the same time, without admitting it, to find or to devise some hidden solace for the tragedy beyond solace that is exploding in the world today. Millions of actors; heroes dominated by unknown, unfathomable passions; Fate pouncing on them, making them blind and deaf, gripping them and pushing them with both its hands toward the abyss. Fate must have encountered some old impediment to rage against.

What might the impediment be? Perhaps the old spiritual and moral impulses have failed and turned to matter. Perhaps it is these that are now obstructing the ascending power. Perhaps new impulses have been born and are wandering about angrily, unable to fit into contemporary reality. A dreadful method, but the ascending power does not seem to care very much about human life.

Unconsciously I was nourishing the following hope inside me. If I could find some ray of light in the horrendous darkness of Shakespearean tragedy, if within the slaughter let loose by those two consorting allies—blind

Fate and the soul of the hero—I could discover some consolation, even though it might be a superhuman one, then perhaps I could feel the fearful war now breaking out among the human flocks. For the war too is the work of Fate and the soul. And if I could feel it, perhaps I could justify it. And—who knows? (the human soul in its essence is ruthless, pure and hard as a diamond, indifferent to happiness)—perhaps I could even love it.

Some voice within us, the voice of man, naturally feels compassion for humanity and is repelled by blood. But there is also another voice inside us which is not concerned with security, comfort, or human happiness, knowing that without Father War life would stagnate like water that does not flow. This inhuman voice within us is not our own. It belongs to some demon lurking in the human soul; inhuman, superhuman, still better, beyond-the-human, the demon cries and fights for superhuman ends. And this voice "hopes" that the war will go on forever.

I read the beloved tragedies over and over, leafing through these works that are the free man's Bible, trying to see Fate with clarity, and not only to feel it but to love it as well. Seeing clearly, introducing order into the anarchy of the heart, looking horror straight in the eye—there is no other salvation. This is the only way man can conquer fear: by abandoning the absurd, undignified pattern of the ostrich, and instead of burying his head in his own indolence, or in some comfortable theory, or in the sky, calmly looking up and staring straight into the eyes of Fate.

IV. After a time the present-day landlady came down to Susanna's garden and we began to converse. Then my mind was distracted with more lowly and more pleasant concerns and I found a little relief from my turmoil.

This marvelous woman was over eighty years old, finely

made, slender, supple, with bright blue eyes, a powerful jawbone, a smile all severity and thoughtfulness. I had never seen such vitality, such an insatiable urge to see and hear, such a triumph of the human being in conquering time. She had moved from India to Europe, from Europe to America, all alone, hurrying impatiently on, as though she feared that her eyes might suddenly close forever and she wouldn't have time to see and feel everything. An unappeasable thirst for learning, a mind as avid as a child's, ever ready to ask and to take. "Learning is my religion," she herself said with a smile for this inexhaustible, unquenchable need of hers.

She had a much-loved home on the Ganges, rising pure white alongside the tomb of Vivekananda. In this house she used to take refuge in order to concentrate. Not, however, according to the Oriental method of remaining motionless and allowing the thoughts to collect around a fixed point. That manner of concentration was utterly alien to her own active, irrepressible nature. This rare woman concentrated by acting.

She was economical in her everyday life to the point of parsimony, never wasting anything in unimportant matters. But once, after concentrating, she had made a decision and determined what she had to do, then she would suddenly expend huge amounts for works that she thought should be done. Thus she had founded valuable organizations for public welfare in India, in the name of Vivekananda.

She often told me about how she had met the fiery Hindu missionary with the athletic body and the jet-black eyes:

"One day in New York I heard him preaching in his deep, melodious voice," she said. "He was explaining how human beings can cleanse themselves of their passions and feel that they are all brothers and so be saved.

He believed that all the religions worship the same God, except that there are different faces, according to the times and the peoples. That was his message and I listened to him carefully, weighing his every word. And when he'd finished, I got up and said, 'I agree. I'll go with him!'"

She gave him money immediately so that he could dedicate himself wholly to his mission. A throng of men and women had gathered around him, and they listened to him openmouthed. No one but this indomitable woman stood up to him as a free and clear-sighted human being. And often in her smilingly independent way she would poke quiet fun at his little human failings. Is there any surer sign of indissoluble friendship?

"I loved and honored him very much," she said to me one day, "and I knew that he could take my teasing even when it stung the most."

She came down to the garden again today to look at the flowers and sit in her favorite place, beneath the Gothic Madonna and the white roses.

"Tell me about Vivekananda," I asked her, with my mind very far away from this well-meaning, rather simple-minded apostle of love. But I liked seeing how the spark of a human being's life can last more than eighty years— eighty years of burning the machine and not having it rust, with the teeth, the feet, the kidneys, the brain all strong at work, able to do their duty, still intact without a falter; able to take in the raw materials of food, drink, air, and the sun's heat, and transform them into spirit. It has always seemed to me that old age is a humiliating habit, a sign that the spirit has declined and is dragging the flesh down with it. For the wrinkles, the faded eyes, the stumbling feet, only the spirit is to blame. It's the spirit that has grown wrinkled and faded and is stumbling.

With her dry voice and cold flame Miss MacLeod began her story:

"Vivekananda was anxious when he first went to his teacher, the great Ramakrishna. He had been brought up in a rich home. Their table was always laid for visitors, and his father lived like an extravagant aristocrat. And now that Vivekananda was with his holy guru, his venerable teacher, he couldn't get accustomed to poverty.

"One day, not being able to bear it any longer, he said to his teacher: 'Teacher, forgive me, but I cannot live in poverty. I need money.'

" 'Go ask the goddess Kali to give you some,' Rama-krishna answered him calmly.

"Happy at having gotten the permission, Vivekananda entered the temple and prayed for hours before the an-cient wooden image of the goddess. When he returned that evening, the teacher asked him: 'Well, did you beg her to give you money?'

" 'Ah, I forgot to!' said Vivekananda, beating his hands in despair. 'It completely slipped my mind.'

" 'Go back tomorrow and beg her!'

"Vivekananda went the next day too, but he got ab-sorbed in his prayer, and again he forgot. He went still a third time, with the same result. And Ramakrishna laughed happily.

" 'Come, give up the money,' he told his young pupil. 'Your heart doesn't accept money, you see? It's ashamed to ask such unworthy things of the goddess. You are made for great works.' "

As she spoke of Vivekananda, the indomitable old lady swung her beautiful, transparent hands serenely as if caress-ing the air. Vivekananda was still the greatest person she had met in her long, much-traveled life. He had given a purpose and a unity to her action, and surely this man who had died so young had helped her to live so long and so correctly. She stroked a white rose, as she con-tinued:

"When they cursed him and slandered him, he remained silent and buried himself in thought. Suddenly his face would light up, and he would murmur softly, as though he were praying, 'Shiva! Shiva!'

" 'But you must answer,' I used to tell him. 'You must defend yourself and get angry—like a man.'

"And he would reply with a smile: 'Why? For what reason, my dear one? Since the one who strikes and the one who is struck are the same? Since the one who praises and the one who is praised are the same? *Tat tvam asi*—we are all one.'

"He was simple like a child, innocent as a saint. His mind never turned toward evil. He laughed with us and played. There were many women around him and beautiful ones, but he never got misty-eyed for a single moment. If he had, I would have been the first to notice. It wouldn't have escaped me."

She laughed and tossed her snow-white head. "What momentous, meaningful days!" she said, glancing far, far off in the direction of India.

But soon she returned to Stratford, to her sun-bathed garden, to the atmosphere of war. "And these days are very momentous and meaningful too," she said. "But those days were altogether different. We had a simple, wise holy man with us. And whatever he said penetrated into our whole hearts. He was very fond of recounting to us tales about his fatherland, and he would extract from the simplest folk myths the loftiest moral doctrines. One day he told us a story that had a decisive influence upon my life:

" 'Once upon a time a birdcatcher caught a great number of doves and shut them up in a big net. The doves immediately began trying to squeeze through the holes and get free, but they were too big. So they submitted to their fate. Every day the birdcatcher came and fed them.

He threw them food in abundance so they would get fat quickly, and he could slaughter and sell them. All the doves ate with a great appetite, not realizing that the more they ate the fatter they got and the fatter they got the closer they came to death. Only one dove refrained from eating. It got thinner and thinner, and finally one day it was able to get out of the net and fly away . . .' "

I listened to the marvelous woman with my own mind far away. I very much enjoyed these idyllic stories which convey difficult abstract conceptions with such Oriental charm. When a thing is said in a perfect and vivid way, I reflected, it can fool even the most alert mind, so that a beautiful image becomes metamorphosed into an intellectual or moral certainty. There is a point where the form, if it is perfect, can create the essence.

Miss MacLeod understood that my mind had wandered and she smiled. "Your mind is elsewhere," she said. "But I will make you bring it back. You'll see!" She took a yellowed sheet of paper out of her pocket. "I never read you the last letter Vivekananda wrote. He sent it to me from California on the eighteenth of April, 1900." She unfolded the yellow paper and read me the following:

" 'I am well, and indeed especially well in my spirit. I care more about my spirit's serenity than my body's. Battles are won and lost. I have collected my baggage and am awaiting the Great Deliverance. Shiva, O Shiva, guide my boat to the other shore.

" 'I am now just the boy who listened in ecstasy and wonder to the fascinating words Ramakrishna spoke beneath the giant tree of Daksinesvar. That is my true nature. The work, the activity, the philanthropies were all later additions. And now I hear his voice again. Always the same voice, bringing quivers to my soul. The bonds are loosed. Love dies. Work has ceased to have significance now. Life has lost its luster. Now there is only the voice of the Teacher calling to me: "Here I am, Lord, here I am! Let the dead bury their dead, and follow me! . . . Here I am, dearly beloved Lord, here I am!"

" 'Yes, here I am, I am coming. Nirvana is opening up before me. Sometimes I feel it, the same boundless ocean of calm, without a ripple, without a breath of air.

" 'I am content to have come into the world. I am content that I suffered so much, content that I made grave mistakes, content that I am entering into peace. I am not leaving behind me any one in chains. I am not taking any chains with me. The venerable Teacher is gone, gone forever, never to return. The guide, the guru, has departed, while the young one, the student, the slave, has lingered on.

" '. . . The sweetest moments of my life were those when I let myself drift with the stream. And now I feel once more that I am drifting. I see the sun before me, hot and brilliant, and dense trees all around me. Everything is so quiet and peaceful in the heat, and the stream is bearing me gently towards the tender bosom of the great river. I do not dare to stir the water with my hands or feet, lest I interrupt the sublime silence.

" 'In back of my work was ambition; in back of my love was personality; in back of my innocence was fear; in back of my activity the guiding force was thirst for power. Now all these things have vanished, and I am being carried by the stream. Here I am, Mother, here I am! I am coming to your warm bosom. I am letting myself float where you guide me, to the strange and speechless land of miracles. Here I am now. I have become a spectator, no longer a person who acts.

" 'What peace reigns! My thoughts seem to come from very far away, from the depths of my own heart. They are liked muffled murmurs in the distance, and peace descends upon everything, a sweet peace, devoid of fear, devoid of love, devoid of emotion, like the peace we feel when we are alone and surrounded by paintings and statues. Here I am, Lord, here I am; I am coming. . . .' "

As Miss MacLeod read this farewell letter, so heart-breaking in its tranquillity, there was no tremor either in her hand or in her voice.

"Do you ever pray?" she asked me when she had finished. "When you are very happy or in deep despair, do you pray?"

"Never!" I answered. "I never pray."

"What do you do then?"

"I write. That's how I find relief."

"I don't ever pray either," said Miss MacLeod. "When I'm very much moved, I go for a walk—not in the country, but in the city—and I look at the people. Or I do something that I think is a good act. Or else I read this letter. That's how I find relief."

V. In this precious moment, this golden now, I am sitting sunning myself in the Poet's Garden behind Shakespeare's house. Red and yellow flowers, hedges trimmed with a master craftsman's shears in the shape of ducks, swans, peacocks. The poplars rustling, the water gurgling, and two little girls rolling about, scratching each other and playing like a pair of affectionate white kittens in the grass.

All your mighty cares and anxieties are silenced, lose their venom, bask in the sun like lizards in the Poet's Garden. You have only to stretch out your hand to grasp the moment—full, cool, round like a rose. In such a garden, on such a sun-caressed day, the world seems otherworldly. The air is flooded with lofty presences. And if you open your eyes slightly, you might see sitting next to you on the bench the master of the garden, with his towering forehead, his shiny bald head, his melancholy eyes and his thick sensuous lips.

He is holding a big register. He opens it and flicks through the pages. If you bend down, you will see not tragic verses or love sonnets, as you had hoped, but bills and figures, so many pounds, so many shillings, so many pence, to so-and-so on such-and-such a date. He turns the pages—so much rent from the houses, so much wheat; the fields, so much wool from the sheep, so much milk. . . . He turns more pages—a confusion of hen-scratches, disjointed phrases, helter-skelter. He doesn't understand any of it. For a second you are overcome by an impulse to start a conversation with him. You start to open your mouth, but Shakespeare, pale, tired, fifty-two years old, this warm day in March has fallen asleep on his bench.

Now you are free to bend over the open account book, and after a thousand frustrations you manage to decipher a few of the scratches:

"In the name of God, Amen. I, William Shakespeare, gentleman of Stratford, in perfect health and memory . . ."

And further on:

"To my daughter, Judith, one hundred and fifty pounds (150). To my sister, Joan, twenty pounds (20), To my granddaughter, Elizabeth Hall, my dishware except for the big silver platters."

Rows and rows of incoherent scratches follow. The hand that penned them was trembling and in haste. The pen rebelled, and the paper filled with smudges. In one corner you can still make out:

"To Thomas Combe, my sword. To Mr. Collins, 13 pounds, 6 shillings, 8 pence. To my daughter Susanna . . ."

Shakespeare gives a start, sighs, opens his eyes, looks

about him. He sees no one, not even his little granddaughter Elizabeth, who is rolling and playing in the grass. He sighs again, and takes from his belt a high bronze inkwell with a heraldic device carved on it—a silver spear in a gold field, and a hawk with its wings outspread. He takes out a quill, bends down and begins to write:

"To my wife, my second-best bed." He thinks a moment, hesitates, but finally comes to a decision and adds: "With the furnishings."

He is tired. He pauses again. It is the month of March; one month later, he will die, the twenty-third of April. He feels his life ebbing away, as though his veins are opening and his blood flowing out.

> *I am dead, Horatio. . . .*
> *You that look pale and tremble at this chance,*
> *That are but mutes or audience to this act,*
> *Had I but time—as this fell sergeant, death,*
> *Is strict in his arrest—O, I could tell you—*
> *But let it be. . . .*

A crow comes and sits on the poplar tree over the way. The branch bends. The ominous bird turns round and looks at the master on the bench. It stares, stares greedily, shakes its head, lowers its beak, as though already smelling the carrion.

Shakespeare lifts his hand. Does he want to welcome it? Does he want to chase it away? Who knows? . . . He lifts his hand, but with the effort he makes, he gets dizzy. His body dissolves and scatters like a tremulous springtime frost over the grass. It keeps getting more and more diffuse and takes on different shapes. Each shape it loses in turn. Then a sudden cold breeze blows and Shakespeare settles on the earth like dew.

■ ■

I turned around. The two little girls had disappeared. The crow had nested in the poplar tree and now began to caw. My companion was still sitting next to me on the bench. He was a retired Englishman whom I had met here in Stratford. He had been a teacher for forty years, and played at being a poet too. Last year he came back to die in this little town where he was born. He had white, silky mustaches, carefully trimmed, and his little eyes were like cool violets.

He had taken me the rounds of all the shrines that morning. "This is where Shakespeare was born; here was his house; this is his bed, this his will, this his signature; here where the pastry shop stands at present, used to be his daughter Judith's house; here the arched bridge where he used to rest and watch the sunset . . ."

The whole city limps along, living and trading beneath the great shadow. Now he dominates them all like the Pantocrator. He became their happy ruler too late, after he had wrenched the most tremendous sighs from his bosom.

Alas, 'tis true I have gone here and there,
And made myself a motley to the view,
Gored mine own thoughts, sold cheap what is most
*   dear, . . .*

A mediocre actor, his most successful role was playing the ghost in *Hamlet*. An unsuccessful lover, he used to tag along behind the "black" Mary Fitton, who cuckolded him and had children by other men, younger, richer, and more handsome than he.

He is contented thy poor drudge to be,
To stand in thy affairs, fall by thy side

He attached himself to various young lords and humbly dedicated his works to them. And these proud lords, if their names still live, owe it to this lowly man of the theater who condescended to record them with his pen. "The love I dedicate to your Lordship," runs one of these encomiums, "is without end. . . . What I have done is yours; what I have to do is yours." Or else he would sigh and write them brokenhearted sonnets:

> No longer mourn for me when I am dead,
> Than you shall hear the surly sullen bell
> Give warning to the world that I am fled
> From this vile world, with vilest worms to dwell:
> Nay, if you read this line, remember not
> The hand that writ it; for I love you so,
> That I in your sweet thoughts would be forgot,
> If thinking on me then should make you woe.

He was tender and sensitive, his contemporaries assure us, honest, openhearted, soft-spoken, possessed of a feminine kind of grace—the "Sweet Swan of Avon," as his friend Ben Jonson called him. He entered into the human soul and felt all its joys and griefs with his own heart. This was his abiding secret. Shakespeare might have said of himself what Dante said in those splendid lines:

> One am I, who, whenever
> Love doth inspire me, note, and in that measure
> Which he within me dictates, singing go.

And yet from the Swan's tender bosom there flew rapacious, carnivorous birds: savage spirits that with intrepid hands killed innocence, kindness and sleep. His great heroes were dragons: Othello, Coriolanus, Richard III, Macbeth. And they have been let loose into the world, never to leave it again. They return at midnight, in our own brains, enriching the subterranean areas of our souls, heightening the terror of our solitude.

The same bosom was simultaneously giving birth to other spirits, delicate, innocent, incorruptible: Juliet, Desdemona, Ophelia, Imogen, Cordelia, Virginia, Miranda. These figures adorn the upper floor of the spirit, Paradise. Thanks to Shakespeare, woman acquired new marks of nobility, and we are not able to make love now without having Ophelia's loosened hair sway on the water behind our beloved's shoulders, or without catching a sudden glimpse of Desdemona's bloodstained, perfumed handkerchief.

An infinite spirit, from the depths of hell to the summit of Paradise. If the whole of humanity was to send a single representative to speak for its rights before God, it would send him. He is also the only one who could represent our planet at some giant interplanetary conference. No one ever used human speech with such power and at the same time such sweetness as Shakespeare, with such harshness and at the same time such melody and so magical an aura.

In his earliest works Shakespeare's language was still fumbling and rhetorical, but in a few years' time, with A Midsummer Night's Dream and Romeo and Juliet, it had acquired an inexpressible sweetness and music. The lovers do not talk to each other; they warble, caught like nightingales in the flowering branches of April. Later, in Julius Caesar, his language became more dense and its rhythm attained greater power and sharpness. With Hamlet, the ever-increasing richness of his powers of utterance revealed itself in new qualities of passion and a faster tempo, gained without any diminution of the previous sweetness. In each of the great tragedies the verse was renewed, the flame waxed stronger, and the mind became more profound. The expression grew more integrated; there was a heavy, seething passion, saturated in bitterness, horror, scorn for humanity, and a heart-rending cry. Finally in *The Tempest* he found his peace and sweet temper again, but the peace and sweetness were utterly different from the lovely music that warbled in his early works. In *The Tempest* you feel that in order to attain the peace, his soul had been compelled to live through all the tempests, and that the sweetness is a product of human toil, of some alchemical manufacturing process, in the course of which a man's heart gathered all the poisons and made them into honey.

Who but Shakespeare, then, could represent humanity in its wholeness—the men and women, the mind's dreams, the swans and the monsters—if every star were to send its representative to God?

VI. Suddenly, at the very moment when he had mastered the language and when his power of expression had reached its peak of magic, this man who had created more souls than any other creator except God came back to his birthplace, this second-rate town of Stratford. He bought a few pieces of land, lived on the interest from his pounds, and at this most productive point in his development—he was just turned fifty—he yielded to the insipid, senile pleasures of a successful man. A good pew in church, a comfortable house with a garden, silver platters, good food, leisurely strolls, rambling conversations, deep bows in the street . . .

"So, had he really set out to make money and not to find glory?" I asked myself. "Had he really become an immortal in spite of himself, as that slyest of all English poets, Pope, suspected?"

"I don't understand it at all," I said aloud, abruptly breaking my silence. "I simply don't understand it."

The affable pensioner, who was sunning himself next to me and leafing drowsily through his book, was shocked. He looked at me. "What is it you can't understand?" he asked me in his sugary, disagreeable voice.

"Why he gave up creating. He had steeped himself in joy and sorrow; his heart was full of abundant good things, like those rich ships that used to sail back from the exotic islands of the Indian Ocean. So why did he come back here to Stratford like a shipwrecked galley?"

"Shipwreck!" The Shakespeare devotee was outraged. "Are you talking about Shakespeare? You call that shipwreck or apotheosis?"

"Apotheosis? I don't understand you."

"He'd left his home town, gone to the big city, done his duty more than anyone else in the whole world, and then like a good workman he came back to the land, his own village, to spend the last few years of his life in peace and quiet—to enjoy a good sleep, good food, Sunday church services, an evening stroll, the respect of his fellow townsmen. In a word, to live on the fruits of his own labor. What more perfect cycle could a human life follow? That's the cycle that the sun follows itself."

I didn't answer. How could you argue with a retired schoolteacher-poet whose defense of Shakespeare was really just a concealed, dignified, feignedly naïve way of defending his own petty existence, which he thought was following the same curve?

But inside me, the question remained painfully unanswerable. For I have never been able to make up my mind whether man's duty ever ends; whether we have the right until death, or even beyond death, to give up the struggle.

"What I like best of all," continued the schoolteacher, "is the humane and characteristically English ending that Shakespeare gave to his demonic life. He bought houses and land, and became the pillar and pride of the little town where he was born. He became a gentleman, bought his own coat of arms with his own money (a silver spear, a gold field, and a hawk with wings outspread) and then he was entitled to carve them over his doorway, on his carriage, on his seals and rings, to put them on his plates and forks and knives, on his handkerchiefs and his underwear. And on his tombstone. That's how happy heroes—I mean, the really enviable heroes—always end."

I laughed.

"What are you laughing at?" the pensioner asked, his goatee shaking menacingly.

"Please forgive me," I answered, "but as you were talking just now, the strangest image popped into my mind. You know how it is when you kill a chicken and scrape out its entrails, and you find a row of yellow yolks inside, big ones and little ones, that haven't had time to become eggs. You've killed the chicken too soon, and you feel upset, you know."

"Well?" my interlocutor queried nervously.

"Well, I was just thinking, if we had opened Shakespeare like that when he died, wouldn't we have found a whole stack of tragedies, like unhatched eggs?"

The pensioner shrugged his shoulders, and out of politeness refrained from making a reply. These Orientals! he must have been thinking to himself, they just have no sense of hierarchy, no respect. I talk to him of Shakespeare and he's reminded of a chicken without its stomach, and chicken eggs! Their god, the Sun, must be the most shameless of all the deities.

He leafed through the book he was holding, put on his glasses, and found a page.

"With your permission," he said. "Listen to the words of one of our great writers, Carlyle."

He is the grandest thing we have yet done. For our honour among foreign nations, as an ornament to our English Household, what item is there that we would not surrender rather than him? Consider now, if they asked us, Will you give up your Indian Empire or your Shakespeare, you English; never have had any Indian Empire, or never have had any Shakespeare? Really it were a grave question. Official persons would answer doubtless in official language; but we, for our part too, should not we be forced to answer: Indian Empire, or no Indian Empire; we cannot do without Shakespeare! Indian Empire will go, at any rate, some day; but this Shakespeare does not go, he lasts forever with us; we cannot give up our Shakespeare!

He was silent. If Shakespeare could have heard these praises, how he would have shaken his head in irony and sadness! What could this life-loving man do with glory after death, he with his delicately wrought, hungry five senses, which in his most passionate erotic moments, when they were fully alive, had to feed on leftover foods?

> When, in disgrace with fortune and men's eyes,
> I all alone beweep my outcast state,
> And trouble deaf heaven with my bootless cries,
> And look upon myself, and curse my fate,
> Wishing me like to one more rich in hope,
> Featured like him, like him with friends possessed,
> Desiring this man's art and that man's scope,
> With what I most enjoy contented least . . .

"What are you thinking about?" the teacher asked me, peering at me from underneath his eyeglasses.

"That this adoration came too late," I answered.

"Better late than never!" commented the practical-minded old pensioner. "When a great man reflects, in the midst of his suffering, that recognition and glory will come some day, he suffers less."

"How do you know?" I burst out, getting angry in spite of myself. "Who told you? For the spirits that love life—the whole of life, old wine, good food, women, traveling, honors—and suffer very deeply because they don't have anything of what they long for, and yet are proud, better never than late! What's it worth to be starving all your life long and to have sumptuous tables laid for you when you die?"

"Why do you get angry?" the teacher asked, smiling condescendingly at this crude, inflammable Oriental.

"Because his friends, the lords—Pembroke, Essex, Montgomery, Southampton—scorned him a little and stole the women he loved from him, and there was no one to guess the identity of this humble man of the theater, 'sweet William' who put up with the society of these noble lords.

"He wrote *Hamlet*, laid bare his heart, showed all his wounds, cried out. No one listened to Hamlet. One hundred seventy-nine years had to pass after Hamlet first cried out and turned to clay, before an ear was found to listen. In 1780 a certain Henry Mackenzie was the first to speak of the 'inexpressible charm' of Hamlet. He was the first to guess that some great, spine-tingling enigma lay hidden behind the pale youth. And from then on the enigma began to become entrenched, simply because each generation that passed loaded its own enigmas onto Hamlet."

The pensioner closed his eyes. He wanted to hear no more.

And I went on reflecting inwardly about the gradual crystallization of the Shakespearean legend. As long as the pseudoclassical period lasted, the measured phrase, the cold descriptive term, the chiseled pattern, Shakespeare was considered a monster, without head or tail, a barbarian. But as soon as the romantic era burst loose, the molds were broken. The spirit came gushing out with passionate and angry shrieks. Hyperbole, a flow of colorful terms, daring incongruities, boundless yearnings, were regarded as the new dictates of art, and Shakespeare as the lawgiving prophet who had descended from the Mount Sinai of his mind, bearing the new Ten Commandments.

Ever since then it has been, alongside the Bible, the pride of every English home to have another big book open and much perused: the *Collected Works* of Shakespeare. And yet—and this is the amazing thing—there is no human type so different from the Shakespearean hero as the contemporary Englishman. You look into Shakespeare, and all at once it seems as though you had opened the gate of some wild menagerie. Shrieks and bellows, violent gestures, impulse that defies restraint, a primeval force reveling in its own freedom. This untamed Elizabethan beast still lives inside the present-day Englishman, but it is imprisoned behind the iron bars of Victorian dignity.

One day in London I talked with an English writer on the subject. "How can modern Englishmen," I asked him, "understand spirits that are so different as Shakespeare's heroes? Today the Shakespearean jungle has been moved to warmer zones."

"No one," he replied, "has as much capacity to understand and appreciate Shakespeare as the modern Englishman. Not because he belongs to our race and speaks our own language, but because, while we are hearing him, we feel at last that the chained Saxon beast inside us is unleashed and can bellow at will. We feel that our five senses are opening at last and enjoying everything that they haven't dared to enjoy. For us Shakespeare is the safety valve. It lifts a little and saves us from cutting loose. He is like the wanton dreams that come to ascetics and bring enough compensation so that they can preserve their virginity."

The sun had already set when I got back home after ambling along the peaceful green bank of the river. As the first blue shadows of nightfall descended upon the banks, I could see the swans luxuriating in their evening bath, proudly arching their snakelike necks and pecking their fluffy breasts and curly bellies with their broad yellow beaks. They cleaned and combed and plucked themselves, and the falling feathers collected like foam at the edge of the water.

They had played well, eaten, flown about, and swum all day long. And now the evening had come and they were preparing themselves for sleep. Once again, I was reminded of their big brother, the Swan of Avon.

VII. Sometimes a painter will paint his own face in a corner of his canvas, as though he had been suddenly overwhelmed by compassion for this ephemeral raiment of his soul, doomed to vanish, and had felt a craving to save it from total extinction. He places it, like an extra with nothing to do, in one of his great scenes, among heroes and kings; or, if it's an ikon, among the saints. Thus, somewhere in the painted throng, you can find the beckoning figure of El Greco, pale, other-worldly, like an aura.

Shakespeare too must have inserted his own face among the tragic kings and heroes of his work of a thousand faces. Of course, all his heroes are flesh of his own flesh, the most bloodthirsty of them as well as the most ethereal. All these monsters and lilies he had inside him, and in order to find relief and escape he incarnated them, dressed them in words and dispatched them into the world as independent organisms. But without any doubt his own face is crystal-

lized more faithfully in some forms than in others. Or, to
be more accurate, his own faces. For a spirit with such sensitivity as his must have gone through extreme torment from
hope to hope, and from despair to despair; and he must
have changed his face many times. If we could find them,
we could follow the sanguinary traces of his spirit over the
earth stage by stage.

I pored over Shakespeare's densely populated work,
longing to single out his own face among the thousands of
shapes. To see how he was as a young man, how he was
after he had been sprayed with all the poisons, and how he
found his way to the tranquility of *The Tempest*. Poetry
gives us great joy. But man doesn't always need joy, and
what I sought in Shakespeare with a more insistent interest
was to find, amid the thick forest of his work, the narrow
path of his salvation.

In four different places I thought I could clearly detect
the face I was looking for. It was always the same, but
sometimes youthful and gay, sometimes mature and despairing, sometimes quiet and gray-haired. I could hear the
name of William Shakespeare, concealed but unmistak-
able, behind four different names: Romeo, Jaques, Hamlet, Prospero.

How his spirit had begun to warble those days from the
balcony of the Capulets! As though it was the dawn of the
world. With what youthful freshness and innocence, with
what charming awkwardness his spirit broke out that damp
spring night! Extravagantly, with teeming images, poetry
overflowed, began, began again. In vain did the erotic passion struggle to achieve a pure form of expression that
would afford it relief . . . like the nightingale. Youth was
intoxicated. Romeo believes in woman's innocence, in
the eternity of the moment. "He jests at scars that never
felt a wound." The youthful Shakespeare, thirty years old,

still in the first ecstatic phase of inexperienced happiness, still unhurt by fate, still weighted down with unsquandered riches and youthful melancholy, was stirring behind the face of Romeo and speaking confusedly through Romeo's mouth. He had not yet encountered the truth (what we consider the truth to be) and his lips were still smeared with milk and honey.

Three years passed, only three years, and Shakespeare's face changed, grew pale and tear-stained. We can see it clearly behind the diaphanous mask of Jaques in *As You Like It*. Now he was pierced by invisible arrows. He was wounded. He no longer mocked at the wounds, and the lightest touch gave him pain. He wanted to escape from humanity; to hide away in solitude. He laughed when others wept and wept when others laughed.

I have neither the scholar's melancholy, which is emulation; nor the musician's, which is fantastical; nor the courtier's, which is proud; nor the soldier's, which is ambitious; . . . but it is a melancholy of mine own, compounded of many simples, extracted from many objects, and, indeed, the sundry contemplation of my travels, in which my often rumination wraps me in a most humorous sadness.

All the world now seemed to Shakespeare like a stage. He had ceased to believe in sincerity or purity. Now he could see, blown up to four times life-size, the comical tragedy and the tragical comedy in the fate of man. He no longer isolated the joyful moment to make it eternal. He envisioned things in depth, took in instantaneously a face in three dimensions, the trinity of Joy, Grief, and Nothingness.

> *All the world's a stage,*
> *And all the men and women merely players:*
> *They have their exits and their entrances;*
> *And one man in his time plays many parts,*
> *His acts being seven ages.*

A crying baby; a lagging snail of a schoolboy; a burning lover; a truculent, blaspheming soldier; a pot-bellied, bearded judge; a bony old man with slippers, spectacles and a bulging purse; and finally, as the last and seventh act, a little handful without teeth, without eyes, without taste, without anything!

Three or four more years passed. The sweet and melancholy Jaques grew angry, sometimes biting his lips and gnashing his teeth, sometimes getting splashed with blood, sometimes letting loose shouts of irony, hissing like a snake—or sometimes laughing a laugh that was far more bitter than his dirge. He became Hamlet. At this time grief brought Shakespeare to the edge of madness. The words for the first time change rhythm. The phrase often whizzes like a whip. The monologues multiply because the solitude increases. Unbearable bitterness seeps out everywhere through this new mask of Shakespeare's. Bitterness and at the same time an indestructible sullen pride in the infiniteness of the human soul, surrounded as it is by beasts and worms and condemned to dissolution.

This delicate, sensitive hero—like all the other masks behind which Shakespeare's face is concealed—believes in beauty, kindness, love. And suddenly a woman, his mother . . .

> *O! that this too too solid flesh would melt,*
> *Thaw and resolve itself into a dew!*
> > *O God! O God!*

How weary, stale, flat, and unprofitable
Seem to me all the uses of this world.
Fie on't! O fie! . . .

And a little later:

> . . . I have of late—but wherefore I know not,—
> lost all my mirth, forgone all custom of exercises;
> and, indeed, it goes so heavily with my disposition
> that this goodly frame, the earth, seems to me a
> sterile promontory; this most excellent canopy, the
> air, look you, this brave o'erhanging firmament, this
> majestical roof fretted with golden fire—why, it ap-
> pears no other thing to me than a foul and pestilent
> congregation of vapours.

The moral crisis that Shakespeare endured during the
years between 1601 and 1610 must have been frightful.
That was when he wrote the great tragedies. His spirit was
in a state of violent turbulence. Passion wore a hideous
black mask. He had abandoned all hope, as though everyone and everything had betrayed him—men, women,
ideas . . . Cries came from his heart, sometimes through
the mouth of the jealous Moor, sometimes through King
Lear, sometimes through Antony caught in the toils of the
fatal siren, sometimes through the fierce wide mouth of
Coriolanus. The indomitable, deeply wounded soul of the
poet stumbled from precipice to precipice, shouting, assuming a multitude of faces, changing masks, wounds, and
martyrdoms, struggling, living all the passions in order to
find release from all the passions.

Superhuman passions, at the farthest extreme of human
capacity, transcending logic and proportion, and driving
the heroes to the abyss, into which they fall as noiselessly as
giant clouds, or else bellowing like buffaloes. The boun-

daries of beauty crumble, of logic and of madness and of hope, and we confront the harsh, steep, breathtaking ascents of towering terror.

But by giving flesh to his grief, making it into comedies and tragedies, Shakespeare found relief. In order not to kill, he had to fashion out of words men who kill. In order not to be killed, he had to make imaginary creatures who get killed.

O coz, coz, coz, my pretty little coz, that thou didst know how many fathom deep I am in love!

These words that he put into one of his comedies represent things Shakespeare said in his own life. He loved enormously, got hurt enormously, got ruined enormously by his love of life. And he had to find a way to escape.

If he placed his hopes in living people, his friends, the women he loved, or in ideas and great moral laws, he knew that they would betray him; he knew, for he had experienced it. Instead of finding relief, he too would collapse like his heroes, who were naïve enough to entrust their spirits to these shifting sands. There was only one safe refuge. After cruel humiliations, deeply wounded by his experience of this world, which passes for solid, and this reality, which passes for indubitable, he reached man's unique refuge, the realm of imagination. Since this world is inferior to our own heart, let us create a world for ourselves, on the model of our heart, just as we see it—imaginary, ethereal, absolutely our own, unassailable.

And thus the beleaguered great man grew wings and became free. Free, as we see so clearly in his last work, *The Tempest*. Prospero, the magician, makes a world all his own out of air, thought and dreams. He blows and this world rises up out of the sea. He blows again and it vanishes. The mind exults in its omnipotence. The heart finds

relief at last, because it perceives the truth. The truth that
it is all a dream. Prospero had all-powerful imagination to
do his bidding. The airy demon of the wasteland came
and fell at his feet:

> All hail, great master! grave sir, hail! I come
> To answer thy best pleasure; be't to fly,
> To swim, to dive into the fire, to ride
> On the curl'd clouds—to thy strong bidding task
> Ariel and all his quality.

After so many years of struggle and turmoil, Shakespeare
had become liberated from every hope. And once he was
entirely liberated from hope, he was also entirely liberated from fear. He became free, as though all his work had
been a series of labors—bandits, lions, Lernaean hydras
and Stygian stables—which he had passed through in
order to find salvation. Like all genuine creators, Shakespeare had one aim, and only one, in mind when he created: to free his own soul. He journeyed through the whole
of hell and the whole of purgatory—there is no other road
to paradise. And Shakespeare's paradise is far more sub-
stantial than the paradise of Dante. For Shakespeare's
is made not out of theological convictions, but out of the
mists of dreams.

▪ FREEDOM

You do look, my son, in a moved sort,
As if you were dismay'd: be cheerful, sir.
Our revels now are ended. These our actors,
As I foretold you, were all spirits, and
Are melted into air, into thin air:
And, like the baseless fabric of this vision,
The cloud-capp'd towers, the gorgeous palaces,
The solemn temples, the great globe itself,
Yea, all which it inherit, shall dissolve
And, like this insubstantial pageant faded,
Leave not a rack behind. We are such stuff
As dreams are made on; and our little life
Is rounded with a sleep.—Sir, I am vext;
Bear with my weakness; my old brain is troubled:
Be not disturb'd with my infirmity:
If you be pleased, retire into my cell,
And there repose: a turn or two I'll walk,
To still my beating mind.

And, since the revels were ended, he withdrew to his cave in Stratford. He had left this green, river-washed village in the flower of his youth, his spirit weighted down with flesh, and his five senses heavy with desires. The external world seemed to him then more trustworthy than the imagination, more true than thought. Like all the exuberant and voracious organisms of the Renaissance, Shake-speare had more confidence in his hands and lips than in the incorporeal play of the mind.

For this alluring delusion he seems to have been se-verely punished. He slipped into all the traps that life in its ever resourceful sportiveness sets for us: the traps of friend-ship, of sexual love, of virtue. He expected too much from passion. He trusted woman more than that charming but wretched creature merits. He yielded blindly to sensual involvements. He got enmeshed in the thick and diaboli-cally tangled web of things. He did his human duty.

He completed his military service in hell. He fought, got wounded, and was taken prisoner. He cried aloud and found relief, created wounded souls to cure his own wounds, and created spirits blinded by passion in order to bring discipline and enlightenment to his own passion. Ariel, the ether within him, did his work well. In con-densing, the ether gave being to a multitude of souls, and in returning to vapor, it annihilated them, playing all the time. Shakespeare must surely have been satisfied with his spirit; and if Ariel had asked him, as he asked Prospero, "Sir, all this service have I done . . . Was't well done?" Shakespeare would have replied in the same way:

> *Bravely, my diligence. Thou shalt be free.*
>
> . . . .
>
> *then to the elements*
> *Be free, and fare thou well!*

In the creator's life there is nothing he can count on to give him steady and effective support, except his imagina-tion. Without that he is lost. At the end of his life Shake-speare perceived that Ariel was leaving him. And sud-denly all his powers became paralyzed.

Now my charms are all o'erthrown,
And what strength I have's mine own,—
Which is most faint . . .
                                   now I want
Spirits to enforce, art to enchant,
And my ending is despair . . .

But Ariel was not leaving him midway. He had remained faithful to him up to the end of the journey. He led him to the farthest reach of despair, to the very edge of the abyss, and then blew on his eyes and, with his finger laid over his mouth, said to him with a smile: "Look!" And he saw that this world is a dream, a mist falling on nothing, with a thousand shapes and a thousand colors covering nothing. And that reality is the anthropomorphic mask of nothing, there to frighten us. At the extremity of despair, Ariel, the last and most ethereal creation of his imagination, stood and smiled at him—at Prospero, the omnipotent magician, the mind of the free man. Shakespeare and Prospero merged, as two clouds merge. A gentle breeze blew and they dissolved.

Even with the highest gifts and the best of fortune, a human being hardly has time to refine all the matter assigned him as his lot and to finish converting it into spirit. Rarely can he prove, on the basis of his own murderous experience, that matter (let's define matter as impediment plus weight) does *not* exist. Or rather, that though it does exist, a great spirit has the capacity to extinguish it by transforming it. And by extinguishing it, to extinguish joy and grief, hope and fear, good and evil and all finite things, and thus to arrive at the great freedom.

How many mortals have achieved it so far? Pythagoras? Plato? Leonardo? Surely Buddha. Perhaps Shakespeare. His heart was a miracle-working chemical workshop, where meat and beer and women and hope and tears were tossed in and spirit emerged. In Shakespeare's wounded being, the voice of freedom could not be silenced. Although stifled at first, it rose up, ever more ethereal in tone. And that was what Shakespeare followed; that was his road, passing through all the forms of slavery. His spirit, like all great spirits, was a Jacob's ladder. It was anchored deep in the ground, amid stones and muddy soil, and its top rested in the sky.

Whatever the poet Pope said, Shakespeare did not go to London just to make money. Of course, the practical Anglo-Saxon in him did want to make money, to buy a coat of arms, to become a gentleman, and to go back to his home town as a respectable village elder. This was the lowest and crudest level of his spirit—the ground floor, getting rich. But there were floors above, and they were constructed of progressively lighter materials. The second floor: escape from the provinces, contact with the wide world, loving and being loved; in a word, living. The third floor: writing plays, outdoing Marlowe, Greene, Fletcher, Beaumont, Ben Jonson, and winning fame. The fourth floor: finding words to embody his inner desires; singing his joy to keep from going mad and his grief to keep it from killing him. He was not writing here in order to vanquish his rivals; he was creating in order not to suffocate, in order to find liberation. The fifth floor: invisible, made of dreams and noiseless summer lightning . . . freedom!

Having reached the tip of the highest peak of the English spirit, we can gaze out at this island rising out of the green sea like some giant ironclad tower afloat through the ages.

From the first megalithic monuments in Wiltshire and the clumsy stone implements going back two or three thousand years before Christ, up till September 3, 1939, and the outbreak of the new war that will decide the fate of England, humanity waged three decisive battles on this green island, and won them.

1. *The Gentleman*. The individual fought to free himself from enslavement to the neighbor, the lord and the king; to mark out around himself the widest possible sphere of human liberty; to create a new type of human being, free, at ease, proud and gentle, brave and modest, taciturn, self-controlled—the Gentleman. And in this he succeeded.

The individual carried on a simultaneous struggle to emancipate his religious conscience, which had been terrorized by the Catholic priests. And he shook off the yoke of the papacy. Freedom.

2. *Magna Carta*. The polity fought to acquire political and economic privileges, "liberties" as they were called; to limit the arbitrary will of the king; to judge through its own representatives, and to let the whole decide in the interests of the whole. The polity fought and won. People and king became linked together in the parliamentary system, the monument of England's victory. Freedom.

3. *Shakespeare*. The supreme spirit created by the four races—Celts, Saxons, Vikings, Normans—wrestled to liberate itself from the appearances that enslave the essence; to lay out the path of freedom through the passions and the interests, the virtues and the vices.

Without consciously pursuing such an aim, Shakespeare fought for freedom by following the impulse of his island. The essential nature of a race manifests itself in its greatest spirits. For the struggles of a thousand years become concentrated in these spirits and so are made visible to us. Innumerable unseen efforts are brought to completion by them, and like an unlooked-for miracle, they suddenly present us with the victory which had been in preparation for centuries.

All the rest—the mediocre spirits—represent the unsuccessful endeavors of the race to give body to its greatest desires. These are the miscarriages of the race, and the heroes only are its sons. Hence, if we want to ascertain the deepest ambitions and the highest capabilities of a nation, the only infallible way is to scrutinize its heroes. The hero is the unsullied and faithful mirror wherein the race can see the reflection of its own countenance.

England sees her face in Shakespeare, and she glories in him, because she realizes that this son of hers has perfectly reproduced and crystallized all her own characteristics within his own individual person: Anglo-Saxon practicality; Celtic daydreaming; the Viking's piratical bravery; and the discipline of the Norman; and above all, in the heart of it all, freedom.

In my walks along the coasts of England, I had pondered on a tormenting problem. Every great people has its own bluebird, the supreme and mystical ideal in which all its urges coalesce. Ancient Greece had beauty; Rome, the state; the Jews, divinity; the Hindus, Nirvana; Christianity, the everlasting kingdom. What, then, is the bluebird pursued through the ages by Great Britain? And now, after patient and persistent study, we can descry the blue wing flitting through the English air. It is the beloved bluebird, bloodstained but immortal, that first on this planet built its nest in Greece—freedom.

■ EPILOGUE*

THE ANGELS OF CYPRUS
(*The Fate and Honor of an Empire*)

These very days, a great people are crossing the Bridge
of Trika. [This is the site of a heroic battle in the Greek
War of Independence, 1821.—TRANSLATOR.] It is not only
Cyprus' fate that is being judged. It is not the fate of
Cyprus alone that is at stake. For the just rock is sure to
devour the unjust mountain. What is at stake, what is
being judged at the present moment is the fate and honor
of a whole empire! The nation that had risen with such
national pride and moral exaltation, as one man, to save
the honor of the world in those critical hours of the war, is
now undergoing one of the fateful apocalyptic trials that
will reveal whether its value is genuine or counterfeit.

And at a still deeper, broader level, the fate and honor of
the entire Western world is being judged. Always until
now, it has boasted that it was fighting for the justice and
freedom of other nations. But now we will see whether
that world is worthy of using these sacred words, whether
the soul of any honorable man at the present time can have
confidence in world leaders such as these . . .

In a major island, 400,000 spirits are raising a hue and

---

* This section was first published in *Nea Estia*, September 25, 1954.
It seems expedient to include it here, inasmuch as it adds a new
facet to the author's point of view on England.—EDITOR.

cry, demanding their liberty. And the thrice-noble nation where liberty and light were born is raising a cry along with them. From the four corners of the earth (and even from English throats) voices of anger and protest are exploding. By now it is no longer possible for violence and injustice to stifle a whole people in secret, without protest. Apparently, this world we thought had gone rotten, still has spirits that dare to rear their head against hypocrisy, injustice, arrogance.

It is a critical moment. The moral salvation of the whole world depends on the answer given to the Cyprus question. And on this moral salvation the political, social, cultural salvation of the world has always depended. Cyprus is no longer a detail now, a mere island at the extreme tip of the Mediterranean. It is becoming the fate-marked center, where the moral value of contemporary man is at stake.

How is the British Empire facing this tragic moment where its own value is on trial? Alas! With means unworthy of a great nation; with unmanly silence at first; and then with deceit, sycophantism, violence. Shame has hidden its face, far off from the disgraced quarters of the Foreign Office.

The genuine people, though, are not despairing. They know that in this dishonorable, inconsistent world, certain fundamental principles still live and reign, daughters of man, whom he has created with his own sweat, blood, tears. And these are the immortal ones. Most of them were born in Greece: freedom, human dignity, the thirst for justice.

Great mysterious forces are multiplying and bearing fruit even while they are being pursued. Hear the words of an age-old myth: An angel came down to earth, and the ruler of the world was enraged on seeing it. And he lunged at it with his sword and split it in two. And at once the one angel became two. And again, the ruler of the world lunged at them and split these two angels in two. And the two angels became four, and the four eight, and the eight sixteen, and soon the earth had filled with angels.

Who was this angel? The angel of freedom? Cyprus will soon be full of angels. And the ruler of the world will be crushed, disgraced in Tartarus, his sword shattered.

There is some mystic law in this world (for if there were not, this world would have been destroyed thousands of years ago), a harsh, inviolable law: in the beginning, evil always triumphs, and in the end it is always vanquished. Apparently, for man to buy this privilege, much effort, much sweat, many tears are imperative. And freedom is the most expensive good that can be bought. It is never given for nothing, either by human beings or by the gods. It goes from land to land, wherever it is summoned, from heart to heart, unsleeping, unsubduable, uncompromising. At this moment we can watch it traversing the soil of Cyprus with steady momentum. And soon its limbs will be spattered with blood. For this is the way freedom always forges its path.

For us this is a good moment to forget our passions and our petty cares; for each man of us with his own God-given gifts to follow the path of freedom throughout the land of Cyprus. And we must share her grief, her upsurge, her danger, insofar as we are capable, and surely later on (for this is the law, we said) her great joy as well.

I myself represent nothing. I am not anything. Only a clear conscience. But a clear conscience weighs more in the scale of God and time than an empire. And now that Cyprus has been saved from the waves and is crying out, all clear consciences—from all the quarters of the world; wherever they may be—can hear this cry and see the injustice and cast the stone (the curse) against the ruler of this world, the wrongdoer. The ruler laughs and acts in a cynical manner. He has power on his side, soldiers and fleets, lethal birds of the air, vast wealth and traitors—and great *hubris*. He laughs and acts in a cynical manner, but one day (such has always been the omnipotence of man when wronged)—one day, Clear Conscience will hurl this stone at it and it will hang around the neck of the empire and sink it. Thus great empires have always sunk.

Several years ago I went back to Cyprus, enchanted by her Greek light and pleasant air. An old man emerged from a peasant house near Famagusta. We picked up a conversation. He was discussing (what else!) the union, and his eyes flashed. And suddenly a broad smile flooded his sunburned face. He put his hand over his heart, and he said, slowly as though confiding some great secret to me:

"The foundation stones of England are shaking! They are shaking, because the human heart has stirred."

Yes, the human heart has stirred, O great Empire!